AGRICULTURAL
PRODUCT
PRICES

AGRICULTURAL PRODUCT PRICES

William G. Tomek
Kenneth L. Robinson

CORNELL UNIVERSITY PRESS
ITHACA AND LONDON

First published 1972 by Cornell University Press.
Published in the United Kingdom by Cornell University Press Ltd., 2–4 Brook Street, London W1Y 1AA.

International Standard Book Number 0-8014-0748-6
Library of Congress Catalog Card Number 72-4872

Printed in the United States of America by Vail-Ballou Press, Inc.

Librarians: Library of Congress cataloging information appears on the last page of the book.

Preface

The decision to write this book was motivated by two considerations. First, we believe that the behavior of agricultural product prices is sufficiently unusual as to require special treatment. Second, we saw a need for a more up-to-date text, which would combine principles of price determination, information on pricing institutions, and an introduction to selected quantitative techniques as applied to agricultural prices.

This book is designed for an intermediate-level course in agricultural prices and marketing. Students would benefit from a prior course in microeconomic principles, although Chapters 2 through 5 provide some of the essential material. For the most part, no mathematical competence beyond ordinary algebra is assumed. The very limited use of differential calculus is confined almost exclusively to footnotes and appendices. Some students may find the discussion of futures markets and prices (Chapters 12 and 13) at a somewhat more advanced level than the earlier chapters. Chapters 15 and 16 have been written with the assumption that students will have had an introduction to statistics, including some knowledge of regression procedures.

Students and colleagues, too numerous to mention individually, provided comments and suggestions on selected parts of the initial manuscript. Paul Farris, Richard King, Lester Manderscheid, and Ian Sturgess reviewed the entire manuscript, and we gratefully acknowledge their help. We owe a special debt to James P. Houck for an unusually thorough review and for comprehensive suggestions.

We especially appreciate the encouragement to carry through with this project given by B. F. Stanton, and we are grateful for the accurate typing and secretarial assistance of Nancy L. Brown.

                                                      WILLIAM G. TOMEK
                                                      KENNETH L. ROBINSON

Ithaca, New York

Contents

Figures

Tables

AGRICULTURAL PRODUCT PRICES

CHAPTER 1

Introduction

The principal objective of this book is to provide students with an understanding of the complex array of forces that influence the level and behavior of agricultural product prices. A secondary objective is to introduce students to empirical studies and analytical techniques that are useful in predicting price changes or the economic consequences of price changes.

Agricultural product prices are important both economically and politically since they strongly influence the level of farm incomes, the welfare of consumers, and, in many countries, the amount of export earnings. The incomes of nearly half the world's population are determined principally by the prices received for agricultural commodities. A decline of only a few cents per pound in the prices of such internationally traded commodities as sugar, coffee, and cocoa can have serious political and economic repercussions in such countries as Mauritius, Colombia, and Ghana. Even in the United States, both farmers and consumers are politically sensitive to changes in the prices of farm products. The continuing economic importance of agricultural prices is reflected in the fact that agricultural commodities, processed foods, and feed still account for slightly more than one-fourth of the value of all items which make up the Wholesale Price Index.

Distinguishing Characteristics of Agricultural Prices

Agricultural commodities provide an exceptionally interesting vehicle for the study of price-making forces. The manner in which commodity prices are determined ranges over the entire spectrum from almost complete government regulation to perhaps the closest approximation that now exists to the textbook example of pricing under freely competitive market conditions. Thus, in examining agricultural prices, one is inevitably led to a study of a wide range of models of price determination and of pricing institutions.

Agricultural commodity prices are much more volatile than are the prices of most nonfarm goods and services. It is not unknown for the price of a commodity like eggs or pork to drop by as much as 50 per cent within a period of twelve to eighteen months. Between February 1970 and February 1971, for example, the price of hogs dropped from nearly $30 per hundredweight to less than $20. Over the decade of the 1960's, the price of sugar traded on international markets ranged from less than 2 cents to over 9 cents per pound, while the price of cocoa in the mid 1950's fell within two years from 58 to 27 cents per pound. Very few nonfarm goods and services, except possibly ship charter rates and the prices of nonferrous metals, can match the amplitude of the swings in agricultural commodity prices.

The biological nature of agricultural production is, of course, a principal cause of price instability. Unlike most nonfarm industries, actual production in agriculture may exceed or fall short of planned production by a considerable margin. Yields vary from year to year because of unusually favorable or unfavorable weather and the presence or absence of disease or insect infestations (e.g., the failure of the monsoon in Asia or the occurrence of corn blight in the United States). Seasonal variations in production likewise contribute to price instability from month to month. Many crops are harvested only once a year and some of these cannot be stored, and livestock products like fluid milk also are perishable.

The sequential events in producing farm products are separated by significant time intervals. Thus, many farm products are not suited to an assembly-line type process, and substantial time lags exist between a decision to produce and the realization of the final output. These lagged relationships are especially important in agriculture. Relatively high or low prices may persist for considerable periods because of the inability of farmers to respond promptly to a change in price signals. At least a year is required for producers to change hog production, two years to change the supply of beef, and five to ten years for growers to change production plans for tree crops, such as apples, in response to price changes. In the case of livestock, an increase in the price of meat may lead to a further rise in the short run as farmers reduce the number of animals sent to market and withhold female stock for breeding.

Brewster (1950) states that the time separation of farm operations also is an important factor in making family-operated farms competitive with larger-than-family units in numerous situations. The mechanization of farming *per se* was not sufficient to determine the dominance either of family or larger-than-family farms.

The decentralized nature of farm production and its geographical dispersion complicate the problem of price determination. Agriculture is still an industry in which relatively small-scale units predominate (Nikolitch, 1970). While farms are becoming larger, it still requires production from thousands of units to account for 80 per cent of the total supply. In contrast, only a half dozen firms or fewer will often account for 80 per cent or more of the total output in many nonfarm industries such as automobiles, aluminum, rubber tires, and farm machinery. However, both food processing and food distribution are characterized by a core of a few large firms, each with a fringe of a large number of small firms (Handy and Padberg, 1971). The geographical dispersion of production in agriculture also makes it costly to assemble commodities and to estimate accurately the supplies available.

Price-making forces in agriculture are not confined to national boundaries. For many commodities, a world view is essential to understanding why prices change. An increase in the price of soybeans, for example, may be due to drought or an early frost in the USSR which cuts sunflower, hence sunflower-oil, production. Grain prices in the United States are influenced by what happens to production in Canada, Argentina, Australia, and even such countries as Thailand, which is now an important exporter of corn to Japan.

Role of Prices

Prices play a central role in economic theory in guiding production and consumption.[1] The authors are under no illusion, how-

[1] Bowman and Bach (1946, pp. 35–41) provide a simplified model of a free price system and explain how such a system would work to register consumer preferences, get desired goods produced, and distribute the products of eco-

ever, that either the production decisions of farmers or the buying
decisions of housewives are governed solely by prices. Government
programs, including land-retirement or acreage-control measures,
as well as personal preferences, the limits of climate and soils, and
the availability of equipment, obviously exert a strong influence on
what farmers plant each year. Consumers are likewise influenced
in their decisions by advertising, the display space given to foods
in supermarkets, personal whims, packaging, and convenience, as
well as by prices.

Some economists argue that prices no longer serve the function
they once did of coordinating production and consumption (Breimyer, 1962; Collins, 1959). This view has been challenged by others (e.g., Gray, 1964). We take an intermediate position. Prices,
especially relative prices, influence human behavior. Consumers do
respond to changes in the price of beef relative to the prices of
pork and chicken. Farmers, likewise, have demonstrated repeat-
edly that they will produce more onions, potatoes, cabbage, or
pork in response to relatively favorable prices. Thus, an understanding of the concepts of economic theory does provide valuable
insights into human behavior and to the way prices are determined.

However, neither consumers nor producers respond to price
changes in a mechanical way. The degree of responsiveness of
quantity to given size price change may itself change with the passage of time. As consumers become more affluent, their purchases
of individual food products may become less responsive to changes
in prices, and as farmers tend to have higher fixed investments,
their output also may become less responsive to price changes.[2]

National governments have played an increasingly important
role in pricing farm products since the 1930's. Agricultural price-

nomic activity. In addition, they provide a brief description of the American
economy.

[2] These statements illustrate possible changes in the degree of responsiveness of producers and consumers to price, and they should be treated as hypotheses subject to empirical verification. Since economic development implies
the development of new substitutes and since increases in the number and importance of substitutes imply greater sensitivity of quantity to price, increased
affluence could lead to greater rather than less responsiveness by consumers to
price changes.

support policies now strongly influence the prices of commodities which make up about half the value of all farm products sold by farmers in the United States. Government programs also influence the prices of about 80 per cent of all agricultural commodities produced in the United Kingdom and in the European Common Market countries. The prices of such internationally traded commodities as coffee, sugar, and butter are influenced by international commodity agreements or the joint decisions of several governments. The prices of still other commodities are influenced by marketing boards (for example, in Canada, Australia, New Zealand, Uganda, and Nigeria). In the United States, federal and state marketing orders also have been used to divert supplies and to fix minimum prices for such commodities as potatoes and milk. Clearly, many agricultural commodity prices are no longer determined by the free play of market forces. But pricing decisions, whether made on the basis of market forces or political or welfare considerations, have important economic consequences. For this reason, tools of analysis that will help one to anticipate the economic effects of pricing decisions are still important.

Farmers, marketing and supply firms, and government officials have to make many decisions which require a knowledge of what will happen if the price of a particular commodity rises or falls. Meat packers, for example, want to know how much the production of hogs will change in response to the price of hogs or, more importantly, to the price of hogs relative to corn. Government officials need to know how much storage holdings will rise or how much land will have to be kept idle if the support price of wheat or cotton is raised 10 per cent. Apple growers and storage operators need to be able to anticipate the effect of controlled atmosphere storages, which lengthen the storage life of fruit, on seasonal price changes. The student of prices can help to answer these questions.

Plan of the Book

The first section of this book is devoted to a review of the economic concepts that underlie price determination, particularly as they apply to agricultural commodities. This is followed by a section dealing with price variation and the linkage between prices at the retail, wholesale, and farm levels, at different points in time, and in different locations. The third section is devoted to a description and analysis of alternative pricing arrangements for agricultural commodities, such as commodity exchanges, auctions, pricing formulas, collective bargaining, and government-support programs. The final section provides an introduction to analytical methods and empirical studies of demand and supply relationships for agricultural commodities.

References

Breimyer, Harold F. 1962. "The Three Economies of Agriculture," *J. Farm Econ.*, 44:679–699.

Brewster, John M. 1950. "The Machine Process in Agriculture and Industry," *J. Farm Econ.*, 32:69–81.

Bowman, Mary Jean, and George L. Bach. 1946. *Economic Analysis and Public Policy.* New York: Prentice-Hall.

Collins, Norman R. 1959. "Changing Role of Price in Agricultural Marketing," *J. Farm Econ.*, 41:528–534.

Gray, Roger W. 1964. "Some Thoughts on the Changing Role of Price," *J. Farm Econ.*, 46:117–127.

Handy, C. R., and D. I. Padberg. 1971. "A Model of Competitive Behavior in Food Industries," *Am. J. Ag. Econ.*, 53:182–190.

Nikolitch, Radoje. 1970. *Our 31,000 Largest Farms.* Econ. Res. Ser., USDA, Ag. Econ. Report No. 175.

I

PRINCIPLES OF
PRICE DETERMINATION

Selected elements of the principles of price determination are reviewed in this section. In addition, some topics not ordinarily discussed in introductory economics courses are considered. Principles of demand theory and their application to the demand for agricultural products are discussed in Chapter 2, and elasticity and flexibility concepts are described in Chapter 3. Principles of supply theory with special reference to the supply of farm products are discussed in Chapter 4. Principles of demand and supply are combined in selected models of price determination in Chapter 5; models of particular interest in agricultural economics are stressed.

Demand for Agricultural Products

An objective of this chapter is to review elements of demand theory, relating these principles to the demand for agricultural commodities. An understanding of demand theory is essential, not only because it helps to explain price behavior, but also because it provides the framework for empirical studies of demand.

Logical Basis of Demand Theory [1]

The basic unit of demand theory is the individual consumer. Each consumer is confronted by a problem of choice. He has a large number of wants arising from basic needs (e.g., food and shelter), personal characteristics, and his social and physical environment. On the other hand, the consumer usually has a limited income. Thus, the problem is to choose the specific goods and services that "best" satisfy his wants within the limits imposed by income.

Economists usually define "best" in terms of the consumer's attempt to maximize utility (well-being). The utility approach to the theory of demand can be stated mathematically. This involves the maximization of a utility function subject to an income constraint. The theoretical concept of a utility function could be given empirical content *if* we knew the algebraic form and the coefficients of the function. Then, the classical mathematics of constrained optimization could be used to derive explicit demand relations for the

[1] This section presents an intuitive, rather than rigorous, argument. The student may wish to consult an intermediate price theory text for more detail and alternative approaches (e.g., Leftwich, 1966).

consumer. In practice, this is not done, and the utility function is used mainly as a conceptual device.

On the basis of such theory, we can conclude that a consumer tends to prefer more to less of a commodity but that he will buy more only at a lower price. That is, there is an inverse relationship between quantity demanded and price. Also, a number of useful, general theorems about relationships among elasticities have been derived from the idea of maximizing a utility function subject to a constraint. These topics are discussed in Chapter 3.

Consumer and Market Demand

Consumer demand is defined as the various quantities of a particular commodity which a consumer is willing and able to buy as the price of that commodity varies, with all other factors affecting demand held constant. The consumer demand relation can be described in two ways: as a table of prices and quantities (a demand schedule) and as a graph or algebraic function of prices and quantities (a demand curve). The demand relation simply defines the pure relationship between price and the quantity purchased per unit of time while holding other factors constant.

Price and quantity vary inversely; that is, the demand curve has a negative slope. This inverse relationship is sometimes called the law of demand, and it can be explained in terms of the substitution and income effects of a price change.

The substitution effect arises because consumers shift their purchases toward the relatively cheaper product as prices change. For example, if the price of broiler-chickens declines relative to beef, consumers tend to substitute broilers for beef.[2] Assuming that the consumer is maximizing utility or satisfaction, as relative prices change, he tends to substitute the relatively cheaper commodity for the more expensive to remain at the highest possible level of utility within the constraint of available income.

The income effect arises because a change in the price of one commodity, all other prices remaining constant, changes the con-

[2] There is an implicit assumption about the nature of the consumer's preferences in this statement. In particular, we assume the consumer is not satiated with chicken.

sumer's real income. A decrease in price increases the purchasing power of a given money income; an increase in price has the opposite effect. For example, at 10 cents per unit, 300 units of a commodity cost $30. A price decline of one cent (to 9 cents) per unit means that a consumer can buy the same 300 units for $27, a saving of $3. The consumer is clearly better off in the sense that he can buy the same 300 units and still have $3 to spend on other items. Stated another way, the consumer would be as well off with the price decline and a $3 reduction in his money income as he was with the original higher price and a higher income. With a fixed money income, changes in prices have the same effect as a change in real income.

 The substitution effect of a price change for a particular commodity is always negative (Wold and Jureen, 1953, p. 103). With an increase in price, the substitution effect is to decrease the quantity taken. The reverse is true for a decrease in price.

The income effect of a price change also is generally negative. An increase in price reduces real income, and hence with the usual positive relationship between quantity and income prevailing, quantity and price will move in opposite directions. An analogous statement can be made for a decrease in price.

There are a few commodities for which an inverse relationship between income and quantity exists. In these cases, a decrease in real income, resulting from an increase in price, will be associated with an increase in quantity purchased. That is, the income effect of a price change would move quantity in the same direction as the price change. If this income effect were greater than the substitution effect, then the quantity demanded would increase with an increase in price and vice versa. This is the rare case of Giffen's paradox or positively sloped demand relation.

Normally, however, the effect of a price change is to alter the quantity demanded in the opposite direction. Positively sloped demand relations are extremely rare.

Market demand is a generalization of the consumer demand concept. It is defined as the alternative quantities of a commodity which all consumers in a particular market are willing and able to buy as price varies and as all other factors are held constant. A market demand relation can be thought of as a summation of in-

dividual demand relations. A change in price results in changes
in the number of consumers buying as well as changes in the quantity purchased per person.

We will be concerned primarily with market demand relations.
This relationship may refer to the demand in a city, region, nation,
or other market area. Estimated demand relations for beef in the
United States in two time periods are illustrated in Figure 2-1.
Quantity is a function of price, but price is conventionally placed
on the vertical axis and quantity on the horizontal axis of diagrams
of demand (and supply) functions.

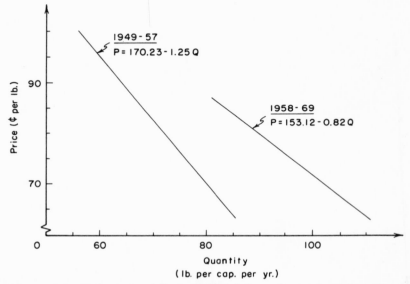

Figure 2-1. Estimated retail demand relations for beef, United States,
1949–1957 and 1958–1969. Estimated by the authors from annual data. The
estimates incorporate the revised retail price data available in 1970. The intercept coefficients are adjusted to reflect the average levels of per capita
disposable income in the two periods. The length of each relationship indicates the range of consumption in the two periods. The retail price of beef
is deflated by the Consumer Price Index (1957–59 = 100).

Static and Dynamic Aspects of Demand

The static concept of demand refers to movements along a demand curve; this is called change in the quantity demanded. It is
static in the sense that we are looking only at quantity response to

price and all other factors (e.g., incomes and the prices of competing products) are assumed constant. With the passage of time, however, other things do not remain constant. Thus, the strictly defined demand curve of economic theory describes the price-quantity alternatives at a moment in time with instantaneous quantity adjustments.

This, in turn, implies that consumers have perfect knowledge about price changes and act instantaneously and rationally on this knowledge. This definition does not allow consumer expectations about future changes in price to influence current purchases. Consumers would not be assumed to defer purchases, for instance, on the expectation that prices will be lower in the future.

The strictly defined, static concept of demand may seem somewhat artificial, but it is useful nevertheless. It isolates the logical relationship between quantity and price, and demand theory provides a logical method of classifying and thinking about forces other than price which influence demand. Hence, the purpose of the *ceteris paribus* assumption is methodological; the consequence of relaxing an assumption that a particular variable is held constant can be studied.

The term "dynamic" is used in two ways in demand theory. First, it may refer to changes in demand which are usually associated with changes in income, population, or other variables influencing demand and which occur with the passage of time. Second, it may refer to lags in adjustment. Quantity adjustments do not take place instantaneously because of imperfect knowledge, the time required to make changes, and so on. The concept of delayed adjustments associated with the passage of time leads to differentiating between short-run and long-run demand. The latter is sometimes defined as the quantity that will be purchased after sufficient time has been allowed for all adjustments to be completed.

Changes in Demand

It is important to distinguish between a change in quantity demanded and a change in demand (i.e., between movements along a demand curve and shifts in the level of the curve). The major factors influencing the level of demand may be grouped under four headings:

   (1) population size and its distribution by age, geographic area, etc.,
   (2) consumer income and its distribution,
   (3) prices and availability of other commodities and services,
   (4) consumer tastes and preferences.

These factors are sometimes called determinants of demand. As emphasized previously, these factors are assumed constant for a given level of a demand function, but with the passage of time, changes in demand are an important aspect of price changes.

Before discussing the specific effects of various determinants of demand, a distinction also needs to be made between simple or "parallel" shifts in the demand curve and "structural changes" in demand.[3] The difference in the concepts is most easily demonstrated by an example. For this purpose, we assume a simple demand equation in which quantity (Q) is a straight line function of its price (P) and of consumer income (Y).

$$Q = \alpha - \beta P + \gamma Y,$$

and α, β, and γ are parameters which indicate how the variables are related.

A graph (demand curve) of Q and P can be plotted for a fixed level of Y. If the level of Y changes, then the P-Q function shifts to a new level. This illustrates a parallel shift in the demand function. However, it is also possible that the parameters—α, β, and γ—may change; that is, the coefficients relating the variables may change. A change in one or more of the parameters is a structural change. In addition, a structural change may result in a change in the algebraic form of the equation, say from a straight line to a curve.

A demand curve assumes a given set of tastes and preferences. As long as tastes and preferences remain unchanged, relationships between price and income and quantity also remain unchanged (in the simplified case where these are the only relevant variables). For a consumer demand curve, the obvious source of a structural

---

[3] The term "parallel" is used in a loose way since demand relations need not be straight lines.

change is a change in consumer's tastes and preferences. The consumer's demand curves are, in theory, derived from his utility function. If the utility function changes, then the demand curves change. For a market demand curve, other sources of structural change include changes in the distribution of the determinants of demand (e.g., income) and the introduction of an entirely new commodity or group of commodities.

A simple shift in demand is illustrated in Figure 2-2. The estimated demand functions for beef suggest a structural change (Figure 2-1); of course, the level of the function also has shifted with increases in income. For simplicity of exposition, we will usually refer to both as a "change in demand" or a "shift in demand."

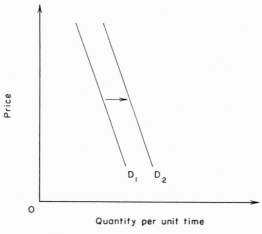

Figure 2-2.   A shift in demand

An increase in demand means that the demand curve has moved to the right (Figure 2-2). Consumers are willing to buy more of the commodity at the same price, or they are willing to buy the same quantity at a higher price. A decrease in demand (shift to the left) has the opposite effect.

Increases in demand both for food in the aggregate and for individual products are closely linked to the rate of population growth. The age distribution of the population also influences total demand as well as the demand for different commodities. A teen-age popu-

lation obviously consumes more calories than one made up of a
high proportion of persons over sixty-five. Baby food manufacturers
gain relative to those selling soft drinks during the early stages of a
population boom, but as the population grows older, suppliers of
the latter gain relative to the former. Changes in the regional distribution of the population or the proportion living in urban areas
likewise may influence the demand for certain types of food. For
instance, rural families tend to consume more milk than those living in urban areas. A shift in the demand for commodities such as
rice or pork also may occur as a result of changes in the racial
composition of the population.

For most agricultural commodities, income and demand are positively related; that is, an increase in income shifts demand to the
right. But for a few commodities the reverse is true. These are
called "inferior goods," not because of nutritional inadequacies, but
simply because consumers buy less as incomes rise. Bread and dry
beans are among the commodities for which demand is likely to
decline as incomes rise. Thus, in principle, the relationship between income and demand can range from positive through zero to
negative.

Changes in demand also can occur as a result of redistributing
income from the rich to the poor. It is possible to increase the demand for meat and citrus fruit by transferring income to families
near or below the poverty line without changing the total or average level of income. In most cases, very little of the marginal tax
dollar collected from upper-income families would have been used
for food, while a substantial proportion of the increase in income
going to lower-income families in the form of welfare payments or
"food stamps" is likely to be used to purchase more food or to up-
grade diets. However, an income redistribution scheme may reduce
the demand for certain farm products such as high-quality wines or
avocados.

In general, the quantity of a commodity (other than an inferior
product) purchased rises with increases in income, but at a decreasing rate. Total expenditures usually rise even more rapidly
because families shift to higher grades or buy foods with more
built-in services. The relationship between total income and the
quantity purchased or the amount spent on a particular food or

commodity group is sometimes referred to as an Engel curve.[4] Such curves are also called consumption functions; consumption, as measured by quantity or expenditure, is a function of income. An empirical relationship of this type is shown in Figure 2-3. Average per capita daily milk consumption for the U.S. population as a whole (based on a household survey conducted in 1965) rose from about 0.5 pounds for the lowest income group to approximately 0.8 pounds for the highest income group (Miller, 1970). Note that the level and the rate of increase was much greater for twelve- to fourteen-year-old males than for the population as a whole. Both relationships are curvilinear, and this is typical of most foods.

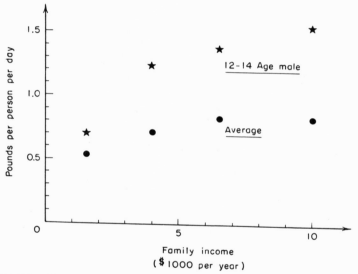

Figure 2-3. Consumption of milk and milk drinks by income groups, sample households, United States, one day in spring 1965. The observation on the highest income category represents the range $8,000 and over. Data from Robert R. Miller, "Milk Consumption by Age, Sex, and Income, Including Away-from-Home Use," Dairy Situation, DS-331 (July 1970), pp. 25–31.

[4] The German statistician Ernst Engel was among the first to undertake empirical studies of the proportion of income spent on food and other items such as clothing and housing as incomes rise (Burk, 1962). One relationship, which he observed, has persisted and has become known as Engel's law. Essentially, it states that as consumer incomes increase the proportion of income spent for food decreases. This implicitly assumes other things remain constant. With the passage of time, services are added to food; food prices change; and so forth.

Changes in tastes and preferences obviously contribute to shifts in the demand for agricultural commodities although their effects are often difficult to isolate because they appear to be associated with changes in income or other variables. For example, the demand for table wine seems to have risen markedly in the United States during recent years, but it is not clear whether this is the result of changes in tastes or income or both. Long-run trends in per capita consumption are sometimes used as an indicator of changes in preferences; however, such trends are not necessarily a reliable guide to shifts in demand. A downward trend in per capita consumption may simply reflect changes in per capita production. For instance, if growers produce fewer apples, per capita consumption will decline, regardless of what happens to demand. Thus, per capita consumption figures can reflect mainly the decisions of producers (i.e., shifts in supply with movements along a demand curve) rather than changes in demand.

The demand for each commodity is a function, not only of its own price, but of the prices of every other commodity and service. All prices, in theory at least, are linked together in an interdependent system. A change in the price of one commodity brings about shifts in the demand for other commodities. The direction of change in demand depends on the direction of change in the price of the related commodity and on whether the related commodity is a substitute or a complement. For substitutes, the change in the price of the substitute and the change in demand are usually positively related.[5] If, for instance, the price of beef decreases, then the demand for pork can be expected to decrease. Consumers tend to shift from pork to the relatively cheaper beef. Most agricultural products are substitutes, some much more so than others.

For complements, the change in the price of the related commodity and the change in demand are usually inversely related. Assuming cranberries and turkeys are complementary commodities, an increase in the price of turkeys would decrease the demand for cranberries. The price of turkeys and the quantity of cranberries move in opposite directions. While all prices in an economy

[5] We say "usually" because there are exceptions to the statement. For an explanation see the discussion of cross elasticities in Chapter 3.

are technically interrelated, some commodities can be treated as being independent. Presumably, there is no measurable influence on the demand for beef of a change in the price of cranberries.

An important shifter of demand for some agricultural products has been the development and introduction of new products. Artificial fibers have substituted for natural fibers such as cotton and wool. Detergents have tended to replace soap, which is produced from animal fats, thereby causing a decline in demand for this animal by-product. The demand for natural rubber and sugar also has been influenced by the development of synthetic products. On the other hand, the total demand for oranges used for processing has probably been increased by the development of frozen orange juice concentrate.

Speculative Demand

The reader perhaps has thought of demand concepts only in terms of demand by consumers for current use. Speculative demand represents a type of demand related to anticipated use and prices (relative to current prices). Since numerous agricultural products are produced seasonally but are consumed throughout the year, the concept of speculative demand is of particular interest to agricultural economists. Inventory holders, for example, provide the service of carrying stocks from harvest throughout the marketing season, and they are speculating, at least to some extent, that price will rise from harvest through the year by enough to provide them with a profit.[6]

A demand function can be interpreted as including both demand for current use and for speculative purposes. Assuming speculative demand is incorporated in the demand function, additional factors may contribute to shifts in demand (hence, to changes in prices). For instance, the prospect of a small crop for next year would increase speculative demand for current inventories. Crop prospects for substitutes, the expectation of war, and the possibility of a dock

[6] Inventory positions can be hedged through the use of futures contracts for some commodities (discussed in Chapters 12 and 13). This transfers risk to speculators who do not have physical control of the inventory. Also, inventories are carried for purposes other than speculation. Thus, one cannot classify all inventories as speculative positions.

strike, which would restrict imports and exports, are other examples of factors that could change speculative demand.

Speculation is sometimes viewed only as increasing the amplitude and frequency of price fluctuations. If an increase in speculative demand occurs, it is added to the demand for current use, and for a given supply, prices increase. If speculators' anticipations are *not* realized, then from an *ex post* viewpoint the price fluctuation was unnecessary. For example, commodity prices would be increased by a "war scare," and if war does not materialize, prices would subsequently decline. The price rise followed by a decline increased the amplitude of price change beyond what it would have been without the incorrect expectation.

However, speculation which correctly anticipates future events reduces the amplitude of price fluctuations. The purchase of stocks by warehousemen at harvest time increases price over the level that would otherwise have prevailed. Likewise, the sale of stocks during the year keeps prices below levels that would have prevailed with little or no inventory. Hence, the amplitude of the seasonal price pattern is reduced. In an analogous way, if speculators correctly anticipate a relatively small crop for the next crop year, then the carrying of additional inventory into the new year helps ameliorate the price effects of the small crop.

In sum, a demand function can shift with changes in speculative demand. Speculation that incorrectly anticipates future events may increase price variability, but speculation that correctly anticipates the future reduces price variability.

Lengths of Run in Demand Theory

We turn now to a second aspect of the dynamics of demand theory—namely, the concept of length of run. Simple, static theory assumes instantaneous adjustments to price changes. In the real world, however, there are a number of reasons why we do not expect instantaneous adjustments; the quantity demanded at a given price is likely to change gradually over time. The impediments to quick adjustments in the quantity demanded in response to a price change include such factors as imperfect knowledge, consumer uncertainty, technological and institutional barriers to changes in use, and rigidities in consumer habits.

The consumer cannot be expected to react to price changes of which he is not aware. Thus, lack of knowledge can prevent rapid adjustments. Uncertainty or anticipated changes in prices also may affect consumer behavior. If the consumer is uncertain about future price changes, purchases may be postponed or accelerated. If the price of an item falls, the consumer may even defer purchases anticipating a still further price decline. He may react in the opposite fashion if the price goes up.

Technological impediments cover several related ideas. Consumers tend to wear out durable goods before replacing them. A consumer is not likely to buy a new refrigerator simply on the basis of a price change if his current refrigerator is relatively new. This is a matter of stock or inventory adjustment.

A second type of technical impediment is the lack of complementary goods needed to take advantage of a relative price change. A farmer cannot instantaneously adjust the fuel used in his tractor in response to a price change; nor is a homeowner likely to change his furnace immediately to take advantage of price changes for various types of fuel.

In the short run, consumers' incomes are largely committed. They have installments due, rent, insurance premiums, electric and other utility bills to pay. Thus, the consumer's discretionary income (i.e., the income remaining after deducting all cash commitment including debt repayment) may be small, and he cannot take advantage of a price change. For example, a consumer may observe a decline in the price of carpeting, but he will not be able to act on this if he does not have the income or is not able to borrow at the moment to take advantage of the lower price. After some time lag, the consumer's discretionary income may increase and the purchase can be made.

Consumers may continue to make purchases on the basis of habit even though price has changed. The consumer habitually buys certain quantities of a commodity, and consequently he does not immediately respond to a price change. Houthakker and Taylor (1970, p. 62) report that food consumed in the home is subject to some habit formation but that habit wears off quite rapidly.

A distinction is made in demand theory between the "short run" and the "long run." The long run is usually defined as the time required for a complete quantity adjustment to occur in response to a "one-time" price change. The long-run time period corresponds to the adjustment period for each commodity, but since the time required for adjustment (because of the lags or impediments outlined above) is likely to vary among commodities, the long-run time period will necessarily differ for different items purchased by consumers. For example, the time required to complete the adjustment process is likely to be greater for durable goods which are purchased infrequently than for food items which are purchased daily or weekly.

The estimation of long-run demand relationships from empirical observations is difficult because prices and other factors affecting demand do not remain constant for a long enough period of time for the full effects of a given combination of variables to work themselves out. Further changes in prices or other variables are likely to occur before the adjustment to the initial price change is completed.

The short-run demand schedule is simply a "snapshot" of demand at a given point in time, before complete adjustment has occurred. Since the short run may refer to any time period of shorter duration than the one required for full adjustment to occur, it cannot be uniquely defined.

Pasour and Schrimper (1965) suggest that adjustments in the very short run should be distinguished from those that occur over a longer period of time for commodities that can be stored. In the very short run, the response to a price decrease may be somewhat greater than in the intermediate run simply because some buyers are willing to purchase a commodity in order to hold it for speculative or other purposes (as discussed in the previous section). The demand for use may change very little, but when the demand for storage is superimposed on the demand for use, the response to a short-run price change may be substantial. The housewife, for example, may buy additional cuts of meat to place in the freezer if the local supermarket announces a "special" on beef. Thus, in the very short run, storage demand must be considered in addition to purchases for consumption, while in the long run, demand will be determined almost entirely by use. During the intervening period, the response to price changes may be very difficult to predict because of the possible liquidation of stocks previously acquired.

Concept of a Distributed Lag

The idea of a delayed adjustment to a price change leads rather naturally to the concept of a distributed lag. The lapse of time between a cause and its effect is called a lag. In demand theory, the price change is specified as the "cause" and the quantity change as the "effect." The effect is likely to be spread through time rather than occurring instantaneously at a point in time. Hence, the term distributed lag arises from a delayed response which is spread over time.

Given a change in the causal variable (e.g., price), there are many alternative paths of adjustment that the other variable (quantity demanded) might follow through time. A simple adjustment path for quantity response to a price change is depicted in upper Figure 2-4. In this example, adjustment is assumed to follow a smooth, geometric path. Alternatively, there may be a large initial adjustment followed by a lower rate of adjustment as shown in lower Figure 2-4. One of the problems of empirical analysis is that many alternative paths of adjustment are theoretically possible. The price analyst has little basis on which to select one in preference to another unless special knowledge is available about the product.

Nonetheless, econometric models have been developed to estimate economic relationships for which distributed lags are thought to exist (Nerlove, 1958; Tomek and Cochrane, 1962). Their intent is to take account of possible lagged responses in economic relationships. Distributed lag models often, though not always, assume a geometric form for the lag (as in upper Figure 2-4). In empirical work, distributed lag models have been used more frequently in estimating supply relations in agriculture than demand relations.

Derived Demand

The ultimate consumer is the one who determines the shape and position of the demand function. For this reason, consumer demand relationships are often referred to as "primary demand." In empirical analysis, retail price and quantity data are customarily used to determine primary demand relationships.

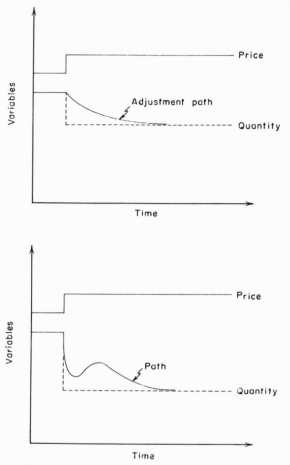

Figure 2-4.   Examples of a lagged quantity adjustment to a price change

The term "derived demand" is used to denote demand schedules for inputs which are used to produce the final products. Corn, for example, is an important input in the livestock industry, while wheat is used to make a variety of bakery goods. Thus, the demand for wheat and corn is derived from the demand for end products. Similarly, one can say that the demand for soybeans is derived from the demand for soybean meal and soybean oil, the major products produced from crushing soybeans. Demand schedules for inputs such as labor and land, likewise, can be derived indirectly from the demand for commodities which are produced with these inputs.

The term "derived demand" may be extended to most wholesale- or farm-level demand functions. Derived demand differs from primary demand by the amount of marketing and processing charges per unit of product. The demand for meat animals at the farm, for example, is based on the retail-level demand function for meat minus marketing costs such as slaughtering, processing, and transporting meat. The concept of derived demand can be carried even further. For example, the demand for feeder calves on the part of feed-lot operators is ultimately derived from the retail-level demand for beef.

A derived demand curve can change either because the primary demand curve shifts or because marketing margins change. Empirically, derived demand relationships can be estimated, either indirectly by subtracting appropriate margins from the primary demand schedule, or directly by using price and quantity data which apply to the appropriate stage of marketing (e.g., wholesale prices and quantities can be used to approximate the derived demand at an intermediate level, while farm prices and sales data may be used to estimate the demand curve confronting producers). The relationship between primary and derived functions is discussed more fully in Chapter 6.

References

Burk, Marguerite C. 1962. "Ramifications of the Relationship between Income and Food," *J. Farm Econ.*, 44:115–125.

Houthakker, H. S., and L. D. Taylor. 1970. *Consumer Demand in the United States: Analyses and Projections*. 2d ed. Cambridge, Mass.: Harvard Univ. Press.

Leftwich, Richard H. 1966. *The Price System and Resource Allocation*. 3d ed. New York: Holt, Rinehart and Winston. Chapters 4 and 5.

Miller, Robert R. 1970. "Milk Consumption by Age, Sex, and Income, Including Away-from-Home Use," *Dairy Situation*. Econ. Res. Ser., USDA, DS-331 (July). Pp. 25–31.

Nerlove, Marc. 1958. *Distributed Lags and Demand Analysis*. USDA Ag. Hb. 141. Pp. 1–20.

Pasour, E. C., and R. A. Schrimper. 1965. "The Effect of Length of Run on Measured Demand Elasticities," *J. Farm Econ.*, 47:774–788.

Tomek, William G., and Willard W. Cochrane. 1962. "Long-Run Demand: A Concept, and Elasticity Estimates for Meats," *J. Farm Econ.*, 44:717–730.

Wold, Herman, and Lars Jureen. 1953. *Demand Analysis*. New York: John Wiley and Sons. Chapter 5.

CHAPTER 3

Demand Elasticities
and Related Coefficients

One objective of this chapter is to review the concepts of own-price, cross-price, and income elasticities of demand. Interrelationships among these coefficients as implied by theory are described. In addition, the relationship between own-price elasticities at different market levels is discussed. Two additional concepts, total elasticity and price flexibility, are introduced.

Price Elasticity

Definition

The concept of a demand schedule or a demand curve has been defined. It provides a description of the relationship between price and the quantity buyers are willing and able to buy, other factors remaining constant. Price theory suggests an inverse relationship between price and quantity, but the inverse relationship by itself says nothing about the responsiveness of quantity demanded to a price change for a commodity. This responsiveness is likely to vary from commodity to commodity.

An explicit demand curve is defined by its algebraic equation, assuming it is known. The quantity variable is normally expressed in physical units while price is expressed in monetary terms per physical unit. But since different units of measurement are often employed (bushels, pounds, kilograms), it is difficult to make direct comparisons from algebraic equations of the impact which a given change in price will have on different commodities. To facilitate comparisons, economists frequently make use of percentage relationships which are independent of the size of units used to measure price and quantity. The most common of these relationships is the concept of own-price elasticity of demand. This is simply a ratio which expresses the percentage change in quantity associated with a given percentage change in price.

Price elasticity is defined for a point on the demand curve, and hence for most demand curves the magnitude of the elasticity coefficient varies along the curve. Let Δ equal a very small change, then a mathematical definition of price elasticity is

$$E_P = \frac{\frac{\Delta Q}{Q}}{\frac{\Delta P}{P}} = \left(\frac{\Delta Q}{\Delta P}\right)\left(\frac{P}{Q}\right) .^{1}$$

An alternative equation for defining price elasticity is the arc formula

$$E_P = \frac{\frac{Q_0 - Q_1}{Q_0 + Q_1}}{\frac{P_0 - P_1}{P_0 + P_1}} = \left(\frac{Q_0 - Q_1}{Q_0 + Q_1}\right)\left(\frac{P_0 + P_1}{P_0 - P_1}\right).$$

The subscripts represent two different points on a demand curve. The arc equation is mainly a device for computing an elasticity at an average between the two points—not the average of the elasticities on the arc between the points. The smaller the arc or segment the more nearly the elasticities computed from the arc and point formulas approach each other. Remember, elasticity is strictly defined only with respect to a particular point.

Interpretation

The own-price elasticity-of-demand coefficient for any commodity can be interpreted as the percentage change in quantity de-

[1] If the demand function is written as $Q = f(P)$, then the slope of the function is dQ/dP, and the price elasticity at a point $(\overline{Q}, \overline{P})$ is $E_p = \frac{dQ}{dP}\left(\frac{\overline{P}}{\overline{Q}}\right)$. Since graphs of demand functions have price on the vertical axis, the equation may be written $P = f(Q)$. In this case, the slope is dP/dQ, and $E_p = \frac{1}{dP/dQ}\left(\frac{\overline{P}}{\overline{Q}}\right)$.

⟡manded given a very small percentage change in the price of that commodity, other factors held constant. A convenient way to think of a price elasticity is as the percentage change in quantity corresponding to a one per cent change in price. Since the slopes of demand curves are negative, price-elasticity-of-demand coefficients have a negative sign.

The range of the price-elasticity coefficient is from zero to minus infinity. This range is traditionally divided into three parts. (1) If the absolute value (neglecting sign) of the coefficient is greater than one, demand is said to be *elastic*. The percentage change in quantity demanded is greater than the corresponding percentage change in price. The limiting case is the horizontal demand curve —demand is perfectly elastic (coefficient is infinite). (2) If the absolute value of the coefficient is less than one, demand is *inelastic*. The percentage change in quantity is less than the corresponding percentage change in price. Quantity demanded is relatively unresponsive to price changes. The limiting case is an elasticity of zero—demand is perfectly inelastic. (3) A coefficient of -1 represents the case of *unitary elasticity*. The percentage change in quantity equals the percentage change in price.

The elasticity coefficient varies along the demand curve for most functional forms of the curve. If a straight-line demand function is extended to the two axes, the elasticity varies from infinity on the price axis through various (negative) values to zero at the point on the quantity axis. This may be verified by referring to the definition of price elasticity (point equation) and noting that price is zero when the demand function intersects the quantity axis and that quantity is zero when the function intersects the price axis. A few special cases exist where the elasticity is a constant over the range of the curve. These cases include a straight horizontal line, a straight vertical line, a power function, and a rectangular hyperbola.[2]

Since in general the elasticity coefficient varies in magnitude along the demand curve, it is not technically correct to say that the demand for a commodity is elastic or inelastic. Demand is elastic (or inelastic) only within some range of prices. However, it is con-

[2] Letting $Q =$ quantity demanded and $P =$ price, the power function is $Q = \alpha \, P^\beta$. A rectangular or equilateral hyperbola is $QP = \beta$, or $Q = \beta \, (1/P)$; in this case $E = -1$.

venient to categorize and speak of the demand for a commodity as being either elastic or inelastic. This shorthand reference should be interpreted as referring to the elasticity within the *usual* range of prices. In making empirical estimates, a common procedure is to compute the elasticity at the mean of the observations.

Price Elasticities and Total Revenue

Total revenue is defined as price multiplied by quantity; it has two components. Since these two components are inversely related, it is not obvious how changes in price will influence total revenue. For example, the question whether a given percentage increase in price will increase or decrease total revenue depends on the magnitude of the corresponding percentage change in quantity. The question is answered by the magnitude of the price-elasticity-of-demand coefficient.

If demand is elastic in the relevant range of prices, then price and total revenue vary inversely. A price increase will decrease total revenue, and a price decrease will increase total revenue. This follows from the definition of an elastic demand, which means that the percentage change in quantity demanded is greater than the percentage change in price. A decrease in price, for example, results in a more than offsetting percentage increase in quantity taken. Hence, total revenue increases as price decreases. However, it does not follow that total revenue will increase indefinitely as price decreases. At some point, price would presumably move into an inelastic range of the demand relation.

If demand is inelastic in the relevant range of prices, then price and total revenue vary directly. A price increase will increase total revenue and vice versa. The reader should reason out why this is true based on the definition of an inelastic demand.

The price elasticity of demand for hogs at the farm level in the United States is estimated to be about −0.5 (inelastic). Thus, other things being equal, we would expect farm price and total revenue to vary directly. When hog production increases and consequently prices decline, total revenue falls. In 1968, for example, 21.1 billion pounds of hogs were produced and cash receipts were $3.8 billion. The next year hog production declined to 20.4 billion pounds but cash receipts increased to $4.5 billion. Since the demand for pork is not constant from one year to the next and since the elasticity of -0.5 relates to a point on the demand function, the change in revenue cannot be entirely related to a particular elasticity. Nonetheless, the example suggests the approximate effect of volume changes on total revenue for a commodity with an inelastic demand, and it is a phenomenon common to many agricultural commodities. This was recognized at least as early as 1915 when Henry A. Wallace wrote, "The Demand Laws . . . indicate to me that the farming class as a whole is penalized for over-production and rewarded for under-production" (as cited in Stigler, 1962, p. 17).

Farm policy measures which attempt to limit supply assume that the demand for the commodity is inelastic. Otherwise, reducing volume would lower the total revenue received by farmers. Also, reducing production reduces total costs.

The price elasticity concept measures responsiveness *along* a demand curve. This, of course, is implicit in the discussion of elasticities and total revenue. If, for example, demand increases, then total revenue and quantity may increase even though demand is inelastic. This is a function of the shift in demand and not of the elasticity of one demand relation. The effect of an increasing demand for apples on the total value of apple production in the United States is illustrated in Figure 3-1. The size of crop and value of the crop are inversely related within a period of a few years, but with the passage of time, the value of a given size crop has increased.

Income Elasticity

Income elasticity of demand is a measure of the responsiveness of quantity to changes in income, other factors held constant. The income-quantity relationship, of course, can be expressed algebraically. This relation is sometimes called a consumption, or Engel, function. The income elasticity is defined at a point on the function and typically varies along the range of the curve. The income elasticity for food in the aggregate, as well as for many individual food products, is thought to decrease as incomes increase. Some empirical evidence exists to support this hypothesis (Goreux, 1960; Rock-

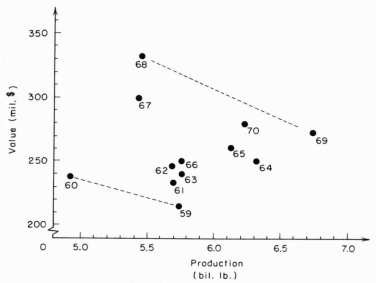

Figure 3-1. Apples: Production and value of production, United States, 1959–1970. Data from Statistical Reporting Service, *Fruits Noncitrus by States, 1959–64, Production, Use, Value,* USDA Stat. Bul. No. 407, 1967 and subsequent annual supplements.

well, 1959), and an illustration is given in Figure 3-2.[3] Purcell and Raunikar (1967) found that income elasticities for some foods declined while for other cases income elasticities remained constant over the range of income between \$3,000 and \$10,000 per year per household.

Let Y represent income, then the definition of income elasticity at a point is

$$E_Y = \frac{\frac{\Delta Q}{Q}}{\frac{\Delta Y}{Y}} = \left(\frac{\Delta Q}{\Delta Y}\right)\left(\frac{Y}{Q}\right).$$

It may be interpreted as the percentage change in quantity corresponding to a one per cent change in income, other factors held constant.

[3] This implies that, in empirical analyses, the consumption function for foods should be in a form that permits a declining income elasticity as income increases (for further discussion see Leser, 1963).

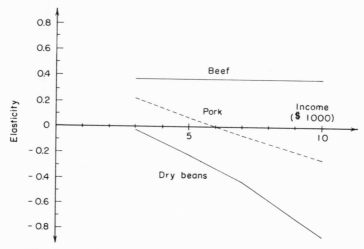

Figure 3-2. Estimated income elasticities as related to level of household income per year for selected foods, Atlanta consumer panel, 1958–1962. Data from J. C. Purcell and Robert Raunikar, "Quantity-Income Elasticities for Foods by Level of Income," *J. Farm Econ.,* 41:1410–1414, Dec. 1967.

In most cases, the coefficient is positive. This is consistent with the idea that as income increases a consumer buys more of most products and when income decreases the opposite occurs. There are a few commodities which have negative income elasticities in the usual range of incomes. As indicated above, a commodity may have a positive income elasticity over some range of incomes and a negative elasticity over larger incomes. Since income elasticities are used in making demand projections (i.e., to estimate the impact of increasing income on the demands for specific commodities) and since the elasticity itself can change as incomes increase, the researcher must exercise great caution in making projections using a single coefficient.

In empirical analyses, "income elasticities" are sometimes estimated from observations on expenditures rather than observations on physical quantities and on incomes. Expenditure on a particular commodity is made a function of total expenditures. Observations on income obtained in sample surveys often contain errors and do not correspond to the economic concept of income. For instance, evidence exists that income earned by household members other than the respondent in the survey is frequently overlooked. Also, observations on expenditures are sometimes more easily obtained than observations on physical quantities. This elasticity represents the percentage response of expenditure on an individual commodity to a one per cent change in total expenditures. Occasionally, individual expenditure is made a function of household income. Coefficients which measure the responsiveness of expenditures to a change in income (total expenditure or other measure) are sometimes called expenditure elasticities. These elasticities generally are larger than those based on physical quantities. Expenditures are usually more responsive than quantities to changes in income. This is reasonable since consumers with higher incomes probably buy higher-quality items (hence higher-priced items) as well as larger quantities. Thus, the expenditure change in response to an income change includes a price effect due to quality as well as the quantity effect (Klein, 1962).

Cross Elasticity

Cross-price elasticities of demand are measures of how the quantity purchased of one commodity responds to changes in the price of another commodity. More precisely, the cross elasticity of commodity i with respect to commodity j is defined as

$$E_{ij} = \frac{\frac{\Delta Q_i}{Q_i}}{\frac{\Delta P_j}{P_j}} = \left(\frac{\Delta Q_i}{\Delta P_j} \right) \left(\frac{P_j}{Q_i} \right).$$

This may be interpreted as the percentage change in the quantity of i given a one per cent change in the price of j, other factors held constant.

In practice, three types of cross-relationships can be identified: the commodities may be substitutes, complements, or independent. The definition of the three types of relationships is based on the *substitution effect* of the price change of j (see Kuhlman and Thompson, 1965).

The substitution effect is positive for substitute commodities; the price of j and the quantity of i move in the same direction. If the price of j increases, then consumers tend to substitute i for j. If the price of j decreases, then consumers tend to substitute the relatively cheaper j for i. In both cases, there is a positive relationship between the price of j and the quantity of i.

The substitution effect is negative for complementary commodities; i.e., the price of j and the quantity i move in opposite directions. An increase in the price of j means that the quantity demanded of j decreases and hence the quantity of the complementary commodity i also decreases. A similar argument can be made for a decrease in the price of j, and in both cases there is a negative relationship between the price of j and the quantity of i.

The substitution effect is zero for independent commodities. Independence means that no substitution or complementary relationship exists between the two commodities.

On the basis of the reasoning outlined above, economists generally say that substitute commodities have positive cross elasticities; complementary commodities have negative cross elasticities; and independent commodities have zero cross elasticities. However, from a technical mathematical viewpoint, these generalizations need not be true. There is also the *income effect* of the price change for j. The income effect on the demand for i is generally, but not always, negative for cross elasticities. A decrease in price increases real income and hence tends to increase quantities purchased. An increase in price decreases real income and tends to decrease quantity.

The income effect may "outweigh" the substitution effect resulting in a net reduction in the demand for commodity i when the price of commodity j increases. Consumers will normally substitute i for j if the price of j increases; but an increase in the price of j is equivalent to a reduction in real income. This will adversely affect consumption of both i and j. Thus, the real income effect on consumption of i will be negative, while the substitution effect will be positive. If the former exceeds the latter, the net effect may be negative even though the two commodities are substitutes.

The income effect usually tends to reinforce the substitution effect for complementary commodities. However, two commodities could be independent from the viewpoint of substitution and still have a negative cross elasticity from the income effect of the price change. The interpretation of cross elasticities is further complicated by the fact that the income effect is not always inversely related to price. There are inferior commodities, which means some commodities have negative income elasticities. This implies a positive income effect which would reinforce or add to the substitution effect for some commodities.

The importance of the income effect depends on the size of expenditure on the commodity relative to total expenditures. Typically, the expenditure on one commodity is a small fraction of total expenditures, and hence the income effect usually does not "outweigh" the substitution effect. Thus, the generalizations economists make about the signs of cross elasticities usually hold, that is, a positive cross elasticity implies that the commodities are substitutes while a negative cross elasticity implies the commodities are complements; and a coefficient near or equal to zero implies the commodities are independent.

Butter and margarine are examples of substitute commodities. Hot dogs and buns are complementary. In practice, economists have found the measurement of cross elasticities very difficult. Substitution relationships have been somewhat easier to identify than complementary relationships.

Reversing the commodities in the cross-elasticity equation does not necessarily give the same coefficient. The cross elasticity of sugar with respect to coffee probably is not the same as the cross elasticity of coffee with respect to sugar. A change in the price of coffee is likely to have a modest influence on the use of sugar, but a change in the price of sugar probably will have very little influence on the use of coffee.

The explicit relationship between cross elasticities can be spelled out mathematically. The substitution effect (whether for complements or substitutes) is symmetric, but the income effect is not. The exact relationship is given in the next section.

Relationships among Elasticities

Consumer Demand

A great deal of effort has been devoted in recent years to the implications of demand theory for relationships among elasticities and to the application of these concepts to the estimation of elasticities for food products (Brandow, 1961; George and King, 1971; Wetmore, et al., 1959; Wold and Jureen, 1953). The important relationships include the homogeneity condition, the Slutsky condition, and the Engel aggregation condition; each of these conditions is discussed in this section.

The theory from which these interrelationships are derived makes certain assumptions regarding individual consumer behavior. Thus, the elasticity conditions hold for an individual consumer with a given utility function, which satisfies certain assumptions including the assumption that the individual's tastes and preferences are in some sense reasonable.[4]

While the theory has been developed in terms of the individual consumer, the empirical uses of the elasticity conditions have been for market (aggregate) elasticities. A limited number of studies, such as one by Barten (1967), seem to justify this type of extended application. In any case, the elasticity conditions provide a theoretical basis for the intuitive arguments about differences in elasticities for different products.

Homogeneity condition. Equation (1) states that the sum of the own- and cross-price elasticities and the income elasticity for a particular commodity is, taking account of signs, zero.

(1) $E_{ii} + E_{i1} + E_{i2} + \ldots + E_{iy} = 0,$

where $E_{ii} =$ own- (or direct-) price elasticity

$\begin{matrix} E_{i1} \\ E_{i2} \end{matrix} =$ cross-price elasticities

.

.

.

$E_{iy} =$ income elasticity.

[4] To be precise, the axioms must be stated in mathematical terms, and this is not within the scope of this book. Roughly, the consumer is assumed to be able to rank commodity bundles in an order of preference and the ranking must avoid ambiguity and be consistent (transitivity). Moreover, the consumer is assumed not satiated and prefers more to less. A further assumption is required about the nature of the utility function to assure that the usual conditions for a constrained maximum (from the calculus) are necessary and sufficient. The reader may refer to George and King (1971, pp. 33 ff.) or to Wold

Wold (1953) calls this equation the Slutsky-Schultz relation; it has also been called the row constraint.

The meaning of the homogeneity condition is that the substitution effect and the income effect of an own-price change must be consistent with the cross and income elasticities for the commodity. A large income elasticity tends to imply a large (in absolute value) own-price elasticity. A large number of substitutes (hence a large number of significant cross elasticities) and/or some very close substitutes (implying large positive cross elasticities) also suggests a relatively large own-price elasticity for the commodity.

The relation is illustrated using estimated retail-level elasticities for beef (Brandow, 1961, p. 17).

own-price elasticity	-0.95
cross-price with veal	0.06
cross-price with pork	0.10
cross-price with lamb	0.04
cross-price with chicken	0.07
all other cross elasticities	0.21
income elasticity	0.47
sum	0

Economists argue that commodities with many substitutes or some close substitutes have price elastic demands. This is implied in equation (1) which says that if E_{i1}, E_{i2}, etc. are collectively large and positive then E_{ii} must be large and negative (i.e., elastic). Viewed in another way, the sum of the cross elasticities is equal to the difference between the price and income elasticity (assuming income elasticity is positive and price elasticity is negative). If this difference is small, then the "cross effects" are collectively small. This suggests few substitutes. If the difference is large, then the reverse reasoning would apply. Thus, given information on the own-price and income elasticities for a commodity, some inferences can be made about the cross elasticities.

The commodity salt has commonly been used as an example of

---

and Jureen (1953, esp. pp. 82 f). The George and King reference provides a recent summary of the literature.

product with an inelastic demand. The intuitive argument is that it has few substitutes and it constitutes a very small proportion of a consumer's total expenditures. From equation (1), we can observe that if the cross elasticities and income elasticities are near zero, then the own-price elasticity will also be near zero (i.e., inelastic).

The homogeneity condition combined with two reasonable assumptions suggests that the absolute value of the own-price elasticity is likely to be greater than the values of the cross-price elasticities. The assumptions are (1) that the income elasticity is positive and (2) that most of the cross relationships are substitute relations and hence the cross elasticities are mostly positive numbers. Consequently, for the sum of the elasticities to be zero, the commodity's own-price elasticity must be large relative to the cross elasticities and negative.

The homogeneity condition also can be used to set a lower limit on the price elasticity and an upper limit on the income elasticity. We again use the reasonable assumption that the sum of the cross elasticities is positive and that the lower limit of this sum is zero. If the sum of the cross elasticities were about zero, then $|E_{ii}| \approx |E_{iy}|$. If the sum of the cross elasticities were positive, then the price elasticity would be larger (in absolute value) than the income elasticity. Thus, the magnitude of the income elasticity tends to set the lower limit of the own-price elasticity. In a similar way, we can argue that the price elasticity, if known, sets an upper limit for the commodity's income elasticity.

For example, suppose previous research indicates that the income elasticity for food grains in India is 0.7, then the price elasticity of demand is implied to be at least -0.7 and because of substitutes is probably slightly higher. Thus, the estimate of one elasticity can provide a general guide to another elasticity.

Slutsky condition. Equation (2) specifies the relationship between the cross elasticities E_{ij} and E_{ji}. Namely,

$$(2) \qquad E_{ij} = \frac{R_j}{R_i} E_{ji} + R_j \left(E_{jy} - E_{iy} \right),$$

where R_i = expenditure on i as a proportion of total expenditures

$R_j =$ expenditure on j as a proportion of total expenditures

$E_{ij}, E_{ji} =$ cross elasticities

$E_{iy}, E_{jy} =$ income elasticities.

This is also called the symmetry relation.

Assuming (1) that the consumer's expenditure on commodity j is a small fraction of total income and/or (2) that the income elasticities for the two commodities are approximately equal, then

$$(2')\qquad E_{ij} \approx \frac{R_j}{R_i}\ E_{ji}.$$

This relation has been called the Hotelling-Jureen relation; it is an approximation of the Slutsky relation.

The Slutsky (or Hotelling-Jureen) relation indicates how cross elasticities are related. If E_{ij} is known, then E_{ji} can be estimated and vice versa. This relation has also been used in applied research in combination with another restriction to place a limit on the maximum admissible values for cross elasticities (Wetmore, *et al.*, 1959, p. 69). This is of interest because cross elasticities have proven difficult to estimate directly from available data. Thus, economists have attempted to combine estimates of a few elasticities with their knowledge of interrelationship among elasticities to infer estimates of other elasticities.

The substitution effect of a price change is in a sense symmetric, but the income effect is not.[5] The income effect of a price change

[5] The "absolute" response of the quantity of i to a price change in j is defined by the partial derivative $\partial Q_i/\partial P_j$. This partial derivative can be divided into the substitution effect and the income effect.

$$\frac{\partial Q_i}{\partial P_j} = K_{ij} - Q_j\ \frac{\partial Q_i}{\partial Y},$$

where $K_{ij} =$ substitution effect

$Y =$ income, and the last term defines the income effect. The partial derivative $\dfrac{\partial Q_j}{\partial P_i}$ can be partitioned in an analogous way. The symmetry is between the substitution effect components of the two partial derivatives. Namely,

$$K_{ij} = K_{ji};$$

and this implies

$$\frac{\partial Q_i}{\partial P_j} + Q_j\ \frac{\partial Q_i}{\partial Y} = \frac{\partial Q_j}{\partial P_i} + Q_i\ \frac{\partial Q_j}{\partial Y}.$$

will be larger for the commodity which takes a larger proportion of total expenditures. We know, for example, that a much smaller proportion of the average consumer's income is spent on lamb than on beef in the United States. Thus, a one per cent change in the price of lamb has much less effect on the consumption of beef (smaller cross elasticity) than the reverse.

Assuming the average consumer spends 2 per cent of total expenditures on beef (b) and 0.1 per cent on lamb (a) and assuming the cross elasticity of lamb with respect to beef (E_{ab}) is 0.6, then from equation ($2'$)

$$E_{ba} \approx \frac{R_a}{R_b} \ E_{ab} = \left(\frac{.001}{.02}\right)(.6) = (.05)\ (.6) = .03.$$

With the assumed conditions, a one per cent change in the price of lamb will result in only a 0.03 per cent change in the consumption of beef. This is true even though a one per cent change in the price of beef will result in a 0.6 per cent change in the consumption of lamb.

Engel aggregation condition. Equation (3) states that the weighted sum of the income elasticities for all items in a consumer's budget is one. The weights are the expenditures on the respective commodities as a proportion of total expenditures (the R_i's). The equation for n items is

(3) $R_1 E_{1y} + R_2 E_{2y} + \ldots + R_n E_{ny} = 1.$

The readers should not interpret relation (3) as meaning that all income elasticities need to be small. The weights are fractions (less than one). A hypothetical example for three commodities with assumed elasticities of 5, 1, and 0.2 illustrates the point:

$$\begin{array}{ccccc} (.1)\ (5) & + & (.4)\ (1) & + & (.5)\ (.2) = \\ .5 & + & .4 & + & .1 \quad\quad = 1.0. \end{array}$$

Wetmore (1959) describes a method of estimating cross elasticities for food groups when estimates of own-price elasticities and the expenditures on each food group as a proportion of total expenditures on food are available. The own-price elasticities are the diagonal coefficients in Table 3-1, and the expenditure proportions are shown in the last column of this table. The sum of any row of elasticities in Table 3-1, excepting the "all foods" column, which is the sum, represents the net percentage change in quantity of the product group heading the row (e.g., meat) resulting from a one per cent change in all food prices. Thus, the weighted average of the row sums is the price elasticity of demand for all food, which is given as -0.2 (Wetmore, *et al.*, 1959, p. 68). Consequently, the admissible values for the cross elasticities (the off-diagonal elements of Table 3-1, which were unknown) are restricted to those which combined with the known own-price elasticities give row sums whose weighted average is -0.2.[6]

Table 3-1. Own-price and cross-price elasticities for six food groups in the United States, 1957

Demand for	Effect of one per cent change in the price of							
	Meat	Dairy products	Eggs	Fruits	Vege-tables	Other	All foods *	R
Meat	$-.60$	.10	.04	.08	.06	.03	$-.29$	.363 †
Dairy products	.21	$-.50$	.02	0	.06	.03	$-.18$	.171
Eggs	.29	.08	$-.58$	0	0	.05	$-.16$	.045
Fruits	.33	0	0	-1.00	.20	.03	$-.44$	.088
Vegetables	.22	.10	0	.18	$-.70$	.02	$-.18$	.098
Other	.05	.02	.01	.01	.01	$-.10$	0	.235

Source: John M. Wetmore *et al., Policies for Expanding the Demand for Farm Food Products in the United States,* Part I: *History and Potentials,* Univ. of Minn. Tech. Bull. 231 (April 1959), p. 71, table 18.
* This column contains the sum of the elasticities in each row. The weighted average of the column equals -0.2, the assumed price elasticity for all food.
† R is the proportion of total food expenditures spent on each group. The sum is 1.0.

[6] Another condition used in applied research (e.g., Brandow, 1961) is the Cournot aggregation or column restriction. If a column of price elasticities is viewed as containing the price elasticity of the ith commodity and the cross elasticities of the response of all other commodities to a price change of i, then the restriction states that the expenditure weighted sum of any ith column of the complete set of price elasticities equals the negative expenditure weight of the ith column. For commodity 1 (column 1), this restriction is

$$R_1 E_{11} + R_2 E_{21} + \ldots + R_n E_{n1} = -R_1.$$

Three additional restrictions were used. (1) The cross elasticities are assumed to be nonnegative, that is, zero or positive. This is reasonable since the analysis is restricted to food groups which are presumably substitutes. (2) The sum of the cross elasticities for a specific group (say, meat) may not exceed the absolute value of the own-price elasticity (in the case of meat, -0.6). This means that the sum of the own-price elasticity and the cross elasticities for, say, meat must be zero or negative. It also follows from restriction (1) that none of the individual cross elasticities may exceed the absolute value of the own-price elasticity for the commodity group. (3) The cross elasticities are assumed to be interrelated as specified by the Hotelling-Jureen conditions (equation 2'). This equation in effect reduces the unknowns by one-half and helps place maximum admissible limits on the cross elasticities.

These restrictions limit the number of admissible sets of cross elasticities, but they do not provide a rigorous mathematical means of computing the cross elasticities. Restriction (1) provides the minimum values which may be taken by the cross elasticities (zero). Restrictions (2) and (3) help determine maximum admissible values. However, the final specification of cross elasticities is based on the judgments of the analysts. The final outcome of such a procedure is illustrated in Table 3-1.

Since the Wetmore study was published in 1959, contributions in demand theory have provided additional conceptual bases for computing a complete set (matrix) of elasticities.[7] Frisch's (1959) concept of "want independence" gives a base for computing cross-price elasticities given estimates of income and own-price elasticities and expenditure weights as well as some assumptions about utility functions. Related concepts such as separability in the utility function also help provide a basis for reducing the number of demand coefficients to be estimated directly from data. Exposition of these ideas, however, requires substantial mathematics and is beyond the scope of this book (see George and King, 1971, pp. 20–38, 143–152).

[7] In an economy with n goods, there will be n price elasticities for each commodity plus an income elasticity. This gives $n(n+1)$ total elasticities to be estimated. The symmetry condition, the homogeneity condition, and the Engel aggregation provide restrictions that reduce the elasticities to be estimated to $\frac{1}{2}(n^2 + n - 2)$, still a large number (George and King, 1971).

Derived Demand

Relationships between price elasticities of demand for primary and derived demand relations for the same commodity are discussed in this section. This discussion is applicable to market demand relations. The idea of derived demand is broadly interpreted to include the relationships (1) between elasticities at various market levels and (2) between elasticities for joint products and the commodity from which they are derived.

Market levels. In empirical work, it is sometimes difficult to estimate directly price elasticities of demand for a product at different points in the marketing chain, and the elasticities are likely to be different at the retail than at the farm level. It is possible, however, provided knowledge of marketing margins and of the elasticity at one level (say, at retail) exist to estimate the elasticity at another level (say, at farm). Thus, we turn to relationships between elasticities at two market levels. The comparison is for a given quantity moving through the marketing system (see Figure 3-3).

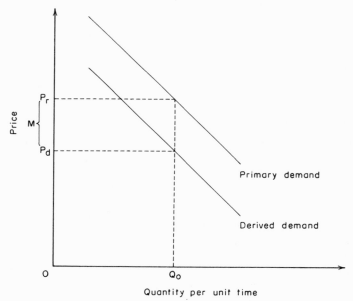

Figure 3-3.   Illustration of primary and derived demand curves

The exact relationship between elasticities depends on how the primary and derived demand curves are related. Since the two curves are separated by a schedule of marketing margins, the problem reduces to one of how the marketing margin behaves. A simple, but somewhat unrealistic, alternative is that the margin is a constant, absolute amount. That is, the margin is a constant regardless of the amount marketed. The two demand curves would be "parallel." In this case, the elasticity at one level can be estimated from the elasticity at the other level from

$$E_d = E_r \left(\frac{P_d}{P_r} \right),$$

where subscript
$$d = \text{derived (say, farm) level}$$
$$r = \text{primary (say, retail) level.[8]}$$

Let c stand for the constant margin: $c = P_r - P_d$. The primary (retail) level price will always be greater than the derived level price. Thus, the price ratio P_d/P_r will always be less than one. This ratio is analogous to the farmer's share of the consumer's food dollar (see Chapter 6). When a constant absolute margin is assumed, the derived-level elasticity will always be smaller in absolute value than the primary-level elasticity. A large margin results in a large difference in the elasticities at the two levels. For instance, if the farm value of a commodity is 50 per cent of the retail price, the farm-level elasticity is one-half of the retail elasticity. Thus, the primary demand for bananas in the United States could be price elastic while the derived demand in Central America is inelastic. The two market levels are separated by a large transportation cost, implying a large marketing margin.

[8] Under the assumptions, the only thing that differs between the two elasticities is the price.

$$E_r = \left(\frac{\Delta Q}{\Delta P} \right) \left(\frac{P_r}{Q} \right) \text{ and } E_d = \left(\frac{\Delta Q}{\Delta P} \right) \left(\frac{P_d}{Q} \right).$$

Thus, if E_r is known, E_d can be computed.

$$E_d = E_r \left(\frac{P_d}{P_r} \right) = \left(\frac{\Delta Q}{\Delta P} \right) \left(\frac{P_r}{Q} \right) \left(\frac{P_d}{P_r} \right).$$

A second alternative is a fixed-percentage marketing margin. This means the margin is a constant percentage of the purchase or sale price. It is highly unlikely that the entire margin would be of this nature, although some marketing firms use percentage mark-ups. Assuming a constant percentage margin regardless of the quantity marketed, the price elasticities at the two market levels would be the same for a given quantity marketed.

In practice, a marketing margin is likely to be a combination of absolute and percentage markups. A further complication is that these absolute and percentage figures may not be constants but may vary with the quantity marketed. The exact relationships between elasticities depends on the nature of the marketing margin. Thus, the economist must have some knowledge of the behavior of the margin to specify the relationship between elasticities.

One fairly simple specification of a margin (M) is the linear combination of a constant absolute amount (c) and a constant percentage (a) of the retail price.

$$M = c + a P_r$$

where $\quad 0 \leq c$
$\qquad 0 \leq a < 1.$

This specification indicates that the per unit margins decrease with lower prices as the quantity marketed increases. Actual margins, of course, may not change in this precise way although some margins behave in a manner consistent with this hypothesis (see Chapter 6).

Using previous notation, the derived-level elasticity is

$$E_d = E_r \left[1 - \frac{c}{(1-a) \, P_r} \right].$$

The constant absolute component in the margin means that the derived-level elasticity is less elastic or more inelastic than the respective primary-level elasticity.

As an example, assume $M = .40 + .20 \, P_r$. If $P_r = \$1.00$ and if the primary-level elasticity is -0.8, then the derived-level elasticity is

$$E_d = -.8 \left[1 - \frac{.40}{(.8)(\$1.00)} \right]$$

$$= -.8 \left[1 - .5 \right] = -.4.$$

The price at the derived level is

$$\begin{aligned} P_d &= P_r - M \\ &= \$1.00 - (.40 + .20 \,(\$1)) \\ &= \$.40. \end{aligned}$$

If $a = 0$, then the equation reduces to the case of the constant absolute margin.

$$E_d = E_r \left[1 - \frac{c}{P_r} \right] = E_r \left(\frac{P_d}{P_r} \right)$$

since $c = P_r - P_d$.

If $c = 0$, then $E_d = E_r$. This is the case of the constant percentage margin.

Joint products. If joint products are obtained in fixed proportions from the basic commodity and if the elasticities are all computed at the same market level, then the price elasticity of the basic commodity (E_x) is a weighted harmonic average of the price elasticities of the joint products (say, E_1 and E_2) (Houck, 1964).[9]

[9] A simple harmonic mean is defined

$$\tilde{X} = \frac{1}{\dfrac{\dfrac{1}{X_1} + \dfrac{1}{X_2} + \ldots + \dfrac{1}{X_n}}{n}} = \frac{n}{\dfrac{1}{X_1} + \dfrac{1}{X_2} + \ldots + \dfrac{1}{X_n}}.$$

For a weighted average, each member $\dfrac{1}{X}$ is multiplied by the appropriate weight and n is replaced by the sum of the weights.

Let $X =$ the basic commodity
                    X_1 and $X_2 =$ the joint products (an example of two)
                    w_1 and $w_2 =$ the fixed yields per unit of X
                    P_1 and $P_2 =$ price per unit of the joint products.
Hence, $X_1 = w_1 X$, and
                              $X_2 = w_2 X.$

Then, the mathematical relationship among the three elasticities is

$$E_x = \frac{P_1\,w_1 + P_2\,w_2}{\dfrac{1}{E_1}\,(P_1\,w_1) + \dfrac{1}{E_2}\,(P_2 w_2)}.$$

The example can be generalized to the case of n joint products (see Houck, 1964).

The weights in the expression are the proportions of X's average value (per unit) attributable to the sales of the joint products. Thus, taking E_1 and E_2 as constants, E_x will vary as the value weights vary. The extreme cases would be $P_1\,w_1$ or $P_2\,w_2$ equal zero; that is, X_2 or X_1 represents the entire value of X and remaining component is, say, thrown away. If X_1 is discarded and $P_1\,w_1 = 0$, then $E_x = E_2$. Or, in a more realistic case, if X_2 represents the major proportion of the value of X, then $E_x \approx E_2$. An example is the division of beef animal into the joint products beef and hide. The hide represents a relatively small proportion of the total value of the animal. Hence, the farm-level elasticity for the animal and for beef would be similar.

Soybeans provide an example. They are processed into the joint products meal and oil. In this case, X is a bushel of soybeans; X_1 is soybean meal; and X_2 is soybean oil. Hence, w_1 equals 47.8 pounds and w_2 equals 10.4 pounds. Meal and oil are obtained in the relatively fixed proportion of 47.8 pounds and 10.4 pounds, respectively, from a bushel of soybeans. Assume for the purposes of this example that the price of meal is 2.9 cents per pound and the price of oil is 12.0 cents per pound at wholesale. If the respective price elasticities are -0.9 and -2.5, then the wholesale-level elasticity for whole soybeans can be computed as follows:

$$= -.8 \left[1 - .5 \right] = -.4.$$

$$E_x = \frac{(2.9)\,(47.8) + (12.0)\,(10.4)}{\dfrac{1}{-.9}\,(2.9)(47.8) + \dfrac{1}{-2.5}\,(12.0)(10.4)} = -1.3.$$

Total Elasticity [10]

Price elasticity of demand provides a measure of the percentage change in quantity demanded in response to a one per cent change in price, assuming all other factors are held constant. However, if the price for one commodity changes, the prices of its substitutes will change as well (unless they are fixed, say by a government support program). The prices of competing products tend to move in the same direction, but by varying amounts. Thus, a change in the price of one commodity sets in motion forces which ultimately result in establishing a new structure of prices. For example, if the price of beef declines, the demand for pork (a substitute) also declines. Given a constant supply of pork, the price of pork decreases, and the change in the price of pork will in turn influence the demand (and hence the price) for beef.

Consequently, one needs to consider more than the price elasticity of demand for beef in order to forecast the net final effect on the consumption of beef of a change in the price of beef. The foregoing discussion assumes that the quantities of the substitutes (in our example, pork) are constant within the period of analysis. The relationship becomes even more complex if one takes account of the possible effects of changes in the relative prices of competing commodities on quantities supplied. To predict the full effects of one initial price change, one needs a knowledge of all own-price and cross-price elasticities of demand and supply for the set of competing products including the commodity in question.

The interrelationship among prices leads to the idea of a total demand response curve and total elasticities. The total demand response curve is defined as the price-quantity relationship resulting when all other important demand variables are "allowed to act and interact as the market structure requires to reach a new equilibrium level" (Buse, 1958, p. 882). The elasticity of total demand response or simply total elasticity is defined as the *net* percentage

[10] This section is largely based on Buse (1958).

change in quantity resulting from a one per cent change in own price, taking account of the interactions of related variables.

Assuming the main interrelationships are substitute relations, then Figure 3-4 depicts the idea of the total response relation and hence illustrates the total elasticity concept. The prices of substitutes are likely to decline as the commodity's own price declines. This would appear as a decrease in demand for the commodity under consideration. The total response curve is less elastic or more inelastic than the *ceteris paribus* demand curve. That is, the net quantity response is less than that indicated by the own-price elasticity of demand. Thus, if the main interrelationships are substitute relations, the total elasticity is smaller in absolute value than the corresponding price elasticity.

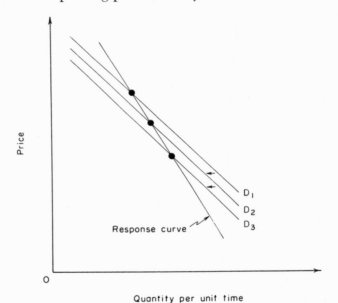

Figure 3-4. Hypothetical total demand response curve

Assuming just one substitute (*j*) for the commodity *i*, the total elasticity for *i* is

$$T_i = E_i + E_{ij}\, S_{ji}$$

where E_i = own-price elasticity

E_{ij} = cross-price elasticity

S_{ji} = the percentage change in the price of j given a one per cent change in the price of i.

Conceptually, the total elasticity coefficient can be viewed as the sum of two terms: the own-price elasticity and a cross elasticity multiplied by the elasticity of the price of j with respect to changes in the price of i. The own-price elasticity is adjusted for the cross effects.

E_{ij} and S_{ji} are usually positive and less than one for substitute commodities (Buse, 1958, p. 889). E_i is, of course, negative and larger in absolute value than the cross elasticities. Thus, T_i is negative but smaller in absolute value than E_i.

For example, if beef is the main substitute for pork, then the approximate total elasticity for pork is

$$T_p = E_p + E_{pb} S_{bp},$$

where the subscript p=pork and b=beef.
Buse (1958, pp. 886 f.) gives the following numerical illustration:

$$T_p = -.94 + (.72)(.29) = -.73.$$

The own-price elasticity of demand for pork was estimated to be -0.94, but the *net* percentage change in the quantity of pork that buyers would be willing to purchase in response to a one per cent change in the price of pork after taking account of the cross effects with beef is -0.73.

Price Flexibility Coefficients

Price flexibility is often treated as the inverse of price elasticity. The flexibility coefficient gives the percentage change in price associated with a one per cent change in quantity, other factors constant.

The price flexibility concept is particularly important for agricultural products. The biological nature of the production process results in many crops being produced annually or only at regular time intervals. Further, some of these commodities are perishable or semiperishable; they cannot be stored for long periods. For such commodities, the quantity available for consumption is largely fixed by the size of production, and the entire quantity must be consumed within a period of months after harvest. Hence, the situation is one of a fixed supply and a given level of demand for a specific time period. Within the time period, the level of production cannot be changed. The remaining question is what price will clear the market of the given supply. The direction of causation is from quantity to price.

Apples produced for fresh use illustrate the point. They are produced annually, and they cannot be stored from one crop year to the next. The level of production is the main factor determining average price for the year. Variations of price within the year have very little influence on the size of production in that year.[11]

The price flexibility coefficient (F_i) is defined as

$$F_i = \frac{\frac{\Delta P}{P}}{\frac{\Delta Q}{Q}} = \left(\frac{\Delta P}{\Delta Q}\right)\left(\frac{Q}{P}\right).$$

Under some conditions it is approximately equal to the reciprocal of the corresponding price elasticity, and like the price elasticity of demand, the direct price flexibility coefficient has a negative sign. A price flexibility of -3.0 means that there is a 3 per cent price response to a one per cent quantity change.

Thus, if demand is inelastic, then the price flexibility coefficient is likely to be greater than one in absolute value. A flexible price is consistent with an inelastic demand; that is, a small change in quantity has a relatively large impact on price. If demand is elastic, then the price flexibility coefficient is likely to be less than one in absolute value. An inflexible price is consistent with an elastic demand.

The price flexibility coefficient implies that price is a function of the quantity of the particular product as well as the quantities of

[11] Price may have a small influence on the level of imports and exports and, in some years, on the quantity harvested.

substitutes. In contrast, the usual demand function makes quantity a function of the price of the product as well as other product prices. Since different variables are held constant in the two equations, the reciprocal of the flexibility is not always a good approximation of the elasticity.[12]

Mathematically,

$$\left| E_{ii} \right| \gtreqqless \left| \frac{1}{F_{ii}} \right|.$$

The reciprocal of the price flexibility sets the lower limit of the price elasticity of demand. If the cross effects are zero (essentially no substitutes), then the reciprocal of the flexibility is a good approximation of the elasticity. If significant cross effects exist, then the reciprocal of the flexibility is less than the elasticity.

Flexibility coefficients that are analogous to the concepts of income elasticity and cross elasticity also may be defined. The price flexibility of income is the percentage change in price in response to a one per cent change in income, other factors remaining constant. It is calculated as follows:

$$F_{iy} = \left(\frac{\Delta P}{\Delta Y} \right) \left(\frac{Y}{P} \right).$$

The flexibility of income is typically expected to be positive. Price moves directly with the shift in demand. A higher income implies a larger demand, and this suggests a higher price for any given level of quantity.

The cross flexibility of i with respect to j is the percentage

---

[12] The derivative dP/dQ from $P = f_1(Q)$ is the reciprocal of dQ/dP from $Q = f_2(P)$. However, demand functions are more complex than this, and we must compare the partial derivatives, say from

$P_i = f_3 (Q_i, Q_j, Y)$ and
$Q_i = f_4 (P_i, P_j, Y).$

Since we are holding different variables constant, we can no longer assume that the partial derivative $\partial P_i / \partial Q_i$ is the reciprocal of $\partial Q_i / \partial P_i$. Houck (1965) provides more details, provided the reader is familiar with matrix algebra.

change in the price of commodity i in response to a one per cent change in the quantity of commodity j, other factors remaining constant. The algebraic relationship is as follows:

$$F_{ij} = \left(\frac{\Delta P_i}{\Delta Q_j} \right) \left(\frac{Q_j}{P_i} \right).$$

The cross flexibility based on the quantity variable of a substitute is expected to be negative. This is in contrast to cross elasticities for substitutes which usually are positive. A larger supply of a substitute results in a lower price for the substitute, which in turn results in a decline in demand for the first commodity. The lower demand implies a reduction in price. Hence, a larger supply of the substitute (commodity j) reduces the price of the commodity under consideration (commodity i).

Houck (1966) has worked out the relationships among flexibility coefficients similar to those developed for elasticities, such as the symmetry relation. His results are derived from equations in which quantity is a function of price, i.e., "normal" demand equations. (If one starts with price-dependent equations, some of the results are different [Waugh, 1964].) It follows that the assumptions which underlie Houck's work are the same as those made for the relationships among elasticities.

Empirical Elasticities

The theoretical concept of a commodity's own-price elasticity is rigidly defined. Economists have attempted to estimate elasticities using empirical data, but these do not always conform to the rigid definition specified by economic theory. An examination of these measured coefficients reveals that there is no such thing as "the" price elasticity of demand for a commodity. The question of why estimates are not unique is discussed in Chapter 16 (see also Manderscheid, 1964), but some examples of empirical elasticities are presented here.

Despite numerous difficulties, reasonably consistent estimates of elasticities have been obtained from a number of studies. The degree of consistency, of course, varies among commodities. There is probably more agreement among price analysts about the price elasticity of demand for beef, for example, than for cotton. One cannot escape making judgments where different estimates have been obtained. Perhaps the most widely used elasticity estimates in agricultural economics to date are from Brandow's study of demand interrelationships among farm products (Brandow, 1961). George and King (1971) have recently provided a similar comprehensive set of elasticity estimates. Some examples are given in Table 3-2. Both the Brandow and the George and King studies use a variety of devices to arrive at a comprehensive set of elasticity estimates. Some coefficients are estimated by statistical procedures; other coefficients are inferred from economic theory based on the relationships discussed earlier. Judgment is an important factor in making the estimates.

Table 3-2. Estimated elasticities of demand, selected foods, United States, 1946–1967

Commodity	Price elasticities		Income elasticities at retail
	Retail	Farm	
Beef	−0.64	−0.42	0.29
Chicken	−0.77	−0.60	0.18
Fluid milk	−0.35	−0.32	0.20
Ice cream	−0.53	−0.45	0.33
Potatoes	−0.31	−0.15	0.12
Apples, fresh use	−0.72	−0.68	0.14

Source: P. S. George and G. A. King, *Consumer Demand for Food Commodities in the United States with Projections for 1980,* Giannini Foundation Monograph 26, Univ. of Calif., Div. of Ag. Sciences (March 1971), tables 5 and 11.

A few estimates of long-run price elasticities of demand are given in Table 3-3. One of the generalizations about the demand for agricultural products, however, is that the demand for most is price inelastic—certainly in the short run and often in the long run. But it is important to keep in mind that empirical estimates are usually made for a point on the demand curve, that elasticities are likely to vary at different points along a demand curve, and hence that estimates made for one point may not hold over other ranges of prices and quantities.

Table 3-3. Long-run price elasticities of demand at retail, United States

Commodity	Elasticity	Adjustment period
Beef *	−1.0	9–12 months
Pork *	−0.75	3 months
Cotton †	−1.84	9 years

* *Source:* William G. Tomek and Willard W. Cochrane, "Long-Run Demand: A Concept, and Elasticity Estimates for Meats," *J. Farm Econ.,* 44 (1962):717–730.
† *Source:* Frederick V. Waugh, *Demand and Price Analysis: Some Examples from Agriculture,* Econ. Res. Ser., USDA Tech. Bull. 1316 (1964), p. 61.

References

Barten, A. P. 1967. "Evidence on the Slutsky Conditions," *Rev. Econ. Stat.,* 49:77–84.

Brandow, G. E. 1961. *Interrelations among Demands for Farm Products and Implications for Control of Market Supply.* Penn. State Univ. Ag. Exp. Sta. Bul. 680.

Buse, Rueben C. 1958. "Total Elasticities—A Predictive Device," *J. Farm Econ.,* 40:881–891.

Frisch, Ragnar. 1959. "A Complete Scheme for Computing All Direct and Cross-Demand Elasticities in a Model with Many Sectors," *Econometrica,* 27:177–196.

George, P. S., and G. A. King. 1971. *Consumer Demand for Food Commodities in the United States with Projections for 1980.* Giannini Foundation Monograph 26, Univ. of Calif. Div. of Ag. Sciences.

Goreux, L. M. 1960. "Income and Food Consumption," *Mo. Bul. Ag. Econ. and Stat.,* 9:1–13 (Oct.).

Houck, James P. 1964. "Price Elasticities and Joint Products," *J. Farm Econ.,* 46:652–656.

——. 1965. "The Relationship of Direct Price Flexibilities to Direct Price Elasticities," *J. Farm Econ.,* 47:789–792.

——. 1966. "A Look at Flexibilities and Elasticities," *J. Farm Econ.,* 48:225–232.

Klein, Lawrence R. 1962. *An Introduction to Econometrics.* Englewood Cliffs, N.J.: Prentice-Hall. Pp. 52–60.

Kuhlman, J. M., and R. G. Thompson. 1965. "Substitution and Values of Elasticities," *Am. Econ. Rev.*, 55:506–509.

Leser, C. E. V. 1963. "Forms of Engel Functions," *Econometrica*, 31:694–703.

Manderscheid, Lester V. 1964. "Some Observations in Interpreting Measured Demand Elasticities," *J. Farm Econ.*, 46:128–136.

Purcell, J. C., and Robert Raunikar. 1967. "Quantity-Income Elasticities for Foods by Level of Income," *J. Farm Econ.*, 49:1410–1414.

Rockwell, George R., Jr. 1959. *Income and Household Size: Their Effects on Food Consumption.* USDA, Marketing Research Report No. 340.

Stigler, George J. 1962. "Henry L. Moore and Statistical Economics," *Econometrica*, 30:1–21.

Tomek, William G., and Willard W. Cochrane. 1962. "Long-Run Demand: A Concept, and Elasticity Estimates for Meats," *J. Farm Econ.*, 44:717–730.

Waugh, Frederick V. 1964. *Demand and Price Analysis: Some Examples from Agriculture*, Econ. Res. Ser., USDA Tech. Bul. 1316.

Wetmore, John M., *et al.* 1959. *Policies for Expanding the Demand for Farm Food Products in the United States*, Part I: *History and Potentials*. Univ. of Minn. Tech. Bul. 231.

Wold, Herman, and Lars Jureen. 1953. *Demand Analysis*. New York: John Wiley and Sons. Chapters 5 and 6.

CHAPTER 4

Supply Relationships
in Agriculture

In this chapter, we are concerned with supply concepts and especially with the role prices play in determining the production decisions of farmers. For this reason, attention is focused first on supply-price relationships. This is followed by a review of the factors which bring about shifts in the supply curve. These and additional concepts are then used to identify the factors that are most important in determining changes in aggregate farm output as well as the production of individual commodities.

Theoretical Basis of Supply Functions

A static supply schedule shows how much of a given commodity will be offered for sale per unit of time as its price varies, other factors held constant. Our interest is mainly in market supply curves which refer to the response of all producers in a particular market area. Logic dictates that a normal supply function should slope upward and to the right. Producers presumably are willing to offer larger quantities as the price rises; however, the amount by which production can be expected to increase for a given increase in price varies with the time allowed for adjustments to take place. In general, the longer the time allowed for adjustment the more responsive the quantity supplied to a given price change.

In the very short run, once the crop is produced and harvested (assuming no reserve stocks or imports and that the current crop cannot be stored), the supply function is a vertical line. The quantity offered for sale can neither be increased nor decreased, regardless of the price offered, until the next harvest comes in. Prior to harvest, the supply can be adjusted by deciding not to harvest a part of the crop if the price is too low. As more time is allowed for farmers to respond to price changes, production can be altered. In the short run, the amount of inputs such as fertilizer applied to crops or feeding rates for livestock can be varied, and in the longer run, the area sown to crops and the number of livestock units can be changed. The tendency for supply curves to become more responsive (flatter) as more time is allowed for adjustments is illustrated schematically in Figure 4-1.

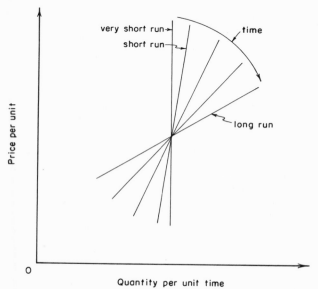

Figure 4-1. Changing supply-price relationships through time

Thus, the time dimension obviously is important in defining supply relationships in agriculture, but it is difficult to define precisely and unambiguously what is meant by the very short run, the short run, the intermediate run, and the long run as applied to supply. The time required for a production response varies from commodity to commodity. It takes more time for production decisions to be altered with tree crops, for example, than for poultry products.

Short-run supply schedules are of particular interest in agriculture, and they assume that some factors of production are fixed, while others can be varied in response to prices. This means a short-run period of one or two years for many farm commodities. The long run is usually defined as that period of time required for all factors of production to become variable: the acreage can be increased, buildings can be altered, additional labor and new machinery can be acquired. In the real world, there is continuous change; hence, the full effect of a particular price change can seldom be observed since additional price changes will often occur before the consequences of the first change are fully worked out.

While it is customary in principles of economics textbooks to show short-run supply curves as straight or slightly concave lines sloping upward and to the right, this sometimes gives a misleading impression of actual supply relationships in agriculture. There is usually some minimum price which must be paid to induce farmers to offer any quantity of a particular commodity for sale. The supply curve intercepts the vertical axis at this price. As prices rise, supply may become very responsive over some range of prices and quite unresponsive over others. The supply curve is likely to be relatively flat if a small change in price makes it profitable to shift from the production of one commodity to another. In contrast, if it is not profitable to shift production to alternative commodities, then the supply curve is likely to be relatively steep.

In general, the shape of a short-run market supply curve for a particular commodity depends on the shapes of the marginal cost curves for farms producing the commodity given the opportunity cost (see below) of producing other commodities. Under the usual profit-maximizing assumptions of economic theory, the optimum level of output on a particular farm is determined by the point at which marginal cost and marginal revenue are equated. Marginal cost is defined as the addition to total cost of producing one more unit of product, and marginal revenue is the added revenue from selling one more unit of product. Clearly, if a firm produced output beyond the point at which marginal cost and marginal revenue are equated, then by definition the added cost of producing the product exceeds the added revenue from its sale.

Hypothetical marginal cost and corresponding average variable and average total cost curves are shown in Figure 4-2. The positions and shapes of these curves are determined by physical pro-

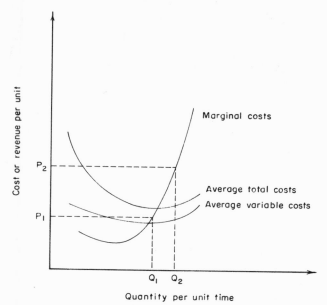

Marginal costs

Average total costs

Average variable costs

Quantity per unit time

Figure 4-2.   Cost curves and optimum output at alternative prices

duction possibilities (the production function) and the cost of factors of production (inputs).[1] Since the individual farmer is assumed to be a price taker, his marginal revenue is equal to the price received for the product; the sales of an individual farmer do not influence price and additional units can be sold at the prevailing price. (Technically, a supply curve can be defined only for the case when individual sellers cannot influence price.) Hence, at price P_1 (Figure 4-2) profits are maximized by producing Q_1 units; at price P_2, the profit maximizing output increases to Q_2.

As long as the price of the product exceeds average variable costs, the supply curve for the individual farm will be determined by the shape of the marginal cost curve. At any point above the low point on the average variable cost curve, the supply schedule

[1] The physical relationship between inputs and output may be defined by a production function. If the production function and the costs of inputs are known, then the various cost curves can be constructed (see, for example, Leftwich, 1966). In practice, empirical production functions sometimes are difficult to estimate. Nerlove and Bachman (1960) provide a summary of alternative approaches to the analysis of agricultural supply.

coincides with the marginal cost schedule—the steeper the marginal cost curve, the more inelastic the supply curve. Assuming profit-maximizing behavior on the part of each producer, the aggregate supply curve for any commodity can be obtained simply by summing the marginal cost curves for all farms.

A farmer will cease to produce a commodity if the price falls below average variable costs of production. Variable costs are those that can be avoided by not producing or not harvesting the commodity. It does not pay a poultryman, for example, to produce eggs if income is not sufficient to cover feed costs; however, in the short run it does pay to remain in production at prices exceeding average variable costs, even if all fixed or overhead costs are not covered. In the long run, of course, a producer will continue to produce only if all costs are covered.

The concept of "opportunity cost" is important in determining the point at which farmers will switch from the production of one commodity to another. The opportunity cost of producing commodity A is the income foregone by not producing commodity B. Thus, if the income foregone (the opportunity cost) of producing A exceeds the revenue from that crop, it does not pay to continue to produce A. The opportunity cost of continuing to produce a particular commodity such as wheat may include revenue foregone from working off the farm as well as the earnings from commodities that could have been produced with the same resources such as barley or grain sorghum.

Price Elasticity of Supply

The price elasticity of supply is defined in a manner analogous to the price elasticity of demand. It expresses the percentage change in quantity supplied in response to a one per cent change in price, other factors held constant. In algebraic terms, it is expressed as follows:

$$E_s = \frac{\frac{\Delta Q}{Q}}{\frac{\Delta P}{P}} = \left(\frac{\Delta Q}{\Delta P}\right)\left(\frac{P}{Q}\right),$$

where Q refers to the quantity supplied. Since an increase in quantity supplied is normally associated with a rise in price, the sign of the coefficient usually is positive. A zero elasticity means that supply is fixed; there is no quantity response to a price change. This is called a perfectly inelastic supply. An *inelastic* supply refers to the range of elasticities between zero and one. Quantity supplied is relatively unresponsive to price changes. An *elastic* supply refers to coefficients greater than one. The percentage change in quantity is larger than the corresponding percentage change in price.

As is the case with demand functions, the elasticity coefficient typically varies in magnitude along the supply function. It is convenient to speak of "the" price elasticity of supply, but such a coefficient usually is measured at the arithmetic mean of prices and quantities. In empirical research, supply equations are often specified as straight lines, but this particular specification places special restrictions on the magnitude of the elasticity (Houck, 1967). As the quantity supplied is increased along the function (that is, as it approaches infinity), the price elasticity of supply approaches one. Specifically, if the linear supply function with a positive slope intersects the origin (intercept equals zero), then the elasticity is a constant equaling one. If the quantity dependent function intersects the price axis first (horizontal intercept negative), the elasticity is always greater than one but approaches one as quantity supplied becomes large. If the function intersects the quantity axis first (horizontal intercept positive), the elasticity is always less than one but approaches one as quantity supplied becomes large.

Empirical estimates of the elasticity of supply are useful to those who have the responsibility of forecasting future supplies or making policy decisions. If the supply schedule for a commodity is relatively elastic, a modest reduction in the support price, for example, may be sufficient to solve a surplus problem, but this would not be true if the supply is inelastic.

The problems of obtaining reliable empirical estimates of supply elasticities are similar to, though somewhat more complex than, those discussed in connection with demand elasticities. (Learn and Cochrane, 1961; Nerlove and Addison, 1958; and Nerlove and Bachman, 1960, discuss methods commonly used in empirical supply analysis.) It is sometimes difficult to isolate the effect of a change in the product price from other factors, such as changes in the prices of inputs or alternative crops which compete for the same resources. Time lags compound the problem of obtaining reliable estimates. Usually an attempt is made in empirical analysis to distinguish between short-run elasticities (based on responses which occur within one or two production periods) and long-run elasticities (based on the full effects of a price change allowing whatever time is necessary for all adjustments to occur).

Empirical estimates of short-run elasticities of supply for selected agricultural commodities produced in the United States are shown in Table 4-1. The elasticity estimates are highest for livestock products with short production cycles such as eggs and broilers. The production of these commodities can be altered quite readily within a few months. Elasticity coefficients also tend to be higher for crops which are produced as a sideline enterprise on many farms and planted on only a small portion of total acreage. Potatoes are commonly cited as an example of such a crop although, because of increasing specialization, fewer farmers are now in a position to expand or contract potato acreage as compared with a generation ago. Short-run elasticities tend to be lower for crops such as wheat, which occupy a large proportion of the cropland and are grown in areas where alternatives are limited, and for

Table 4-1. Estimated short-run elasticities of supply for selected commodities

Crops	Elasticity	Livestock products	Elasticity
Potatoes	.8	Eggs	1.2
Soybeans	.5	Poultry meat	.9
Feed grains	.4	Hogs	.6
Cotton	.4	Beef	.5
Tobacco	.4	Milk	.3
Wheat	.3		
Fruits	.2		

Source: Reprinted from Luther G. Tweeten, *Foundations of Farm Policy,* by permission of University of Nebraska Press. Copyright © 1970 by the University of Nebraska Press. The elasticities are derived by the author from numerous sources and are based on an adjustment period of about two years.

commodities such as beef and fruit, which have long production periods. Price elasticities of supply also tend to be low for subsistence food crops grown in less developed countries; however, the acreage response elasticities for such commercial crops as cotton have been found to be much higher, often approaching or even exceeding those in the more developed countries, including the United States.[2]

Changes in Supply

Empirical studies of supply relationships for farm products, both in the United States and in other countries, indicate that changes in product prices typically (but not always) explain a relatively small proportion of the total variation in output which has occurred over a period of years. Short-run changes in output are often influenced by the weather and pests, while long-run changes in supply are attributable to such factors as improvements in technology which result in higher yields. These and other factors which lead farmers to produce more at the same price are frequently referred to as "supply shifters." It is important to know whether changes in output occur as a result of movements along a static supply schedule (change in quantity supplied) or because of shifts in the supply curve (changes in supply).

A shift in the supply curve to the right (an increase in supply) means that a larger quantity will be offered at a given price; a shift to the left has the opposite effect. The principal causes of shifts in the supply curve are

(1) changes in input (or factor) prices,
(2) changes in the profitability of substitute commodities (i.e., those that compete for the same resources),
(3) changes in technology which influence both yields and costs of production or efficiency,
(4) changes in the prices of joint products (i.e., commodities which are produced together such as wool and mutton), and

[2] According to a summary prepared by Krishna (1967), price elasticities of supply (as measured by acreage response) for individual commodities tend to range from 0.1 for subsistence crops to 0.7 for fibers such as cotton and jute.

(5) institutional constraints such as government acreage control programs.

Changes in production resulting from "unusual" weather and insect or disease damage also can be treated as temporary shifts in supply. Oury (1965), for instance, has considered the problem of explicitly incorporating the effects of weather in a supply model. These effects are generally treated as random shifts in the supply function.

As with demand relationships, it is useful to distinguish between a parallel shift in the curve and a structural change (Learn and Cochrane, 1961).[3] To illustrate, a hypothetical supply function may be written as follows:

$$Q = \alpha + \beta P - \gamma X,$$

where Q = quantity

P = price of product (output)

X = price of input (measure of cost)

and α, β, and γ are parameters of the equation.

The output (Q) is a function of the price of the product (P) and costs (X). The static supply function assumes a fixed level of X. A change in the magnitude of X shifts the level of the equation by a constant amount and hence leads to a parallel shift in supply. However, if the parameters or the functional form of the equation change, this is a structural change. Changes in technology, such as the development of a new variety of a commodity, are an important source of structural changes. Structural change may also arise from changes in management skills, changes in the number and size distribution of firms, development of new areas capable of producing the commodity, and changes in government programs influencing supply. Clearly, changes in shift variables (like X) and structural changes may be related.

Input Prices

The most profitable use of all factors of production is determined by the ratio of the price of the product to the price of inputs, such

[3] This is analogous to the distinction made on the demand side, although the sources of structural change are different.

as labor, fertilizer, and machinery. Thus, an increase in the use of inputs (and hence an increase in output of a commodity) may occur as a result of either an increase in the price of the product or a decrease in the price of inputs, sometimes called factors of production. Conceptually, a change in the price of a factor is treated as a supply shifter. An increase in factor prices, other variables constant, shifts the cost curves of each firm, and hence the supply curve, to the left; a decrease in the price of a factor has the opposite effect.

A given percentage decrease in the price of all factors accompanied by an equal percentage decrease in the price of the product results in the same use of quantities of inputs. Thus, there will be no change in output if the product/factor price ratio remains constant. Analytically, this can be viewed as a downward movement along the static supply curve in response to a reduction in the price of the product and a shift to the right in the supply curve as a result of a corresponding decline in the price of factors. This situation is illustrated schematically in Figure 4-3. Production will

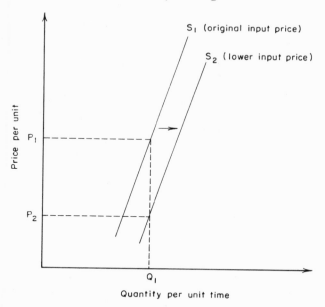

Figure 4-3. Changes in supply associated with a decrease in input prices and a corresponding decline in the price of the product

remain at Q_1 despite the decline in the product price from P_1 to P_2 if factor prices decrease by an amount sufficient to shift the supply curve from S_1 to S_2.

Relative price changes are usually expressed as a price ratio. One of the best-known ratios in agriculture is the hog/corn price ratio which shows the number of bushels of corn required to equal in value the farm price of hogs per hundredweight. It is calculated as follows:

$$\text{Hog/corn ratio} = \frac{\text{price of hogs ($ per cwt.)}}{\text{price of corn ($ per bu.)}} \; .$$

For example, when the price of hogs is $18.00 per hundredweight and the price of corn is $1.20 per bushel the ratio is equal to $18/$1.20 or 15.

An increase in the hog/corn price ratio is usually followed by an expansion in hog production, while a decrease in the ratio leads to a cut in production. The relationship between the hog/corn ratio and subsequent changes in the number of sows farrowing for the period 1956–1970 is shown in Figure 4-4. Note that changes in the number of sows farrowing are relatively small (either positive or negative) when the ratio is between 16 and 17. When the ratio declines to around 13, the number farrowing typically falls from 5 to 10 per cent, while a corresponding increase is likely to occur when the ratio rises above 19.

Corn has become less important in recent years in the total cost of producing hogs. Thus, the hog/corn price ratio probably is a less useful indicator of profits in hog production and consequently has become a less accurate forecaster of future hog production than it was formerly. Nonetheless, the idea of relative price changes is an important one, and price ratios are a useful way to express relative price changes.

Profitability of Competing Commodities

The supply curve for a given commodity will shift to the left if competing or alternative commodities become more profitable; it will shift to the right if other commodities become less profitable.

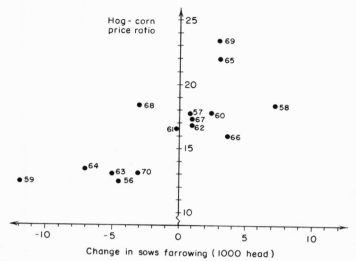

Figure 4-4. Relationship between September—December hog-corn price ratio for north central states and change in sows farrowing the following spring, 1956–1970. Change in farrowings is the increase or decrease from preceding spring. Data from Economic Research Service, *Livestock and Meat Situation,* LMS-181 (Oct. 1971), p. 8, table 2.

Competing commodities are ones that can be produced with the same resources. A competing commodity (B) can become more profitable because the price of that commodity rises relative to the first commodity (A) or because costs of producing B decline relative to A. Thus, relative changes in product prices, yields, or efficiency can change the relative profitability of different commodities.

Corn and soybeans are important alternative crops over much of the central and southern part of the United States. In the 1960's, an increase in the average yield of corn relative to soybeans in the midwestern area made corn more profitable in relation to soybeans at the then prevailing prices. In southern areas, the yield disadvantage of soybeans to corn was relatively less. As a result, soybean acreage increased in the South relative to the Corn Belt (Brown, 1971).

Over time, of course, an initial yield advantage may be offset by a subsequent change in relative product prices. Prices of closely competing products are commonly considered in empirical supply analyses. Changes in the price of B are negatively related to changes in the supply of A.

Technology

Improvements in technology are important causes of long-term shifts in agricultural supply functions. An improvement in technology is defined as something that enables firms to produce more output with the same quantity of inputs as previously. In technical terms, it shifts the production function upward so that producers will find it profitable to increase output at the same ratio of product to factor prices.

Among the more important technical changes which have increased agricultural supply are the development of high-yielding varieties of crops and improved breeds of livestock; better methods of insect, disease, and weed control; mechanization which makes it possible to plant and harvest more promptly; and better tillage techniques. The effects of these changes are well known, but it is often difficult to identify and measure precisely how much of a given change in output is due to technical improvements and how much is due to changes in factor or product prices. Rapid technical changes in agriculture during the 1950's and 1960's in the United States were, for example, accompanied by a substantial decline in the price of nitrogen fertilizer. Both shifted the supply schedule to the right; however, it is difficult to determine how much of the shift was due to technology and how much to the lower price of fertilizer (which, in turn, was the result of rapid technological changes in the fertilizer industry).

Because of the definitional and measurement problems involved, there has been a tendency in empirical analysis of supply to use time or some simple trend variable as a measure of technological improvements without specifically identifying and measuring those factors responsible for shifts in supply. A few economists, however, such as Griliches (1957, 1963) have sought to determine the important causes of technical change in agriculture, including the contributions of public expenditures for research, and to measure the rate of adoption of improved production practices.

Joint Product Relationships

Supplies of a number of agricultural commodities are determined in part by joint relationships. Joint products are those that are produced in approximately fixed proportions, such as soybean oil and soybean meal from soybeans. The supply of wool, for example, is determined by the price of lamb as well as the price of wool. In some cases, crop rotations or particular combinations of enterprises may be fixed largely by technological considerations. This, in turn, leads to the production of joint products. Under such circumstances, an increase in the price of one product can cause the supply curve of the other (joint) product to shift to the right. Such relationships are important for some commodities like vegetable oils, wool, or butterfat, but not for others.

Institutional Factors Affecting Supply

The supply schedule for an agricultural commodity is often influenced by institutional factors such as increases or decreases in acreage allotments, incentive payments to retire land or shift it to alternative uses, zoning or land-use regulations, and bases or quotas. Government programs obviously have had a marked influence on the production of such commodities as wheat, corn, cotton, rice, and tobacco in the United States since the depression years of the 1930's.

Supply Response Relation [4]

A distinction is sometimes made between the traditional supply function of economic theory and a "response relation." The traditional supply curve specifies a price-quantity relation, all other factors held constant. The response relation is more general; it specifies the output response to a price change not holding other factors constant. Thus, the response may involve both movements along a supply curve and shifts in supply.

The response relation is not a reversible function in the sense that a supply curve is reversible. In fact, the supply response elas-

[4] This section is based on Cochrane (1955).

ticity is likely to be different for an increase in price than for a subsequent reduction in price. The traditional supply curve specifies that if price increases and then decreases, the quantity supplied will return to its original level. It is reversible.

The response concept is based on the hypothesis that when price changes, there are likely to be correlated changes in supply shifters. In particular, when prices increase, new techniques of production are more likely to be introduced. This presupposes a backlog of new technologies which may be adopted by the producer. Under conditions of rising prices, firms may be induced to adopt new techniques at a somewhat faster rate than with constant or declining prices. Also, a large proportion of agricultural capital comes from retained earnings, and consequently higher prices may make it possible to finance the adoption of new techniques more rapidly. Under these circumstances, an increase in price can be expected to have two effects. First, it will cause farmers to increase output along the static supply curve; and second, it will lead them to shift to a new supply curve. The resulting increase in supply will thus be greater than one might have anticipated if the forecast were based solely on the static concept of supply.

Once adopted, improved production practices usually are retained even though the price of the product subsequently declines. Farmers are not likely to discard new technologies and thereby shift the supply function to the left once it has moved to the right. Hence, the supply response to a subsequent decline in price is likely to be less than to the previous increase in price.[5] Under these circumstances, the response elasticity is higher for a price increase than a price decline. A hypothetical response relation of this type is shown in Figure 4-5. At a price of P_1, producers offer an output of Q_1, but as the price increases to P_2, output expands along the diagonal between S_1 and S_2, ultimately reaching Q_2. If the price thereafter declines to P_3, output declines along the new supply curve S_2, resulting in the production of Q_3.

[5] It is sometimes argued that farmers increase production in the face of declining product prices to compensate for the loss in income; i.e., the supply relation has a negative slope for price declines. While there is some superficial evidence to support this viewpoint, the explanation is more complex (see next section).

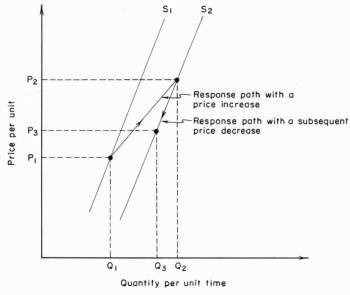

Figure 4-5. Hypothetical supply response paths

Favorable or unfavorable agricultural prices obviously can have a marked influence on the rate at which new technology is adopted, and hence on the rate of change of farm output. Farmers must have an incentive to use new techniques and access to sufficient capital to make the necessary investments. During the 1940's, farmers in the United States experienced these conditions. In contrast, price relationships were unfavorable to agriculture in many of the less developed countries in the 1950's and early 1960's. T. W. Schultz attributes the lag in farm production during this period among the less developed countries to "widespread underpricing of agricultural products and overpricing of agricultural inputs" (1965, p. 51).

Aggregate Farm Output

Changes in aggregate farm output over time have been associated mainly with shifts in the aggregate supply function rather than movements along a static supply curve. The aggregate supply relationship in agriculture in most countries is highly price inelastic in the short run. This is due mainly to the fact that resources once committed to agriculture tend to remain in use, especially when alternative opportunities for employment are limited. This phenomenon is sometimes referred to as "asset fixity" (Edwards, 1959). Land, buildings, family labor, and machinery often have low salvage or alternative use value outside of agriculture. Even when agricultural prices are relatively low, a farmer will find it more profitable to use his labor and equipment to produce another crop when nearby alternative employment opportunities are unavailable or intermittent, rather than to attempt to work off the farm and to sell his equipment at second hand prices. Stated in another way, the salvage value of such resources frequently is below their value in use. Hence, it pays to continue farming, at least until the resources are "used up" or need to be replaced.

The unresponsiveness of aggregate farm output to a fall in product prices was dramatically demonstrated in the United States in the early 1930's. Total farm output was maintained between 1929 and 1932 despite the fact that farm prices fell about 50 per cent during this period. Farmers continued to produce because they had no better alternatives. Their behavior was consistent with profit-maximizing principles as D. Gale Johnson (1950) has pointed out. The optimum use of factors, as emphasized earlier, is a function, not of product prices alone, but of the ratio of product to factor prices. In the early 1930's, feed prices, land rents, and eventually even the wages of hired labor in agriculture fell almost as much as farm product prices. This meant that product/factor price ratios remained approximately constant, and consequently farmers used about as much of these factors after the decline in product prices as before.

The experience of the 1930's is not likely to be repeated in precisely the same way, but it illustrates a very important principle: namely, that input prices in agriculture, especially for land and those items produced by some farmers and sold to others such as seed, feed, and livestock, are likely to decline along with product prices. When this occurs, output will remain relatively stable in the face of a severe agricultural depression. This is less likely to occur as more inputs with inflexible or administratively-determined prices are used in agriculture.

Because of the rigidities which exist in agriculture, including "asset fixity" and the difficulty of changing production plans in the short run, it is not surprising to find that empirical estimates of the aggregate elasticity of supply are quite low. Tweeten and Quance (1969) estimate the aggregate short-run elasticity of farm production in the United States to be no more than about 0.15. This estimate is based on historical data. Their analysis suggests further that the aggregate quantity supplied is less responsive to a price decrease than to a price increase. The elasticity estimate for periods of falling prices is 0.07, while for periods of rising prices it is 0.17.

Understanding Changes in Agricultural Product Supply

Supply relationships for individual farm commodities are often complex. One reason for this is that yields are subject to unpredictable elements. Too much or too little rain, an early frost, or disease damage may cause actual production to deviate substantially from planned production. The biological nature of agricultural production also means that supply cannot respond immediately to a change in prices. Moreover, production decisions, unlike those in many nonfarm industries, are highly decentralized and are made by thousands or even millions of individuals managing small units.

Nonetheless, those charged with the responsibility of predicting changes in agricultural prices would like to have reasonable estimates of supply since short-run changes in farm prices are mainly related to changes in supply rather than in demand. Current consumption for many farm products also is determined principally by current production. This is true of most fruits and vegetables, poultry, eggs, and meat; imports and exports or changes in storage stocks account for only a small proportion of the total supply of these products. But it is not true of grains, cotton, tobacco, oilseeds, and similar commodities produced in the United States which can be stored and are commonly sold abroad in substantial volume. For commodities such as these, supply analysis must take account of potential changes in inventories as well as exports and imports.

In attempting to predict changes in domestic production, it is important to distinguish between those factors of production that can be altered within a short period of time and those that cannot. With increasing specialization in both equipment and skills, many farmers find it difficult to change production plans very significantly in a short period of time. In order to forecast supply changes one needs to identify those regions and types of farms which have the capacity to alter production plans and to estimate the relative returns from alternative enterprises on such farms. One also needs to keep in mind that changes in supplies of livestock products are limited by the availability of female stock and the time required to produce a new generation.

Feeding rates are important and can be adjusted more quickly than the number of female animals. Rates of grain feeding are determined mainly by the ratio of the price of the product to the price of feed or the price of feed ingredients such as corn and soybean meal. For hogs, the critical relationship, as pointed out earlier, is the price of pork relative to corn. Milk production also has been found to be associated with the price of milk relative to dairy feed.

Switches between enterprises also must be considered. The production of milk, for example, is influenced in some areas by the price of beef relative to milk, and in other areas by the price of hogs relative to milk. In Australia, the production of wool or lambs in some regions is influenced principally by the relationship between the prices of these (joint) products and the price of wheat. The relevant price ratio to consider in attempting to forecast the supply of a particular commodity obviously varies from commodity to commodity and region to region, but again it is relative prices that are critical, not the price of one commodity alone.

In forecasting production, an understanding of the prices to which farmers respond is important. For most commodities, except those grown under contract, product prices are uncertain at planting time or when breeding plans must be made. Expected future prices may be based on recent past prices, average prices over a period of years (perhaps with declining weights attached to more distant prices), price quotations on established "futures" markets, government price-support announcements, or outlook statements. For some commodities, there is considerable empirical evidence to suggest that future production plans are based on immediate past or current prices. If this relationship persists, low prices in one year will be followed by reduced production the following year and higher prices, which then will result in increased production the third year. This type of response, with alternate periods of high and low production, sometimes referred to as the cobweb model, is explored more fully in Chapter 9.

A closely related question, as previously mentioned, is the role of time lags in agricultural supply. The biological nature of farm products prohibits rapid responses to price changes. Thus, given a change in expected price, a time period, ranging up to eight or more years for some tree crops, is required for a complete quantity adjustment.

Weather during the planting season also can have a significant influence on the acreage planted to certain crops. Unusually wet weather may make it impossible to plant the desired acreage of the crop which is expected to be the most profitable, thereby forcing farmers to plant an alternative crop with a shorter growing season. In the Corn Belt, for example, a late spring may lead farmers to cut down on the acreage planted to corn and to increase the area planted to soybeans. During the growing season, drought, disease, and pests may influence yields.

Off-farm employment opportunities can affect the supply of some commodities. A rapid increase in employment opportunities during a period of business expansion, for example, may encourage some dairymen to cease production, especially in areas such as the northeastern region of the United States. High unemployment, on the other hand, may slow up the exodus.

In sum, the most important economic factor affecting production of an individual commodity in the short run is the availability of alternatives. The supply relation is much more likely to be price-elastic for a particular commodity when alternative opportunities are available, including work off the farm as well as the production of other commodities. With the passage of time, changes in the supply of farm products are determined principally by shifts in the supply schedule most often associated with improvements in technology.

References

Brown, W. Herbert. 1971. *Soybeans: Acreage Response to Price and Farm Program Changes.* Econ. Res. Ser., USDA, ERS-473.

Cochrane, Willard W. 1955. "Conceptualizing the Supply Relation in Agriculture," *J. Farm Econ.,* 37:1161–1176.

Edwards, Clark. 1959. "Resource Fixity and Farm Organization," *J. Farm Econ.,* 41:747–759.

Griliches, Zvi. 1957. "Hybrid Corn: An Exploration in the Economics of Technological Change," *Econometrica,* 25:501–522.

——. 1963. "The Sources of Measured Productivity Growth: U.S. Agriculture, 1940–1960," *J. Pol. Econ.,* 71:331–346.

Houck, James P. 1967. "Price Elasticity and Linear Supply Curves," *Am. Econ. Rev.,* 57:905–908.

Johnson, D. Gale. 1950. "The Nature of the Supply Function for Agricultural Products," *Am. Econ. Rev.,* 40:539–564.

Krishna, Raj. 1967. "Agricultural Price Policy and Economic Development," *Agricultural Development and Economic Growth.* Ed. H. M. Southworth and B. F. Johnston. Ithaca, N.Y.: Cornell Univ. Press.

Learn, Elmer W., and Willard W. Cochrane. 1961. "Regression Analysis of Supply Functions Undergoing Structural Change," *Agricultural Supply Functions.* Ed. Earl O. Heady *et al.* Ames, Iowa: Iowa State Univ. Press.

Leftwich, Richard H. 1966. *The Price System and Resource Allocation.* 3d ed. New York: Holt, Rinehart and Winston. Chapters 7 and 8.

Nerlove, Marc, and William Addison. 1958. "Statistical Estimation of Long-Run Elasticities of Supply and Demand," *J. Farm Econ.,* 40:861–880.

Nerlove, Marc, and Kenneth L. Bachman. 1960. "The Analysis of Changes in Agricultural Supply: Problems and Approaches," *J. Farm Econ.,* 42:531–554.

Oury, Bernard. 1965. "Allowing for Weather in Crop Production Model Building," *J. Farm Econ.,* 47:270–283.

Schultz, Theodore W. 1965. *Economic Crises in World Agriculture.* Ann Arbor: Univ. of Michigan Press.

Tweeten, Luther G. 1970. *Foundations of Farm Policy.* Lincoln: Univ. of Nebraska Press.

—— and C. Leroy Quance. 1969. "Positivistic Measures of Aggregate Supply Elasticities: Some New Approaches," *Am. J. Ag. Econ.,* 51:342–352.

CHAPTER 5

Price Determination: Theory and Practice

This chapter is concerned with the determination of prices within alternate market structures. The term "market structure" refers to the number and size distribution of buyers and sellers, the degree of product differentiation, and the ease of entry of new firms into an industry.[1] These "structural characteristics" may be used as a basis for classifying markets. Price behavior, in terms of level and frequency of change, varies with the type of market structure.

Classification of Markets

Markets may be classified as competitive (many buyers and sellers), oligopolistic (few firms), or monopolistic (a single firm). Another category, which is sometimes used, is monopolistic competition (many firms selling similar but differentiated products). In this section, we outline the characteristics of some types of markets.

A *purely competitive market* is one in which the following conditions prevail:[2]

[1] Other market or product characteristics besides these which may affect pricing decisions include the durability of the commodity, the adequacy of grade descriptions (where relevant), bulkiness of the product relative to its value, the ratio of fixed to variable costs in the industry, and the continuity and length of the production process. Additional comments on market characteristics and their influence on pricing decisions are contained in Cochrane (1957). Case studies of market structure in agriculture are contained in Moore and Walsh (1966).

[2] These conditions lead to what is sometimes referred to, alternatively, as atomistic competition (Dorfman, 1964, p. 78).

(1) The number of buyers and sellers is sufficiently large so that no individual can perceptibly influence price by his decision to buy or sell.

(2) The product is sufficiently homogeneous so that the product of one firm is essentially a perfect substitute for that of another firm.

(3) There are no artificial restrictions on demand, supply, or prices such as government intervention or collusion among firms.

(4) Mobility of resources and products exists in the economy; e.g., a new firm should be free to enter the industry.

In a purely competitive market, it is assumed that every producer-seller seeks to maximize profits by selling at as high a price as possible, and that every buyer seeks to maximize utility by obtaining the product at as low a price as possible. The collective actions of buyers and sellers determine prices.

To simplify theoretical analysis, economists use the concept of a *perfectly competitive* market. In addition to large numbers and product homogeneity, the term "perfect" implies perfect knowledge by buyers and sellers, complete divisibility of the product, and perfect mobility of the product within the market. With these assumptions, we can talk about "the" price for a product in a market.

Under competitive conditions, the supply and demand relations faced by the individual differ greatly from the market supply and demand functions. Since each buyer and seller cannot perceptibly influence price, the demand and supply relations appear horizontal to the respective individuals. For instance, the individual farmer typically views the (derived) demand function for his product as being perfectly horizontal. He cannot influence price by the quantity he offers for sale; he is a price taker.

A second type of market, at the opposite extreme from perfect competition, is that designated as *absolute monopoly*. The distinguishing characteristic of this type of market structure is a single seller. The firm's demand schedule coincides with the industry demand schedule. Product differentiation is implicit in this definition, since a monopoly could not exist unless the firm's product were substantially different from the products of other firms.

Monopolistic competition refers to a market in which a large number of sellers offer a differentiated product. These products are presumably close substitutes, but the individual sellers are able to differentiate their product on the basis of a trade name, style, quality, service, location, or other factors. Consequently, the firm has some influence on price, but the number of substitutes is likely to limit the firm's discretion in pricing. The demand relation faced by the individual firms, while not perfectly elastic, is likely to be quite elastic in the prevailing range of prices.

Oligopoly refers to a market with a few large sellers. Each firm produces a large fraction of the industry's total product, and consequently the action of one firm in the industry can greatly influence other firms. In a *pure oligopoly,* the sellers are producing a homogeneous product. The steel industry is an example. In a *differenriated oligopoly,* the firms are producing a similar but not identical product. The U.S. automobile industry is, perhaps, the classic example. Because each oligopolistic industry tends to develop unique interrelationships among firms, this type of market structure is the least susceptible to generalizations .about price and output policies.

This classification of markets emphasizes the number of sellers and implicitly assumes a large number of buyers. Other classifications may be devised with emphasis on the number of buyers in the market. For instance, a market with a single large buyer is referred to as a *monopsony.* A market with a single buyer and a single seller is called a *bilateral monopoly.* Obviously, a large number of market structures could be devised, each involving different combinations of numbers of buyers and sellers and degree of product differentiation.

Many markets do not fit neatly into the categories just described. It is not easy to define an industry or to determine the number of firms which should be included, especially with the growth of large conglomerate enterprises. Measuring the degree of concentration also is difficult. One common measure of concentration is the proportion of total industry sales made by, say, the four largest firms in the industry. If the four largest firms in the industry account for 90 per cent of total sales, then the market may be classified as an oligopoly. Of course, such a single measure does not take account of the degree of product differentiation or other possible monopoly elements. In addition, a global or industrywide measure does not reflect the possible high levels of concentration in a local market area, and conversely a firm may have a large share of the total market but only a small share of some local markets.[3]

Price Determination under Pure Competition

Models of agricultural product price behavior often assume a purely or perfectly competitive market structure. Prices of perhaps one-half of the farm products in the United States are determined under conditions approximating pure competition. Even if the number of firms producing the commodity is fairly small, price behavior may still approach that expected under pure competition. This occurs when relatively free entry of other firms is possible. Thus, one can argue that the prices of many fruits and vegetables, poultry, eggs, and meat animals are determined under competitive conditions. The trading of commodity futures contracts also takes place under conditions of pure competition (see Chapters 12 and 13), although price manipulation or an "imbalance" of use by buyers or by sellers may create conditions that deviate from the competitive model.

The federal government, of course, intervenes in the pricing of grains, cotton, rice, tobacco, peanuts, and dairy products in the United States. But models which assume competitive behavior are still useful as a norm against which actual behavior under government intervention can be checked or evaluated. Hence, price determination in the very short run and in the short run under pure competition is discussed in this section. The objective, however, is not to provide an exhaustive discussion of the theory of price determination (this may be found in, for example, Leftwich, 1966).

[3] Economists have made some attempts to classify firms on the basis of the direct-price elasticity of demand faced by the firm and by the cross-price elasticities between firms. For instance, we argued above that the individual firm in a competitive market faces a perfectly elastic (horizontal) demand function. Hence, evidence that a firm faced a perfectly elastic demand schedule for its product would be evidence that the firm was part of a competitive market. Bishop (1952) shows, however, that a classification system based on elasticities involves great subtlety and does not give a completely mutually exclusive classification of markets.

One of the important concepts in economics is that of an equilibrium price. This is simply the price at which quantity demanded and quantity supplied are equated. If the demand function has a negative slope and the supply function a positive slope, then the two curves will intersect at some price. At prices above equilibrium, the quantity consumers are willing to buy is less than the quantity producers are willing to sell, while at prices below equilibrium, quantity demanded exceeds the quantity that will be supplied. Thus, statements such as "demand exceeds supply" are meaningless unless clearly qualified. Quantity demanded exceeds quantity supplied at relatively low prices, is equal to quantity supplied at another price, and falls short of quantity supplied at still higher prices.

Actual market prices tend to approximate equilibrium prices under purely competitive market conditions. However, with imperfect information concerning supply and demand, prospective future supplies, and possible future demand, actual market prices may deviate from the equilibrium price. Price determination is a trial-and-error process.[4] Thus, transaction prices are not always equilibrium prices, but the latter represent a norm or central tendency toward which transaction prices tend to converge. Acting on incomplete or poor information is different from acting irrationally. Also, as we shall see, valid economic reasons exist for differences in prices for different lots of the same commodity (e.g., due to quality differences) under competitive conditions.

Very Short Run

Some farm commodities are harvested periodically and are perishable (e.g., watermelons). The commodity's supply function at harvest is perfectly inelastic, a vertical line. The intersection of the vertical supply curve with a sloping demand curve determines the equilibrium price, say P_1 in Figure 5-1, for that time period. This equilibrium price rations the available supply. The quantity supplied cannot respond to price changes, by definition, in the very short run.

[4] A distinction is sometimes made between the theory of price determination and "price discovery." Price discovery refers to the actual institutional method of arriving at prices and is discussed in Chapter 11.

The level of the very-short-run supply function, of course, can shift from one harvest period to the next. Poor growing conditions in one year would result in a small quantity available for sale, such as S_1 in Figure 5-1, while good growing conditions would result in a large quantity for sale, such as S_2 in Figure 5-1. Total production could be so large that if the entire crop were harvested and marketed, the resulting price would be below harvesting and marketing costs. In this case (not shown in Figure 5-1) a part of the crop would be abandoned.

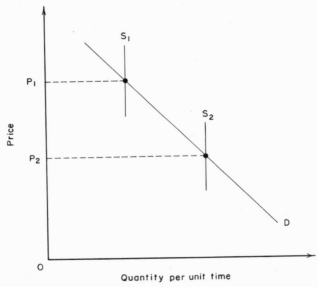

Figure 5-1.   Illustration of equilibrium prices for perfectly inelastic supply functions

The real world is obviously more complex than the simple model depicted in Figure 5-1. Demand functions also shift, and a farm-level price would be related to derived, rather than primary, demand. Nonetheless, an elementary model can be a useful first step in understanding agricultural product price behavior.

For example, red tart cherries must be harvested and used within a few weeks of when they ripen; most are canned or frozen. The quantity processed each year is closely related to production, and for a given year, the supply of cherries is essentially fixed (by carryover of processed products and production). Cherries have highly variable yields and therefore highly variable production. Thus, while supply can be treated as fixed for a particular year, this very-short-run relation can be viewed as shifting from year to year (as in Figure 5-1).

The dots in Figure 5-2 may be viewed as approximate, "average" equilibrium points for each year between a fixed supply and the farm-level (derived) demand. Since no adjustment was made in the data for factors shifting demand, the wide scatter of observations reflects both changes in demand and in supply. The supply of tart cherries, however, has been more variable than demand, giving a scatter with a generally negative slope.

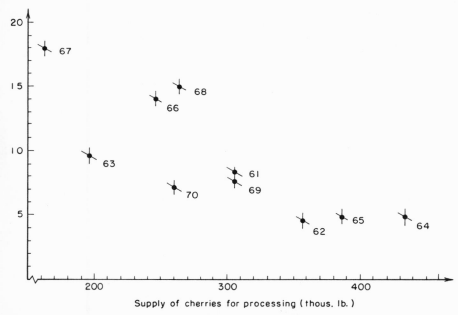

Figure 5-2. Red tart cherries: Relationship between total supply for processing and farm price of sales for processing, Great Lakes region, United States, 1961–1970. Supply is defined as the sum of farm sales for processing and the farm-weight equivalent of July 1 stocks of canned and frozen cherries. Data from Donald J. Ricks and David Smith, *Economic Relationships in Tart Cherry Marketing 1958–70,* Mich. State Univ. Ag. Econ. Report No. 195 (June 1971).

The idea that the points in Figure 5-2 represent equilibria must be qualified. First, tart cherry prices are determined prior to and during harvest, and errors may be made in estimating crop size or other variables influencing price. Actual prices reflect these errors, and consequently the observed average price may not reflect precisely the true demand relation. Second, cherry growers have the option of not harvesting a part of their crop in years of large production and low prices (note the price floor of about 5 cents a pound in Figure 5-2). In such years, quantity sold is a function of price, and hence the quantity supplied to processors is no longer fixed. The elementary model depicted by Figure 5-1 is not appropriate under such circumstances.

If a commodity is storable, then the supply curve is no longer vertical (perfectly inelastic) over its entire range. Supplies may be drawn from stocks at high prices, or certain quantities may be withheld from current sale for storage at low prices. In this case, the supply curve reflects an estimate of the quantities suppliers desire to hold (or supply) at alternative prices (Figure 5-3). The demand curve D illustrates the demand in a particular time period, say a month. The equilibrium price (P_0) is the price at which the quantity buyers want to purchase exactly equals the quantity suppliers (producers and stock holders) want to offer. In Figure 5-3, the total supply available is OB, and the quantity sold within a particular time period is OA. Alternatively, the quantity AB may be viewed as a measure of the sellers' demand to hold that quantity at price P_0. Shifts in either function would, in general, change the level of the equilibrium price.

Short Run

The short run in conventional price theory is a situation in which some factors of production are variable. Hence, as previously discussed, the short-run supply curve includes production costs. The short-run equilibrium price is depicted as being determined by sloping supply and demand schedules similar to those illustrated in Figure 5-4. It is an equilibrium for a given set of short-run demand and supply conditions.

For reasons described in previous chapters, the supply and demand schedules are likely to become more elastic the greater the

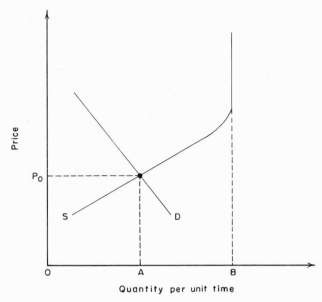

Figure 5-3. Illustration of equilibrium price for storable commodity with fixed available supply OB

time allowed for adjustment to price changes. Thus, in the longer run, the equilibrium price may differ substantially from the one in the short run. The equilibrium price represents that price at which producers will find it just profitable to make the investments necessary to continue producing the marginal unit which will satisfy the quantity demanded at that price.

The conventional supply-demand diagram depicting an equilibrium does *not* imply that price and quantity are constant in a purely competitive market. An equilibrium price is defined for given (static) supply and demand functions. In a dynamic economy, the forces which influence both the level and slope of demand and supply schedules are changing. Hence, the equilibrium price generally changes through time. An increase in income or population typically shifts the demand curve to the right. Changes in the prices and available supplies of inputs or the prices of products competing for the same resources, for instance, cause the supply curve to shift either to the right or to the left. Structural changes in demand and supply may occur as well.

If shifts in demand and supply are equal and in the same direction, the equilibrium price will remain constant. If the demand schedule shifts to the right more rapidly than the supply schedule, the equilibrium price increases; however, if supply increases relative to demand, then the equilibrium price falls (Figure 5-4). In agriculture as a whole in the United States, the latter situation prevailed during most of the 1950's and into the early 1960's. As a result, the average level of farm prices declined.

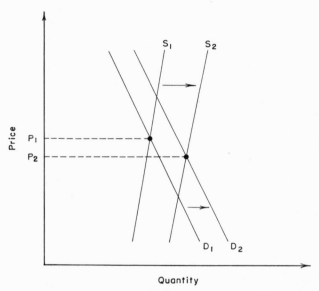

Figure 5-4. Illustration of increase in supply relative to increase in demand

The frequency and magnitude of price changes under purely competitive market conditions depend (1) on the frequency and magnitude of shifts in demand and supply and (2) on the elasticities (more specifically, the slopes) of the demand and supply functions. Wide price fluctuations over short periods of time can be expected if both demand and supply schedules have steep slopes (are relatively inelastic) and if either demand or supply changes sharply from period to period. The typical agricultural commodity has an inelastic demand and a supply which shifts from season to season. An illustration of the sharp annual fluctuations in the price of potatoes is given in Chapter 9 (Figure 9-4).

Price changes will be relatively modest if the demand or supply functions are flat (relatively elastic) and do not shift greatly from one time period to the next. However, even if the demand schedule has a steep slope and shifts from period to period, as long as the supply schedule is relatively flat, price changes will be relatively small. Various combinations of shifts in supply and demand and differences in slopes are possible. This helps explain why different commodities have different degrees of price variability.

The short-run economic model just discussed is most directly applicable in explaining the annual variation of prices and quantities of many farm commodities. (The quantity variable would be represented by an annual total and the price variable by an annual average.) The principal fluctuations in supply often occur from year to year. The reader also should recall that a "typical" supply function may relate current quantity to a lagged price, and clearly much more detail is essential to obtain a more realistic model.

Of course, prices also may vary from day to day (or week to week) under competitive conditions. This occurs with changes in transient factors, which may be viewed as day-to-day changes in demand and supply, and with changing evaluation of information about economic forces by buyers and sellers. Such price changes through time are more fully discussed in several subsequent chapters.[5]

Prices established under purely competitive market conditions should not be considered as inherently superior and therefore sacrosanct. For a variety of reasons, society may prefer to maintain prices above or below those that would prevail with competition. A particular price can be judged "good" or "bad" only insofar as society as a whole considers the consequences of that price desirable or undesirable. Prices established under competitive market conditions do have desirable properties, not the least of which is the avoidance of problems associated with programs to limit production or to ration available supplies. Also, if prices approximate those that prevail under perfectly competitive conditions, the total social product is maximized (resources are optimally allocated). The marginal social benefit of the last unit purchased is just equal

[5] Firms with some control over price are unlikely to respond to transient factors by changing price. Hence, daily price changes are much less likely to occur under market structures with some element of monopoly market power.

to the marginal social cost of producing that unit of output. However, the social product is maximized only if *all* industries operate under competitive conditions. For a more detailed explanation of the conditions necessary to maximize gains to society as a whole see Lerner (1946, pp. 72–88).

If society chooses to use the pricing system, not to allocate resources in a particular way, but to influence the distribution of income, it may do so, provided it is also willing to use nonprice mechanisms to restrain production or to subsidize consumption. Prices may be maintained above equilibrium by such devices as acreage-control programs, land-retirement schemes, or marketing quotas. Likewise, society may choose to keep prices below equilibrium and then use ration cards or other devices to limit consumption. This is frequently done during major wars. Thus, for social or political reasons, actual market prices may be established and maintained above or below equilibrium prices, but this does not make a study of demand and supply relationships irrelevant. It is still essential to know something about the position and slopes of the demand and supply functions in order to ascertain the amount of surplus or deficit that is likely to exist at whatever level prices are established.

Price Determination under Monopoly

Pure, unrestricted monopoly is, in practice, a relatively rare phenomenon. Under the antitrust laws in the United States, monopolies are illegal with exceptions such as public utilities (telephone and electric service). In such instances, rates are regulated by public agencies. Thus, the discussion of pricing under conditions of pure monopoly may seem somewhat academic. However, there are situations in which the theory of pricing under monopoly helps to explain price behavior. A firm, for example, may develop a new product which has few substitutes. In the short run, it may price the product in a manner similar to that of a pure monopolist. There also may be local areas in which the size of the market is such that one firm can operate profitably, but two could not. The existing firm then has a local monopoly, although there are limits to the ability of a firm in this position to raise prices since customers may go elsewhere, or if the price is too high, another firm may find it profitable to enter the market despite the limited scale. Finally, and most important for our purposes, governments sometimes permit monopoly-type pricing by groups or organizations in some sectors of agriculture. Examples include marketing orders in the United States and marketing boards in Commonwealth countries.

The distinguishing feature of a pure monopoly market structure is that the demand schedule facing the individual firm or monopoly organization is sloping rather than horizontal and coincides with the industry demand schedule. Although the monopolist has some discretion in pricing, he must consider the effect of his price policy on sales and net revenue. The more *potential* substitutes available for the product he sells, the more elastic is the long-run demand schedule facing the monopolist. In such cases, if he prices his product substantially above potential substitute products, he could, in the long run, lose a large part of his sales. Thus, the greatest protection society has against the possibility of undue exercise of monopoly power is the potential availability of substitutes, including imported products.

A monopolist can choose any price he likes, but consumers have the final choice of accepting or rejecting the article or service at the stated price. The willingness of buyers to purchase varying quantities at alternative prices is, of course, reflected in the demand schedule facing the firm. The monopolist can establish a price and sell whatever quantities consumers will buy at that price, or, alternatively, he can produce a certain volume and place it on the market. The demand schedule then indicates at what price this volume can be sold. Thus, a monopolist can determine price or the volume of sales, but he cannot simultaneously determine both unless they are consistent with the aggregate demands of consumers.

The monopolist, like all firms, is assumed to maximize profits. This is done by choosing the volume of production (or price) at which marginal costs and marginal revenue are equated. Under monopoly conditions, price does not equal marginal revenue, whereas in perfectly competitive markets, price and marginal revenue are the same. Price is higher than marginal revenue whenever the demand curve facing the individual firm is sloping rather than horizontal. The relationship between marginal revenue and price is expressed by the following equation:

$$MR = P \left(1 + \frac{1}{E}\right),$$

where E is the price elasticity of demand (a negative coefficient).

If elasticity is infinite (horizontal demand curve), the last term $(\frac{1}{E})$ approaches zero as a limit and the equation becomes $MR = P$ $(1 + 0)$ or $MR = P$. The more inelastic the demand curve (i.e., the steeper the slope), the greater the difference between price and marginal revenue. Marginal revenue is positive only if the elasticity of demand is greater than unity. If the elasticity is -1.0 (unit elasticity), the marginal revenue becomes zero, regardless of the price, $MR = P \left(1 + \frac{1}{-1}\right) = P (1 - 1) = 0$; while if the demand schedule is price inelastic (less than -1.0), marginal revenue becomes negative. For example, if elasticity equals -0.2, then $MR = P(1 + \frac{1}{-.2}) = P(1 - 5)$ or $-4P$. It follows that a "rational" monopolist would not set a price in the range of demand that was inelastic.

The profit-maximizing price and volume of output for a monopolist (or for a group of agricultural producers if they were to combine and operate as a single seller) are illustrated in Figure 5-5. In this case, it would never be profitable to sell more than OB units, even if costs of production were zero, since beyond that point the marginal revenue becomes negative. If one takes account of costs, then the optimum level of output is at OA, that is, the volume at which the marginal cost curve intersects the marginal revenue curve. The price at which this output would sell (determined by the average revenue or demand schedule) is P_1.

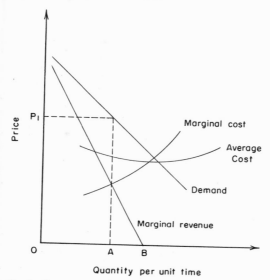

Figure 5-5. Illustration of price determination with a monopoly market structure

The volume of output that will maximize profits for the monopolist obviously will change if either the demand or cost curves change. Prices, however, are less likely to change in the short run under conditions approaching pure monopoly than under purely competitive conditions. The monopolist is more likely to establish a price with long-run rather than short-run profits in mind and to maintain that price for a considerable period of time. If the initial price is high, this may encourage potential competitors to develop new products, or the government may seek to break up the firm or to regulate it. Thus, the monopolist may price below the short-run equilibrium position in an attempt to perpetuate or maintain his long-run profits. However, the firm which has developed a new product (e.g., nylon) may price the product relatively high initially when manufacturing capacity is small, and then reduce the price over time in order to encourage sales as capacity expands. Consequently, at any one point in time, the monopolist's price may vary substantially from that suggested by the pure theory of monopoly pricing.

Price Discrimination

Under some circumstances, it is possible for a monopolist (whether an individual firm or a farm cooperative that has control over a high proportion of the total supply of a particular commodity) to increase its revenue by charging some buyers higher prices for its product than others. The conditions that must exist for a monopolist or a monopoly-type organization to gain from discriminatory pricing are as follows:

(1) It must be possible to identify two or more separate groups of buyers (markets) with different price elasticities of demand.

(2) The markets must be effectively separated to prevent a flow of the commodity among markets and hence permit a higher price to prevail in one outlet than in another.

If these conditions exist, it is possible to increase revenue by charging a higher price in the market with the more inelastic (or less elastic) demand and a lower price in the market with a less inelastic (or more elastic) demand.[6]

The principles involved in maximizing returns by practicing discriminatory pricing can be simply illustrated by assuming just two groups of buyers with different price elasticities of demand. Initially, assuming a fixed supply of the commodity to be sold and that the cost of allocating the supply between markets is zero, marginal costs are zero and can be ignored. The profit-maximizing rule is to shift quantities between markets up to the point where the marginal revenue (MR) obtained from the sale of the last unit in each market is equal. This may be done (provided there is sufficient quantity) up to the point that $MR_1 = MR_2 = 0$. It would not, of course, pay to sell quantities such that the marginal revenue becomes negative in either market.

One condition for successful price discrimination is differences in price elasticities, which implies different demand relations and hence different marginal revenue curves. If the same price were charged to the two groups of buyers, then the marginal revenues

[6] Economists sometimes define three degrees of price discrimination (see Pigou, 1952, p. 279). We discuss "third degree" discrimination, the only degree of practical importance.

would be different. The equalization of marginal revenues increases total revenue by transferring part of the available supply from the market with the lower marginal revenue (raising price in this market) to the market with the higher marginal revenue (lowering price in this market). For example, if reducing sales by one unit in the primary market increased revenue 25 cents per unit and if the added quantity in the secondary market decreases revenue only 8 cents per unit, there is a gain of 17 cents from the transfer. It would pay to continue transferring units until the gain in revenue in one market equals the loss in the other market, that is, until marginal revenues are equal.

In the longer run, where production costs must be considered, the optimum level of output and the quantity sold in each market may change since the monopolist must take account of marginal costs as well as the marginal revenue in each market (Figure 5-6). The optimum level of output is that at which the added cost to the firm (or to the monopoly selling organization) of producing the last unit of product just equals the combined marginal revenue from sales in both markets. The optimum level of output is then allocated between markets in such a way that marginal revenue is equal in all markets and also is equal to marginal costs, that is, $MC = MR_1 = MR_2$.

Under the Robinson-Patman Act it is illegal for firms to charge buyers different prices unless they can prove that the differences in prices are accounted for by differences in costs.[7] Nevertheless, there are cases where discriminatory pricing practices are adopted. In agriculture, this is frequently done with the assistance of the government.

To profit from discriminatory pricing, as pointed out earlier, it must be possible to maintain separate markets. Markets may be differentiated on the basis of

(1) place or location, e.g., domestic and export markets;
(2) time, e.g., seasonal differences in resort hotel prices and higher first-run movie prices;

[7] The courts have held in some cases, however, that a firm may charge buyers lower prices for a particular commodity or service in one market than in other markets provided the lower price is maintained simply "to meet competition" (for additional discussion see Papandreau and Wheeler, 1954).

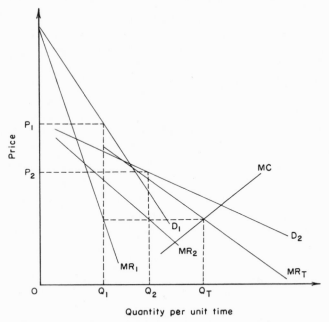

Figure 5-6. A two-market price discrimination model. In this diagram, a monopolist is assumed to be able to divide his market into two parts with demands D_1 and D_2 and his marginal costs are given by *MC*. The profit-maximizing output is Q_T of which Q_1 should be sold in Market 1 at price P_1 and Q_2 should be sold in Market 2 at price P_2. MR_T is the horizontal sum of MR_1 and MR_2.

   (3) form or use of the commodity, e.g., price differences between fresh and processed use of a raw material;

   (4) type of consumer, e.g., residential versus industrial use of a service, charging different fees for medical services by income groups, or different prices for theatre tickets by age groups;

   (5) a combination of the above.

Even if separate markets can be established, gains will be small or nonexistent unless elasticities also differ significantly in the separate markets and a relatively large fraction of the total output is sold in the higher-priced market. The potential methods of separating markets are suggestive of reasons for differences in elasticities. In Chapter 3, we noted that income elasticities may vary with the level of income; the homogeneity condition implies that price elasticities vary with income elasticities, the magnitude of cross elasticities held constant. Thus, it is not surprising that different income groups may have different price elasticities of demand for a particular commodity. Elasticities also may differ among markets because of differences in the availability of substitutes, differences in age level or age distribution of the population, and differences in tastes and preferences. Even if retail demand functions are identical, derived demands faced by the discriminator may still be different.

A large literature has developed dealing with the application of price discrimination concepts in agriculture (Forker and Anderson, 1968; Waugh, 1964). To illustrate, a part of the apple crop is sold at harvest, part in the winter, and part in the spring. These seasonal markets are naturally separated by time, though they are not necessarily independent of each other. If the demand for apples differs seasonally, then the principles of price discrimination could be used to determine the allocation of sales through time in order to maximize revenue to sellers. The implementation of such a scheme, however, would require apple growers to organize and act as a monopoly.

Federal and state marketing orders make it possible for producers of some products to practice price discrimination. Under milk marketing orders, for example, handlers of milk are required to pay higher prices for milk which is bottled for fluid use than for milk of equal quality which is converted into cheese, ice cream, and so forth. Such regulations clearly assume that the demand for fluid milk is more price inelastic than the demand for manufactured dairy products.

Some farm products are exported at lower prices than those prevailing in the domestic market. The demand in the export market is assumed to be more elastic than in the domestic market. The government provides the power for separating markets, subsidizing exports, and maintaining price differences by imposing import quotas or tariffs. Most such schemes probably have increased total revenue, but prices have not necessarily been established at levels which will maximize returns to producers. The possibilities of extracting more revenue from consumers have not been fully exploited. For example, it has been suggested that wheat exporters should sell wheat to developed countries such as the United Kingdom, Japan, and Germany (with high internal price supports and price inelastic demands) at relatively high prices and sell the remainder to developing countries (with more elastic demands) at relatively low prices (Abel, 1966).

The analytics of a price discrimination scheme require a knowledge of the calculus of constrained optimization, which is beyond the scope of this book. The interested student, however, may wish to study Waugh (1964, appendix 6) or a similar reference. We provide here the first steps in setting up the problem.

The simplest problem involves two markets, an unlimited quantity to allocate between the markets, and zero costs of allocation. In this simple case, no constraints exist, and the algebra is relatively simple.

An essential first step is to have reliable estimates of the demand functions for the separate markets. Assuming such functions are available and further assuming they are straight lines, we write them in the form of price (P) as a function of quantity (Q). The subscripts represent the two markets.

$$P_1 = a - b\,Q_1, \text{ and}$$
$$P_2 = c - d\,Q_2.$$

The total revenues (R) for the two markets are

$$R_1 = P_1\,Q_1 = (a - bQ_1)\,Q_1$$
$$= a\,Q_1 - b\,Q_1{}^2.$$
$$R_2 = c\,Q_2 - d\,Q_2{}^2.$$

In this simple case, the optimum point is for the allocation in which the marginal revenues are zero. Readers familiar with calculus will also recall that a necessary condition for a maximum is that the first derivatives equal zero.

The marginal revenues (MR) are defined as the first derivatives of the total revenue functions.

$$MR_1 = \frac{d\,R_1}{d\,Q_1} = a - 2\,b\,Q_1 \text{ and}$$

$$MR_2 = \frac{d\,R_2}{d\,Q_2} = c - 2\,d\,Q_2.$$

Setting these equations equal to zero and solving for the respective Q's gives

$$\hat{Q}_1 = \frac{a}{2b} \text{ and } \hat{Q}_2 = \frac{c}{2d}.$$

The total quantity sold would be $\hat{Q}_1 + \hat{Q}_2$ with the respective quantities allocated to the two markets. The optimizing prices for the two markets are computed from the demand equations.

A somewhat more realistic problem in agriculture is the allocation of a fixed supply to the alternate markets. At harvest, for example, the quantity of apples to be allocated to the alternate seasonal markets is a fixed amount. In terms of an example using two markets, the problem is to maximize total revenue (R) subject to the constraint that the quantities allocated equal the total quantity (Q_T) available. That is,

$$\text{maximize } R = R_1 + R_2,$$
$$\text{subject to } Q_T = Q_1 + Q_2.$$

As previously, the definitions of R_1 and R_2 can be substituted so that R becomes a function of the Q's.

The allocation problem also can be made more realistic by taking account of allocation costs. In the apple example, a seasonal allocation of the crop implies costs of storage. Thus, we could adjust gross revenue for storage costs in such a way as to maximize revenue net of these costs.

It is important to note that—even in the simplest case—the derivation of an appropriate solution is dependent on the quality of the underlying information. Thus, good estimates of the demand functions and cost functions are essential. If the allocation is to be made among four markets, then estimates of four demand functions are required. This is not necessarily a trivial task. The lack of precise estimates may explain why policy programs often use the principles of price discrimination as general guides to allocations among markets but not to find specific optimum points.

Most elementary discussions of price discrimination assume that the various markets are independent, but it is not easy to maintain separate markets, even if they can be differentiated initially. Cheaper processed products, for example, may gradually reduce sales in the higher-priced fresh-use market. Products made from raw materials sold at lower prices in export markets also may eventually undercut sales of domestically manufactured products. This happened in the United States during the late 1950's when cotton was sold abroad at prices substantially lower than those paid by domestic cotton mills. Eventually the textile products manufactured from lower-priced U.S. cotton in Japan, Hong Kong, and Taiwan found their way back into the United States and reduced the sales of domestic mills.

With lack of independence, the profit-maximizing discriminatory prices can *not* be based on the marginal revenues of demand functions that assume independence. Rather, these functions (and the corresponding marginal revenues) must be adjusted for the net effect of possible substitutability among the markets, or more likely, the demand functions must be estimated in such a way as to take account of the interrelatedness (Hoos and Seltzer, 1952).

Finally, one must keep in mind the effect of higher prices on supply of the farm product involved. If discrimination succeeds in raising total revenue, and the additional revenue is paid out to producers, this will encourage expansion. The net effect then may be simply to add to the quantities going into the secondary market, which will subsequently cause average returns to decline. This explains why multiple-price schemes in agriculture may increase returns to producers in the short run, but not in the long run, unless the lower marginal price is reflected back to producers so that there is less incentive to increase output. Monopoly power is required to control allocations of supply to various markets; it also may be necessary to use such power to control or influence production.

In sum, the use of price discrimination concepts to allocate a product among markets assumes some monopoly power, and the resulting allocations tend to equalize *net marginal revenues* in the markets. This allocation, in general, can be quite different from the allocation that would occur under perfectly competitive conditions.

The allocations under competitive conditions tend to equalize *net prices* in the alternate markets. This topic is discussed more fully in subsequent chapters. For example, the relationship of spatial prices under competitive conditions is discussed in Chapter 8.

Price Behavior with Monopolistic Competition and Oligopoly

Monopolistic competition, as previously discussed, is essentially a competitive market structure but with product differentiation. The products involved are close, but imperfect, substitutes, but by definition there are many substitutes. Thus, the demand curve faced by the firm operating in an industry characterized by monopolistic competition is likely to be very elastic.

It is usually assumed that the firms have similar cost structures. Firms with high costs relative to others in the industry presumably could not exist in the long run in a relatively competitive industry. The equilibrium price (and output) is based on equating marginal revenue and marginal cost. Since the products are good substitutes and since similar cost structures are assumed, the prices of the various firms are expected to be similar but not necessarily identical.

Firms operating under conditions of monopolistic competition tend to avoid price competition because of the threat of retaliation by other firms. An individual firm, of course, would gain if it reduced its own price (since its own demand schedule is reasonably elastic), provided other firms did not. But if competing firms also lower their prices to meet the competition, each would gain relatively little. This explains why gasoline stations prefer to avoid price wars. Since price cutting often leads to retaliation, the profit-maximizing price is likely to be similar among firms in the industry and relatively stable as long as costs remain constant.

Similar pressures to avoid direct price competition prevail in industries where a few firms produce or market identical or similar products, i.e. where oligopolistic conditions prevail. In making pricing decisions, each firm must take account of the possible reactions of its competitors. A price change initiated by one firm is likely to be followed by other firms. Often there is a recognized "price leader" in the industry. Competition for sales may take the form of offering more favorable credit terms, advertising or promotion allowances, or even secret discounts or rebates.

It is difficult to generalize about pricing performance under oligopolistic conditions without specific knowledge about the behavior of individual firms. If an aggressive firm is seeking to enlarge its market share, the price established may be very close to that which would prevail under purely competitive conditions. On the other hand, if a tacit agreement exists to maintain market shares and to avoid open price competition, the price established may approximate that which would prevail under conditions of pure monopoly.

Marketing margins for some farm products are determined under conditions which more nearly conform to the oligopolistic or monopolistic competition model than the purely competitive model. A high proportion of the fluid milk sold on retail routes or through chain stores in most cities is processed and distributed by a small number of firms. While these firms usually are compelled to pay producers certain minimum prices under federal or state marketing orders, the distributors are free to establish retail prices (except in a few states which also regulate retail prices). Thus, the behavior of individual firms is an extremely important factor affecting fluid-milk marketing margins. Retail prices (hence margins) are likely to be low in cities where there is one or more aggressive firms seeking to increase their market share; they are more likely to be high in cities where a "live and let live" policy prevails among distributors.

Small processors such as those canning or freezing fruits and vegetables often face a situation best characterized as oligopsony (many sellers and a few buyers). Each produces a small part of the total supply, which must then be sold in competition with similar products offered by other processors to a small number of retail-chain buyers. When supplies of processed products are large, the temptation is for each processor to shave the price to avoid carrying large inventories. Chain-store buyers are then in a position to play off one supplier against another. This can lead to depressed prices for processors, low profits, and little capital for investment in more modern equipment or facilities.

Among agricultural commodities, the breakfast cereal industry offers perhaps the best illustration of what may occur under an oligopolistic structure. Each of the small number of firms which dominates the industry seeks to capture a larger share of the market, not so much through price competition, but by developing new products, by offering coupons or prizes, and through increased expenditures for packaging, promotion, and advertising.

Retail food stores also may seek to increase their sales by building more elegant stores, offering trading stamps, or providing additional services. The net effect of this form of competition is to increase the number and variety of products available and perhaps consumer satisfactions as well, but at the same time, marketing costs are increased. While price competition is still important in the food processing and retailing industry, there is probably greater emphasis today on nonprice competition than when supermarkets were first introduced (see Mori and Gorman, 1966; Nelson, 1966; Padberg, 1968, for additional comments on the role of price vs. nonprice competition in food retailing).

Concluding Remarks

Price performance under alternate market structures is difficult to appraise. Prices established under competitive conditions are likely to be somewhat lower than those that would prevail under monopolistic or oligopolistic conditions. Competitive prices also are likely to vary more frequently and with wider amplitude, especially where demand and supply schedules are inelastic and where either supply or demand shifts abruptly from year to year or season to season.

Economists tend to prefer competitive pricing to monopoly pricing, and obviously there is a greater possibility of farmers being exploited, for example, when only a single buyer or a few outlets are available in a local area. But it is difficult to determine empirically whether or not farmers are being charged higher prices for the things they buy or are being offered lower prices for what they sell than would prevail with a larger number of sellers and buyers.

The economies of scale may be sufficiently large that marketing costs may be lower with a small number of large firms than with a large number of small competitors. Galbraith (1952, pp. 90–99) also calls attention to the fact that where pricing is very competitive, profit margins may be so thin as to limit expenditures for research or capital improvements. He maintains that the most innovative firms have been those that have had sufficient market power to maintain prices above average costs in the short run. By investing in research, they were able to develop improved products and increase efficiency. A substantial share of the benefits of these innovations was subsequently passed on to consumers. In sum, the issue is whether or not the benefits of economies of size, improved products, and so forth when they exist for large firms are more or less offset by higher profits, excessive product differentiation, larger advertising expenses, and other costs.

References

Abel, Martin E. 1966. "Price Discrimination in the World Trade of Agricultural Commodities," *J. Farm Econ.*, 48:194–208.

Bishop, Robert L. 1952. "Elasticities, Cross-Elasticities, and Market Relationships," *Am. Econ. Rev.*, 42:779–803.

Cochrane, Willard W. 1957. "The Market as a Unit of Inquiry in Agricultural Economics Research," *J. Farm Econ.*, 39:21–39.

Dorfman, Robert. 1964. *The Price System*. Englewood Cliffs, N.J.: Prentice-Hall.

Forker, Olan D., and Brenda A. Anderson. 1968. *An Annotated Bibliography on Price Discrimination*. Cornell Univ. Ag. Econ. Res. 241.

Galbraith, J. K. 1952. *American Capitalism: The Concept of Countervailing Power*. Boston: Houghton Mifflin.

Hoos, Sidney, and R. E. Seltzer. 1952. *Lemons and Lemon Products: Changing Economic Relationships*. Calif. Ag. Exp. Sta. Bul. 729.

Leftwich, Richard H. 1966. *The Price System and Resource Allocation*. 3d ed. New York: Holt, Rinehart and Winston. Chapters 6, 9, 10, 11, 12.

Lerner, Abba P. 1946. *The Economics of Control*. New York: Macmillan.

Moore, John R., and Richard G. Walsh, eds. 1966. *Market Structure of the Agricultural Industries*. Ames, Iowa: Iowa State Univ. Press.

Mori, Hiroshi, and W. D. Gorman. 1966. "An Empirical Investigation into the Relationship between Market Structure and Performance as Measured by Price," *J. Farm Econ.*, 48, No. 3 (Part II):162–171 (Aug.).

Nelson, Paul E., Jr. 1966. "Price Competition among Retail Food Stores," *J. Farm Econ.*, 48, No. 3 (Part II):172–187 (Aug.).

Padberg, Daniel I. 1968. *Economics of Food Retailing.* Ithaca, N.Y.: Cornell Univ. Food Distribution Program.

Papandreau, Andreas G., and John T. Wheeler. 1954. *Competition and Its Regulation.* Englewood Cliffs, N.J.: Prentice-Hall. Chapters 6 and 21.

Pigou, A. C. 1952. *The Economics of Welfare.* 4th ed. London: Macmillan.

Waugh, Frederick V. 1964. *Demand and Price Analysis: Some Examples from Agriculture.* Econ. Res. Ser., USDA Tech. Bul. 1316.

PRICE DIFFERENCES
AND VARIABILITY

The focus of attention in this section is on those factors which help to explain price differences associated with the provision of marketing services, with grade or quality, with location, and with the passage of time. Price differences between those paid to the farmer and those paid by the consumer are commonly referred to as marketing margins, and these differences are analyzed in Chapter 6. In the following two chapters, price differences based on quality and on region or location are discussed. Price changes that occur through time are discussed in Chapter 9; particular emphasis is placed on seasonal and cyclical (cobweblike models) variation. In Chapter 10, changes in the terms of trade of farm products (i.e., in the relationship between farm and nonfarm prices) and changes in the general level of all farm prices are considered.

CHAPTER 6

Marketing Margins
for Farm Products

Price theory in its simplest form assumes that buyers and sellers meet directly. Equilibrium prices are determined by the aggregate demand and supply schedules of these buyers and sellers. Elementary textbooks in price theory generally say little or nothing about price differences between producers and final consumers. However, substantial research has been done in agricultural economics on questions related to price differences between farmers and consumers. Nonetheless, unanswered questions remain.

The difference between the price received by producers and that paid by consumers is a marketing margin. Both producers and consumers are concerned about the size of marketing margins, changes in marketing margins, and the incidence of changes in margins. Among the questions frequently asked are the following: Are marketing margins too large? Why do margins differ among products? Why do they change with the passage of time? Are margins larger for small sized crops than for large sized crops? If a margin increases, does this result in a higher consumer price or a lower farm price, or both?

This chapter has several objectives. One is to provide a specific definition of the idea of a marketing margin. A second is to discuss the reasons for changes in margins and the effects of changing margins. Thus, this chapter provides tools of analysis and evidence that will help the student to answer such questions as those posed above. Attention is focused exclusively on marketing margins and not on price differences due to quality, space, or time. Most of the analysis is based on the marketing margin for a single product and assumes a purely competitive market structure.[1]

[1] Some comments are made in the next to last section of this chapter on the potential effects of imperfect competition on marketing margins.

Defining Marketing Margins

Theoretical Concepts

A marketing margin may be defined alternatively as (1) a difference between the price paid by consumers and that obtained by producers, or as (2) the price of a collection of marketing services which is the outcome of the demand for and the supply of such services.

Under the first definition, a marketing margin is simply a difference between the primary and derived demand curves for a particular product. These concepts were presented in Chapter 2. Primary demand is determined by the response of the ultimate consumers. Empirical estimates of primary demand functions are usually based on retail price and quantity data. Derived demand is based on price-quantity relations which exist either at the point where products leave the farm or at intermediate points where they are purchased by wholesalers or processors (see, for example, Daly, 1958).

Primary demand is in some sense a joint demand for all of the inputs in the final product. Thus, a food product at retail may be divided (conceptually) into two inputs: the farm-based components and the processing-marketing components. Given several simplifying assumptions, the derived demand for the farm product is obtained by subtracting the per unit costs (prices) of all marketing components from the primary demand function. Thus, the farm-level function represents the derived demand for the farm component of the final product, and in empirical analyses the farm price usually must be adjusted so that comparable components are being priced at each level. The assumptions are that the final product is made from fixed proportions of the inputs (e.g., one unit of final product is always obtained from one unit of farm product and two marketing units) and that the supply function of marketing inputs is fixed (static) at a particular level (Friedman, 1962).

Under some conditions, marketing margins can be expected to remain constant as the quantity of a commodity marketed is changing, while under other conditions, margins will vary. The manner in which they respond to changes in the volume marketed depends on the assumptions made with respect to the supply function for marketing services. If this supply function is perfectly elastic (horizontal), the margin remains constant as the demand for services (associated with increasing volume) increases. The same marketing margin is subtracted from the primary demand function at all levels of quantity, and hence the derived demand function is parallel to the primary demand function when they are straight lines. This is the situation assumed in Figure 6-1.

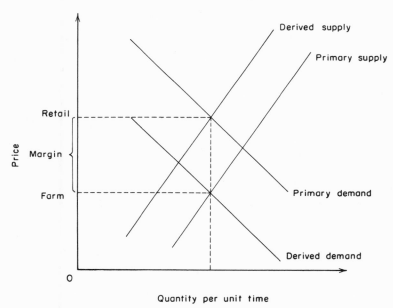

Figure 6-1. Illustration of primary and derived functions and marketing margins

Assuming the supply function for marketing services has a positive slope, then the price of such services would increase as demand increases; hence margins would be higher with larger quantities produced and marketed. But empirical evidence is not always consistent with this assumption (Buse and Brandow, 1960). It may be more realistic to assume that economies of scale in providing marketing services exist. If so, this could lead to a negatively shaped supply curve for marketing services, at least over some range. Under these circumstances, one would expect to find lower margins associated with a larger volume of production. For instance, a small crop may result in an underutilization of marketing facilities while a large crop *may* lead to increased efficiency and hence to lower unit costs. Since many food products undergo a complex transformation from the farm to the consumer, the actual nature of the marketing margins is often difficult to determine.

The concepts of primary and derived supply are analogous to those for demand. Primary supply, however, refers to the relationship at the producer level (Chapter 4). Empirical estimates are based on farm-level data. The supply relation at retail is derived from the primary relation by adding an appropriate margin.

Thus, a retail price is established at the point where the primary demand and the derived supply relation intersect (Figure 6-1). The farm-level price is based on derived demand and primary supply. The difference in the two prices is the marketing margin. The situation depicted in Figure 6-1 is, of course, static; possible changes in these functions are discussed in a subsequent section.

A marketing margin also may be defined as the price of a collection of services. This price is a function of the demand for and supply of all such services. Marketing services include such items as assembly, processing, transportation, and retailing. These services are sometimes classified by time, form, and place utilities (see Waite and Trelogan, 1951). The supply relation for marketing services (mentioned above) is defined in terms of the marginal cost curve for the services, which in turn depends on input prices, etc. In principle, a demand relation for marketing services also may be defined. A particular marketing margin would thus depend on the particular demand and supply relations for services. An attempt has been made to obtain empirical estimates of aggregate service relationships for food (Waldorf, 1966).

Margins differ among products because marketing services differ. Changes in margins may be depicted as resulting from shifts in the supply or demand relations for services. For example, higher input prices for a service with other things the same would result in a decrease in supply and a higher margin (Figure 6-2). Of course, if the supply curve were perfectly elastic, shifts in the demand for marketing services would not change the margin.

In practice, there are many marketing services, and hence empir-

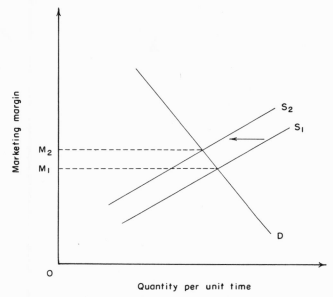

Figure 6-2. Hypothetical demand and supply relations for marketing services

ical analyses require substantial aggregation. Demand and supply concepts, however, can be useful in categorizing variables influencing margins. In the remainder of this chapter, the marketing margin will be defined as the difference between retail and producer prices. It is relatively easy to define empirically the margin for products which retain their general identity as they move through the marketing system (e.g., fluid milk or eggs). However, with the use of more services and with the advent of products like frozen TV dinners, it is becoming increasingly difficult to define marketing margins for many food products.

Empirical Measures

The USDA publishes two commonly used measures of marketing costs, the farm-retail spreads for food products and the farm food marketing bill (see Gale, 1967; Ogren, 1965; Scott and Badger, 1972; Waugh and Ogren, 1961). The farm-retail spreads are computed as per unit (e.g., cents per pound) margins for individual commodities. In addition, the retail cost and the farm value for an aggregate market basket of foods is computed. The marketing bill statistic is a measure of total costs, rather than a per unit margin, but it is briefly discussed to indicate that it represents a different concept.

Farm-retail price spreads are computed as follows. Retail prices are obtained from the Bureau of Labor Statistics for a market basket of foods. These data are based on average quantities of farm-originated foods purchased per household.[2] The spread is computed as the difference between the retail price of the specified quantity and quality of a particular good and its farm value. The farm value is based on prices obtained by the Statistical Reporting Service of the USDA and on computations to obtain the equivalent farm-level quantity of that specified in the retail market basket. The result is an attempt to measure the costs of a fixed bundle of marketing services. The retail-farm spread for choice beef is illustrated in Figure 6-3 (Duewer, 1970).

The familiar "farmer's share of the consumer's dollar" statistic is based on the aggregate market-basket data. The retail cost and the farm value of the total (fixed) market basket are computed. The farmer's share statistic is the percentage computed by dividing the

Table 6-1. Farmer's share of retail cost of a market basket of farm-food products, selected years

Year	Share (%)	Year	Share (%)
1918	51	1955	41
1933	32	1960	39
1945	53	1965	40
1950	47	1970	39

Source: Economic Research Service, Farm-Retail Spreads for Food Products, 1947–64, USDA ERS-226 (1965), and Forrest E. Scott and Henry T. Badger, Farm-Retail Spreads for Food Products, Econ. Res. Ser., USDA Misc. Pub. No. 741, revised (1972), table 1.

[2] These quantities were obtained from a 1960–1961 survey (see Scott and Badger, 1972). The quantities are fixed and are based on purchases by wage earners and clerical workers in urban areas.

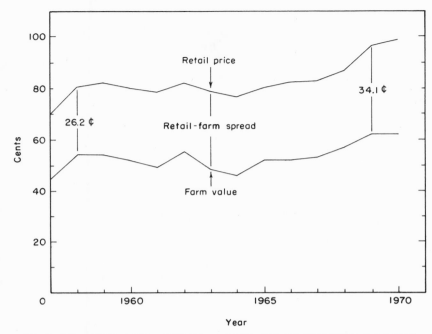

Figure 6-3. Retail price, retail-farm spread, and net farm value per pound, choice grade beef, United States, 1957–1970. Net farm value equals gross value minus a byproduct allowance; gross farm value is defined as the payment to farmers for a quantity of choice grade beef cattle equivalent to one pound of retail cuts. From Lawrence A. Duewer, *Price Spreads for Beef and Pork: Revised Series, 1949–69,* Econ. Res. Ser., USDA Misc. Pub. No. 1174 (May 1970).

farm value by the retail cost. The percentage is sometimes interpreted as the cents received per dollar spent on food by consumers. The retail-farm spread for the market basket of farm foods for a recent period is shown in Figure 6-4.

The food marketing bill is based on the aggregate cost of all marketing services. It reflects changes in the volume of food marketed, changes in the services provided, changes in product-mix marketed, as well as changes in costs of existing services. Consumer expenditures at retail, the marketing bill, and the farm value of domestic farm-food products in a recent period are depicted in Figure 6-5.

The per unit margin (farm-retail spread) statistics and especially the related concept of the farmer's share of the consumer's dollar

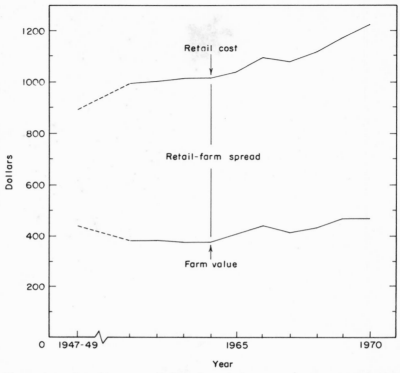

Figure 6-4. Retail cost, retail-farm spread, and farm value for a market basket of farm foods, United States, 1947–1949 and 1961–1970. From Forrest E. Scott and Henry T. Badger, *Farm-Retail Spreads for Food Products*, Econ. Res. Ser., USDA Misc. Pub. No. 741 (revised, 1972).

are subject to misinterpretation. This concept is perhaps the most frequently quoted, but misused, number published by the USDA. There is a tendency to use the number to indicate the "well-being" of farmers or to indicate that marketing costs are "too high." In fact, the farmer's share statistic has little to say about either problem. For example, poultry farmers have received about 55 per cent of the consumer's dollar in recent years, apple growers about 33 per cent, and wheat producers about 12 per cent of the price of white bread. But poultry farmers have not been better off in general than wheat producers.

Farm prices and the farmer's share statistic have tended to move up and down together (Table 6-1). That is, the farmer's share was

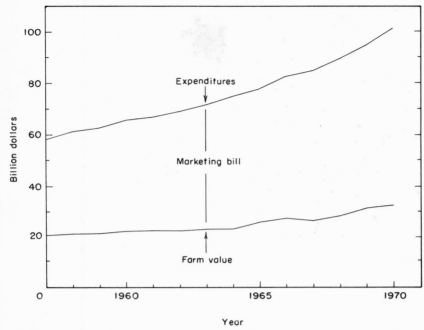

Year

Figure 6-5. Consumer expenditures, total marketing bill, and farm value for domestic farm-food products, United States, 1957–1970. Data from Jeannette Findlay and Leland Southard, "The Bill for Marketing Farm Food Products," *Marketing and Transportation Situation,* Econ. Res. Ser., USDA, MTS-182 (Aug. 1971), pp. 9–16.

high when farm prices were high as in the war years 1918 and 1945. However, this is a function of the relative flexibility of farm prices and the relative inflexibility of the margin, at least in the short run. Hence, when farm prices decrease, they tend to become a smaller percentage of retail prices.

Nonetheless, the farmer's share statistic remained relatively constant at about 39 per cent throughout the 1960's. As pointed out earlier, this tells very little about the welfare of farmers (see also Atchley, 1956). Producers will be better off, regardless of what happens to the farmer's share statistic, if farm costs decline relative to prices. Nor does a decline in the share of the consumer's dollar going to farmers necessarily mean that marketing firms are performing poorly. The decline may simply reflect the increased cost of marketing inputs such as labor. Price spreads provide only a starting point in an attempt to evaluate the performance of the food industry. Measures of efficiency and profits earned by marketing firms also must be examined to determine whether or not margins are excessive (Hammond, 1967; National Commission on Food Marketing, 1966, p. 19).

Changes and Incidence of Changes in Margins

Margin Changes

A margin per unit of product marketed has been defined as the difference between a retail-level and a producer-level (or an intermediate-level) price. These prices, as previously indicated, are determined by particular primary and derived demand and supply relations (review Figure 6-1). Thus, a margin changes because certain of these functions shift relative to others. Of course, the fundamental questions are: What functions shift? and why do they shift?

The derived demand and supply curves shift because the costs of providing existing marketing services embodied in the final product change. Stated another way, the supply function of marketing inputs shifts. Thus, the farm-level (derived) demand for a product may change as the usual determinants of demand change and as the costs of marketing services change. Larger per unit costs, for example, would result in a decrease in derived demand and in derived supply. Marketing costs include waste, loss, and spoilage in the marketing process as well as the more "typical" costs.

Changes in per unit marketing costs (i.e., shifts in the supply curve for marketing inputs), of course, mean changes in marketing margins. The derived demand and supply curves shift relative to the primary curves. A technological improvement in providing marketing services implies a possible structural change in the supply curve of such services. Consequently, the shift in the derived demand curve for the farm product may not be "parallel" to the original level. For instance, the technical change may favor a large volume marketed relative to smaller quantities; the per unit margin may decline more at the larger volumes than at the smaller volumes.

The nature of margins obviously varies among products, and the magnitude of a change in margin depends on the magnitude of the change in per unit costs. There are differences among products in the services provided, such as the amount of processing or transportation included in the product. The degree of perishability also affects margins. Technical improvements may influence the cost of marketing services for one product much more than another.

The primary demand curve shifts with the adoption of new services. When marketing services change, then the product definition at the retail level changes. New inputs or combinations of inputs are used in the final product. Thus, in effect, a new demand curve exists for the at least slightly different product. The addition of new services generally has the effect of shifting the primary demand relation up and to the right (increasing demand). The new service probably means increased costs. In the transition, consumers probably have the alternative of buying the old product or the new higher priced one (with added service). If they are willing to buy the same units of the new product at the higher price, then primary demand has increased. In principle, the demand for certain services also may decline and certain services might be removed, which would result in a decrease in primary demand and a decrease in the margin.

The net effect of an entirely new product on the primary and derived demand relationships for related, substitute products is often very complex. In some instances, the development of a new product, say frozen orange juice, may increase total demand, say for orange products in the aggregate. Primary demand may increase by more than enough to cover additional processing and handling costs, thereby increasing the derived demand for the farm component. In other instances, the demand for the new product may not offset the decline in demand for existing products, at least so that the total derived demand for the farm components is smaller. A consumer in buying a frozen dinner in place of similar products in less processed form is perhaps buying less farm product (and is clearly buying more service). The net effect of this substitution on the derived demand for the farm products is thus difficult to ascertain. In addition, the per unit marketing costs for existing products may increase as the volume sold declines.

In sum, changes in factor prices, efficiency, and services embodied in farm products change marketing margins. Hence, over the longer run, average margins tend to parallel changes in costs (as broadly defined). These costs tend to be "sticky," especially relative to farm prices. Thus, while marketing costs can decrease, the usual tendency is to remain the same or to increase (see Scott and Badger, 1972).

In the short run, there may be temporary changes in margins due to lagged responses in the marketing system to changes in primary supply or demand. Livestock and meat margins "have exhibited a persistent short-run tendency to widen when supplies increase and narrow when supplies decrease" (Breimyer, 1957, p. 691). A larger farm supply, for example, lowers the farm price but is reflected in retail prices only after a lag in time. Hence, the margin rises temporarily but then declines again as competition forces adjustments in retail prices.

Numerous hypotheses to explain the sticky responses of retail prices to changes in farm prices have been advanced. Inertia in the marketing system perhaps accounts for some of the delay in transmitting changes in farm prices through the system. Breimyer (1957, p. 692) argues rather generally that the explanation is "the desire . . . for stability in both prices and volume." Parish (1967) lists arguments both on the cost and demand side. If average unit costs vary sharply as sales vary on either side of some normal quantity, then it would be to a retailer's advantage to stabilize quantity sold. In addition, there are costs associated with price changes. One may also conjecture that the demand facing individual retailers may be more elastic when prices are high than when prices are low. Thus, retailers may be reluctant to move from some established price.

Incidence of Margin Changes

The question of incidence of changes in marketing margins has traditionally been divided into two parts (Waite and Trelogan, 1951): incidence of changes due to the introduction of new service and incidence of changes related to existing services. With a new service and other things the same, the margin is likely to be larger, and the hypothesis is that this change is reflected primarily as a higher retail price. Consumers presumably have the choice of the old product at the old price or the product with new service at a higher price. If they accept the new product, then this appears as a new primary demand at a higher level. Hence, the retail price and the margin are higher, but derived demand and the farm price have not necessarily changed. If consumers do not accept the new service, then primary demand, retail price, and the margin remain unchanged. The incidence of the higher cost of a new service is mainly at the retail level.[3] However, as discussed above, the new service may increase retail demand by more than the cost of the service, thereby increasing derived demand.

If the cost of providing an existing set of services changes, the effect is generally to change *both* retail and producer prices. The change in margin appears as a shift in the derived demand and the derived supply relations for the product. An *increase* in the margin means a decline in derived demand (downward shift) and derived supply (upward shift) with a consequent *increase* in retail price and *decrease* in farm price. Of course, a decrease in margin would have the opposite effect. A competitive market structure is assumed in these statements so that margin changes are reflected through the marketing system.

The magnitude of the price changes at the retail and farm levels, with a given margin change, depends on the slopes of the demand and supply curves. For linear relations, equal slopes (in absolute value) would mean equal, but opposite, changes in retail and farm prices (Waite and Trelogan, 1951). If the slope of the demand relation is steeper than that for the supply relation, then the magnitude of the price change at the consumer level will be greater than at the producer level (Figure 6-6). If the slope of the supply relation is steeper than that for the demand relation,[4] then the magnitude of the price change at the producer level will be larger than at the consumer level. For many agricultural products, the

[3] If farm price is constant and retail price increases, then the farm price as a percentage of the retail price declines.

[4] To be precise, the slope of a function in a price (P)–quantity (Q) diagram is defined as dP/dQ, and the slope of a demand function is negative. Consequently, to say one slope is steeper than another means that the absolute value of dP/dQ for one function is larger than for the other. Let b and c be the absolute values of the demand and supply functions, respectively, then if $b > c$, demand is steeper than supply. Conversely, if $b < c$, then supply is steeper than demand.

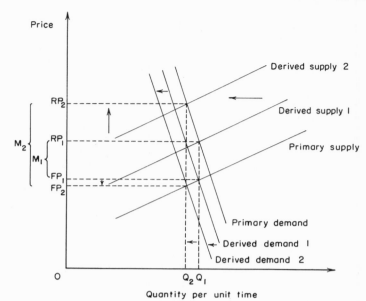

Figure 6-6. An example of a change in margin and the incidence of change on retail and farm prices

supply relation is thought to be more price inelastic than the demand relation. In these cases, to the extent the theory is appropriate, the incidence of a given margin change would be greater at the farm level than at the retail level. Note that, if supply were perfectly price inelastic (a limiting case), then the entire incidence of a margin change would fall on the farm price (Figure 6-7).

A farm price depends on primary supply and derived demand. From the foregoing, we may observe that derived demand changes with changes in primary demand or with changes in the marketing margin. Thus, a lower farm price may be the result of a larger supply or a smaller derived demand, and the latter may be due to a decline in primary demand or to a larger marketing margin. Some attempts have been made to attribute various proportions of declining farm prices to each of these factors (Freeman, 1966; Waldorf, 1966).

The theoretical analysis presented in this section is an example of partial-equilibrium theory. An equilibrium situation for a single product is depicted; one variable—the marketing margin—is

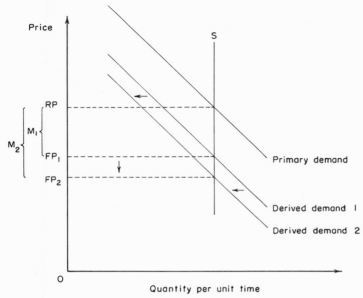

Figure 6-7.   Incidence of a margin change with perfectly inelastic supply

changed; other factors are assumed constant; and the new equilibrium position is observed. This method is useful in illustrating the
influence of a margin change on farm and retail prices, but it may
be somewhat misleading when applied to a "real world" situation,
because other factors are not constant. Under a competitive market
structure, the prices of substitutes will not remain constant as
pointed out in Chapter 3. In addition, the assumption of a competitive market structure may not be appropriate.

For example, an analyst could demonstrate that a smaller transportation cost for apples produced in the Far West would result
in higher prices to growers in that area and lower prices to eastern
consumers. However, the analysis would be incomplete unless it
took into account the substitutability between western and eastern
apples. A lower retail price for western apples in eastern markets
would result in a sympathetic price decrease in substitutes. Thus,
the net effect on price, while it may be in the direction indicated,
may not be as large when secondary effects are considered.

The incidence of changes in marketing margins, as described

above, has to be modified as assumptions underlying the model are modified. For example, some agricultural products have floor prices established by the price-support program. Thus, when the farm price is at the support level, an increase in the margin and the concurrent decrease in farm-level demand would not decrease farm prices. The margin is, in effect, added to the farm-level support price. An increase in margin would result in a higher retail price and hence in a smaller quantity purchased at retail. A smaller quantity would move through the marketing system to the retail level, but farm prices would not decrease. (This implies added government activity to support prices.)

The analysis also assumes a competitive market structure. Imperfect competition may result in different incidence of changes in the margin. This situation is discussed briefly in the next section.

Market Structure, Margins, and Prices

Assumed Conditions

The preceding discussion of the theory of margin changes has been based on the assumption of a competitive market structure. Price is the integrating force between market levels. If primary demand increases relative to supply, then retail price increases. The higher price is reflected through the marketing system to producers, and the eventual result, other factors remaining the same, is a larger quantity supplied.

A change in the marketing margin would be reflected through the marketing system in an analogous way. Prices both at retail and at the farm would generally be affected.

As an example, let us assume that a transportation rate is reduced. For simplicity, we also assume that one type of middleman assembles the product and pays the cost of transportation from the farm to the stores. The lower transportation rate initially accrues to the benefit of these middlemen. However, the assumption of a purely competitive market structure implies that the lower rate will be passed on to producers as higher prices, to retailers as lower prices, or in general as a combination of the two affects. The lower cost (hence higher profit) will induce existing middlemen to do more business and perhaps attract the entry of new middlemen.

However, as they compete with each other for more of the farm product, the result would be higher farm prices, and as they compete to sell more to retailers, the result would be lower retail prices. Competition among retailers would imply that the lower price is passed on to consumers. Thus, the incidence of the lower marketing cost is at both farm and consumer prices (depending, of course, on slopes of functions, effect of price support, etc.).

In practice, the structure of the food marketing system does not fulfill all of the requirements of a purely competitive model. With some monopolistic power, marketing firms may retain all or a part of the benefits of cost decreases as added profits while passing on higher costs to consumers and producers. This suspicion of monopoly power and "unnecessarily" large marketing margins has resulted in studies such as those conducted by the National Commission on Food Marketing (1966).

Some results from studies of the food industry are summarized in the next subsection. However, the incidence of changes in marketing costs remains a controversial question. That is, are marketing margins too large? And, if so, is the impact mainly on consumers or producers?

Current Conditions

Food retailing might be characterized as monopolistically competitive (Holdren, 1964). There are large numbers and relative freedom of entry; furthermore, there is substantial price competition (Padberg, 1968). But retailers do have some degree of spatial monopoly and some discretion over price. A large amount of nonprice competition also exists in the food industry based on product differentiation. Brands for a particular product may proliferate and compete for a limited amount of shelf space. There is often a substantial amount of advertising and promotion related to these brand products, which increases marketing costs. Thus, "imperfect competition" may lead to higher costs but not necessarily to excess profits.

There is fairly high concentration [5] in some segments of the food industry (e.g., breakfast food manufacturing). But, in meat packing,

[5] The Commission defined "high concentration" as a situation in which the four largest firms have more than 50 per cent of the business.

the entry of medium-sized firms has reduced the dominance of the original "big four" (National Commission on Food Marketing, 1966, p. 93). Generally speaking, there has been only a slow increase in over-all four-firm concentration.

The consequences of concentration in food marketing are not entirely clear. With high concentration, firms would seem to have the power to earn larger profits with higher retail prices than would exist with lower concentration. In the breakfast cereal field, "Four firms have 85 percent of the business; advertising and sales promotion amount to 19 percent of manufacturers' sales; retail prices of cereals rose more than other retail food prices between 1954 and 1964; profits are nearly double the average for all food manufacturing; and entry of a new competitor would be extremely difficult" (National Commission on Food Marketing, 1966, p. 94).

However, the Report of the National Commission on Food Marketing (1966, p. 100) was generally favorable to the food marketing system from the viewpoint of efficiency and progressiveness. Their conclusions with respect to farm-retail price spreads are as follows: (a) There are few, if any, unnecessary functions in the *physical* processing and distribution of foods. But, in principle, some *selling* costs could be reduced without reducing the value of final products to consumers. (b) Most marketing functions are performed efficiently, but exceptions exist. (c) Profits are higher in *some* branches of the food industry than necessary to attract capital, but no clear pattern of an upward trend in profits exists in food marketing.

This suggests that lower farm-retail price spreads are possible without reducing services to consumers or reducing profits to unreasonably low levels in the food industry. But, in practice, these reforms are difficult to achieve, and the effect would be small. Farm-retail spreads would remain high because marketing services are costly even when efficiently performed. The incidence of smaller marketing margins would vary from product to product. Presumably, farm prices would be somewhat higher and retail prices lower. The difficulties of eliminating inefficiencies in sales promotion and passing the savings on to consumers is illustrated by the performance of the baking industry (discussed in the next subsection).

The degree of competition may be different at different marketing levels, adding complexity to the analysis. To illustrate, a retail chain may have more market power than the processors of a particular commodity, but competition among processors may result in purely competitive pricing at the farm level. In this situation, the retail chain may be able to maintain a relatively large margin between its buying and selling prices while processors' margins would be relatively small. As pointed out elsewhere, price competition still is important among retail food stores, but it is also true that some commodities have become identified as small (or large) margin items. Food stores follow pricing strategies such that overhead costs are not necessarily allocated proportionately to all items in the store.

What are the conclusions for public policy? Limiting concentration in various parts of the food industry should aid in maintaining competition and hence in keeping margins consistent with the services provided. However, there are problems in arriving at an "optimal" policy on concentration. Economies of size in food retailing do exist. For this reason, it would seem unwise to pursue a policy which keeps a large number of small, uneconomic units in business. Large firms have generally proved to be somewhat more innovative than small firms. On the other hand, an increase in concentration implies more scope for exploiting either consumers or producers.

Vertical Integration

One change in the structure of marketing services that occurs in some parts of the food industry is vertical integration. Vertical integration occurs when successive stages of marketing or of production and marketing are linked together. The usual meaning is that of nonprice linkage through direct ownership or by contract. That is, successive stages of marketing are tied together in some formal way other than by the price system.

A reason for retailers integrating back to processing plants and perhaps to the producer level is to assure a flow of a product with certain specifications and delivery terms. Further, such integration may reduce marketing costs, especially those of selling from one stage to another. These cost savings may, or may not, be passed on to consumers as lower retail prices and to producers as higher farm prices.

The net effect of integration on prices is difficult to test empirically (Walsh, *et al.*, 1964). Some food retailers, for example, have integrated back to bakers. This largely eliminates selling costs for bread, where distribution was largely in the hands of driver-salesmen. But, selling costs for the bakers as a whole may not be reduced. Wholesale bakers, who are selling "brand name" bread, try to maintain their market share in competition with the retailers' private brands by doing more advertising and promotional work (Walsh, *et al.*, 1964, p. 167). Thus, it is not clear whether *total* marketing costs for bread are increased or decreased.

Of course, cost savings are obtained in the integrated sector of the bread market, and thus the question of who gets the savings arises. Private-label bread (sold by integrated retailers) usually sells for two to five cents per pound less than the brand-name bread. However, differences exist by regions with the minimum difference of one cent on the West Coast (Walsh, *et al.*, 1964). Vertical integration may result in lower retail prices, but whether or not benefits are passed on to consumers depends on competition among retailers. In other words, vertical integration may reduce marketing costs, but some firms apparently have sufficient market power to retain these savings as higher profits.

Another interesting aspect of vertical integration, from the viewpoint of economists, is the changing nature of the price system. Vertical integration has changed the locus of price formation, and has reduced the number of points in the marketing chain at which prices are established. Price coordination has been partially replaced by administrative coordination.

This change has several implications. Published prices (from the USDA and other sources) may become less meaningful as a larger volume of a product moves through integrated channels. Thus, the empirical definition of marketing margins between the producer and the retail level becomes more difficult. For example, what is the margin between the retail and farm price of broilers or eggs, when the producers are mainly part of an integrated operation?

Information available to nonintegrated producers is reduced, and they may have fewer alternate markets. Naturally, such producers are concerned when buyers disappear. Producers believe that the lack of buyers may lead to lower prices as the remaining non-integrated producers compete for a smaller share of the market.

Gray (1964, p. 122) argues that vertical integration has eliminated price as a coordinator between market levels when markets were informal or weak. Administrative or engineering coordination, in these cases, does a better job of assuring a given flow of product with a given specification. However, Gray believes that price competition has been strengthened at the remaining price junctures. For example, he argues that price competition is vigorous among retail food stores. Thus, while the role of price is declining in one sense, Gray (p. 126) believes that its role as an allocator at the remaining junctures is strengthened.

Summary

The marketing margin may be defined as the difference between prices at two market levels. But the margin for a particular commodity, like wheat, is often difficult to determine since the form of the commodity changes drastically as it is combined with other products and services in the marketing system. Farm-retail price spreads are computed by the USDA for selected products and for a market basket of farm-food products. These spreads measure the cost of providing a mix of marketing services. They do not measure the effect of adding new products, nor do they indicate the well-being of farmers.

Marketing margins change with changes in factor prices, the efficiency of providing services, and the quantity and quality of services embodied in the final product. Margins obviously vary greatly among commodities. The effect of changes in margins on retail and farm prices under purely competitive conditions depends on the relative slopes of demand and supply relations, when the source of change is in the cost of providing existing services. The incidence of change is more complex when a new service or product is added, though under some circumstances the incidence is primarily at retail. The consequences of changes in margins become even more complicated when the assumption of pure competition is relaxed.

Vertical integration and other forms of concentration in the food industry can result in cost savings, especially for the firms involved. However, the added costs of advertising or other promotional devices related to nonprice competition may increase total marketing costs. Even if there are cost savings associated with concentration, it is not clear that they are passed on to consumers in the form of lower prices. Thus, the net effects of changes in concentration in the food industry on consumer and producer prices are not always clear.

References

Atchley, Frank M. 1956. "Alternate Approaches to the Marketing Margin–Farmer's Share Concept," *J. Farm Econ.*, 38:1573–1585.

Breimyer, Harold F. 1957. "On Price Determination and Aggregate Price Theory," *J. Farm Econ.*, 39:678–694.

Buse, Rueben C., and G. E. Brandow. 1960. "The Relationship of Volume, Prices and Costs to Marketing Margins for Farm Foods," *J. Farm Econ.*, 42:362–370.

Daly, Rex F. 1958. "Demand for Farm Products at Retail and the Farm Level," *J. Am. Stat. Assoc.*, 53:656–668.

Duewer, Lawrence A. 1970. *Price Spreads for Beef and Pork: Revised Series, 1949–69.* Econ. Res. Ser., USDA Misc. Pub. No. 1174.

Findlay, Jeannette, and Leland Southard. 1971. "The Bill for Marketing Farm Food Products," *Marketing and Transportation Situation.* Econ. Res. Ser., USDA, MTS-182 (Aug.). Pp. 9–16.

Freeman, Robert E. 1966. "Roles of Farm Productivity and Marketing Margins in Postwar Decline in Farm Prices," *J. Farm Econ.*, 48:31–41.

Friedman, Milton. 1962. *Price Theory: A Provisional Text.* Chicago: Aldine Publishing Co. Chapter 7.

Gale, Hazen F. 1967. *The Farm Food Marketing Bill and Its Components.* Econ. Res. Ser., USDA, Ag. Econ. Report No. 105.

Gray, Roger W. 1964. "The Changing Role of Price," *J. Farm Econ.*, 46:117–127.

Hammond, Jerome W., *et al.* 1967. "Why the Growing Farm-Retail Price Spread?" *Minn. Farm Business Notes*, Special Issue (Oct.).

Holdren, Bob R. 1964. "The Nature of Competition among Food Retailers in Local Markets," *J. Farm Econ.*, 46:1306–1314.

National Commission on Food Marketing. 1966. *Food from Farmer to*

Consumer. Commission Report. Washington, D.C.: U.S. Govt. Printing Office.

Ogren, Kenneth E. 1965. "Marketing Costs and Margins: New Perspectives in a Changing Economy," *J. Farm Econ.*, 47:1366–1376.

Padberg, Daniel I. 1968. *Economics of Food Retailing*. Ithaca, N.Y.: Cornell Univ. Food Distribution Program. Chapter 9.

Parish, R. M. 1967. "Price 'Levelling' and 'Averaging,' " *The Farm Economist*, 11:187–198.

Scott, Forrest E., and Henry T. Badger. 1972. *Farm-Retail Spreads for Food Products*. Econ. Res. Ser., USDA Misc. Pub. No. 741 (revised).

Waite, Warren C., and Harry C. Trelogan. 1951. *Agricultural Market Prices*. 2d ed. New York: John Wiley and Sons. Chapter 8.

Waldorf, William H. 1966. "The Demand for and Supply of Food Marketing Services: An Aggregate View," *J. Farm Econ.*, 48:42–60.

Walsh, Richard G., *et al.* 1964. "Some Consequences of Bilateral Oligopoly and Vertical Integration in Bread Markets," *J. Farm Econ.*, 46:161–172.

Waugh, Frederick V., and Kenneth E. Ogren. 1961. "Interpretation of Changes in Agricultural Marketing Costs," *Am. Econ. Rev.*, 51:213–227.

CHAPTER 7

Price Differences
Associated with Quality

The specific lots of an agricultural product differ in terms of such attributes as size, color, moisture level, protein content, and the proportion of defects or impurities, and prices often vary depending on alternate grades, classes, and varieties. Price differences based on quality are sometimes referred to as premiums or discounts. These price differences may change through time, but such variations are usually small relative to changes in the average level of prices for the commodity. The prices of all grades of a commodity tend to move up and down together, although price premiums and discounts between grades often change from season to season and may exhibit trends over time. The economic meaning and justification for price differences related to quality variation are explored in this chapter.

In the course of the discussion, two other topics will be briefly considered. One is the relationship among elasticities for different grades; the other is the implications of imperfect competition for price differences related to quality. To simplify exposition, the term "grade" is usually used to refer to all quality differences.

Defining Grades

Grade standards are usually established by governmental agencies in consultation with representatives of producers and marketing firms. Occasionally, grades are informally established by members of the trade. While attributes used to define grades usually vary continuously, a relatively small number of classes must be established for practical use. Two important decisions are required.

First, the optimum number of grades must be determined, and, second, boundaries between grades must be established (Zusman, 1967).

A related problem is the selection of attributes on which to base the definition of grades. Should grades be established on the basis of physical criteria, such as color and size, or on the basis of consumer acceptance? Panels of consumers, for example, seem to prefer the taste of applesauce which grades low on the basis of usual physical criteria (D. G. Dalrymple, 1968; D. J. Dalrymple, 1961). Measurable physical criteria are obviously easier to incorporate into grade standards than concepts like taste, although it is even difficult to specify appropriate combinations of available physical attributes in defining grades. This raises the question of whether conventional grades are an adequate reflection of buyer preferences. While the reader should be aware of these issues, a discussion of them is not within the scope of this book.

Grading facilitates transactions between buyers and sellers. Contracts can be based on grade specifications, and buyers need not inspect each individual lot (which may be graded by an official inspector). Standardization reduces uncertainty between buyers and sellers, and this helps reduce marketing costs (Mehren, 1961).

Grading, of course, is a prerequisite to the establishment of price premiums or discounts for various lots of a commodity. If grades accurately reflect different consumer preferences, price differences will be established which will help determine the composition of future supplies.[1] For example, if premiums are sufficient, farmers tend to produce more lean hogs than overly fat ones.

Grading also makes it possible to practice price discrimination for some commodities. With discriminatory pricing, price differences between grades exceed those that would prevail under competitive conditions.

However, the grading and sorting of commodities is not costless. Thus, the question arises as to whether or not the gains from grading justify the added cost. Grading schemes may not always be

[1] Of course, consumers have imperfect information, and price is often used by consumers as a guide to quality. Incorrect inferences about quality can be made on the basis of price, especially when the seller has some discretion in setting price.

justified, at least on purely economic grounds. Also, a product may
have differences in an attribute (say, color) that does not command
a consistent difference in price. In the discussion which follows, we
assume that grading is economically justified.

Demands by Grades

If grades have economic significance, then it follows that a separate demand schedule exists for each grade. Each such schedule
has the usual determinants. Shifts in each demand curve associated
with income changes probably differ by grades. The income elasticity of demand is thought to be highest for the best or preferred
grade and smaller for lower grades. The reasoning is by analogy
with the superior-inferior product concept. In fact, one method of
defining grades is on the basis of the relative income elasticities.
However, little empirical knowledge exists about quality differences and income elasticities, and for this reason it is difficult to
implement such a concept.

In general, there is great substitutability among grades of the
same commodity, even though each has some unique characteristics. Thus, the main demand shifter for a particular grade is the
change in price of its closest substitutes, and these are typically
other grades of the same product.[2] The various grades typically
have large positive cross-price elasticities of demand with each
other; hence, the demand for each grade is usually more price elastic than that for the entire product.

Wheat provides one example of the price relationships that exist
between grades. Since there is considerable substitutability among
grades, their prices tend to move together (Figure 7-1). High-protein hard spring wheat is preferred in making the flour that is used
in most of the commercial bread in the United States. For this reason, high-protein spring wheat customarily sells at a premium over
other wheats, but the size of the premium varies from season to

[2] This explains the high positive correlation in price changes for various
grades, but the unique characteristics of each grade explain why this correlation is not perfect.

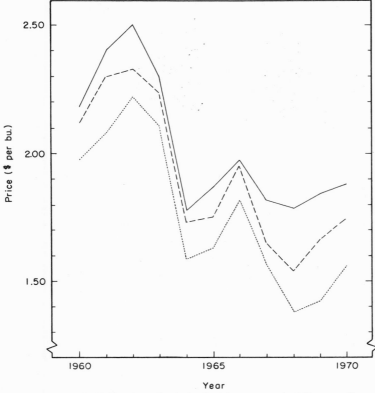

Figure 7-1. Wheat prices, selected grades, United States, 1960–1970. Data from Economic Research Service, *Wheat Situation,* WS-217 (Aug. 1971), p. 14, table 6, and corresponding annual issues for earlier years.

season and sometimes even within a season.[3] The domestic farm-level demand for wheat in the aggregate in the United States is highly price inelastic, perhaps −0.2. The demand for separate grades is much more elastic because of the substitutability among

[3] Variability in premiums and discounts through time is of more than academic interest. For instance, a grain merchant storing grade-one grain and hedging this inventory in a futures contract specifying delivery of grade-two grain is assuming that the prices of the two grades are closely correlated in using the futures market for hedging (see Chapter 13).

grades. Taplin (1969) estimates that the world demand for commercial wheat exports of all grades has a price elasticity of -1.0; the corresponding elasticity for soft wheat is -7.4 and for hard wheat is -3.6.

The separate demand functions for different qualities probably exhibit sharp changes in slope over a range of quantities and prices, at least for some commodities. Demand for a particular quality or variety may be quite price inelastic for relatively small quantities but become elastic for larger quantities. This occurs when a specified amount or a fixed proportion of a particular quality or variety is desired, say, by a processor for a product mix. The flour miller needs a certain proportion of high-protein wheat to achieve a desired protein level in flour (although milling techniques have changed so that this is less true today). When supplies are more than adequate to meet these special uses (i.e., uses for which no good substitutes exist), then price drops into a range where the high-quality product becomes competitive with lower quality products. In this range, demand is likely to be more price elastic.

Logic does not provide a clear guide as to whether the demand for high grades is, on the average, more or less price-elastic than for lower grades. If one assumes that (1) the best grade has the largest income elasticity, (2) the sum of the cross elasticities is the same for all grades, and (3) the homogeneity condition with respect to elasticities prevails, then the demand for the best grades would tend to be more price elastic. But Waite and Trelogan (1951) argue that the best grade typically has fewer substitutes and hence has the smaller (in absolute terms) price elasticity of demand. The critical question in this case is whether the sum of the cross elasticities is equal for all grades.

Generalizations about empirical elasticities must await additional research, and, in any event, the relationship among elasticities for various grades may not be uniform among commodities. Research by Colman (1966) and Taplin (1969) are illustrative of estimates of demand for different grades or classes within a commodity group.[4]

---

[4] Colman (1966) estimated elasticities for two grades of beef, obtaining estimates of -0.54 for low grade and -1.24 for high grade. His analysis, how-

Further, one may argue that estimates of own-price elasticities for separate grades are misleading, or at least subject to misuse. The own-price elasticity, of course, is a measure of responsiveness of quantity to own price, *other factors constant*. But we know that prices of the various grades are likely to be highly related. Other factors are not constant; there are high positive cross elasticities. Thus, the *net* percentage change in a particular quantity depends on the relative movements of a constellation of prices. The net result of these interrelated changes is embodied in the concept of total elasticity (Chapter 3).

Supplies by Grades

While demands for alternate grades can and do change, most year-to-year variations in price premiums are the result of changes in relative supplies. The proportion of various grades produced in any one season is influenced partly by chance factors such as the weather or insect and disease damage. Good weather in the northern Great Plains and excessively wet weather in eastern states, for example, can increase the proportion of hard wheat to soft wheat produced and hence influence the price difference between the two types of wheat. Hail or insect damage may increase the quantity of cull fruit relative to the higher grades.

Through time, the changing profitability of growing alternate varieties or grades also can influence relative supplies. Expected profitability is influenced by price premiums and by relative per unit costs of production. Clearly, other things being equal, a price premium for a particular variety should tend to shift resources toward the production of that variety. But the variety may be more costly to produce and market. Changes in relative yields may in

---

ever, appears to ignore the substitutability between grades. The closest substitute—the other grade of beef—is omitted from the respective equations. An unpublished analysis by the authors suggests average elasticities of -3.3 for high grade and -3.1 for low grade beef. The cross-price elasticity of high grade with respect to the price of low grade beef is an estimated 2.0, and the cross elasticity of low grade with respect to the higher grade price is an estimated 3.3. The analysis is based on quarterly retail-level data for the eleven years 1957–1967. Because of certain statistical problems, however, the results must be treated as highly tentative.

some cases offset the effects of price premiums. For example, new rice varieties developed by the International Rice Research Institute sell at a discount to more "traditional" varieties, but the yield advantage of the new varieties over the old is sufficient to make it profitable for rice producers to adopt the newer varieties.[5]

The relative supplies of different grades of a particular commodity also may vary within a year. For example, the proportion of cattle marketed which grade "good" is likely to increase relative to the proportion which grade "choice" in the fall of the year as cattle are sold directly off pasture without going through feed lots. The proportion of eggs in various size categories likewise varies within the year. Young pullets coming into production tend to produce smaller eggs than older hens, and historically substantial seasonality has existed in the placement of laying flocks and hence in the proportion of various sized eggs marketed. However, seasonality in the placement of young chicks has declined sharply. Commodities in storage also may decline in quality over the storage period. Seasonality in the supplies of various qualities, sizes, or varieties of a product can result in seasonal patterns in quality premiums or discounts.

Price Differentials

Price differentials between grades at a point in time are, of course, the result of particular levels of demand and supply for the various grades. With the passage of time, price differentials change with shifts in the supply and demand functions. The size of the changes in quality discounts and premiums depends on the size of shifts in functions and on the algebraic form and consequent slopes of these functions. Since the demands for each grade typically are closely related through the substitutability among grades, price changes are also closely related.

Generalizations about price relationships among grades are difficult to make because of the many possible combinations of changes in relative supplies and demands by grades and of different slopes

[5] Producers sometimes face difficult economic decisions in determining what particular varieties to grow (see Burt, 1965). Such decisions are complicated by questions like timing of harvest for alternate varieties—hence the impact of the variety on distribution of labor requirements.

for the various functions. For instance, an increase in the supply of one grade depresses the price of that grade and thereby reduces the premium or widens the discount of that grade relative to others. However, the lower price for one grade leads to reduced demands for the other related grades and hence tends to lower prices of these other grades. These lower prices, in turn, influence the demand for the grade with the initial price change. The larger supply for one grade, then, tends to lower all prices as well as change the price difference between grades. The precise size of the changes depends on the size of the increase in supply, the size of the relevant own-price elasticity of demand, and the sizes of the relevant cross-price elasticities with the other grades.

The nature of changes in demands and supplies by grades, as discussed in previous sections, is suggestive of the nature of changes in price differentials. For instance, a small supply of a grade that is required by processors to make a particular product can push the price premium for this grade to a high level. We have also stated elsewhere (Chapter 5) that in years of large production the price of some products may be so low that a part of the crop is not harvested. Under competitive conditions, the lower quality component of the total crop is the quantity typically abandoned. The poorer quality has the lowest price, and this price may not cover harvesting and marketing costs.

The analysis of relationships among prices of various grades is, for the most part, simply a special case of price relationships among substitutes. The prices of close substitutes are highly related. This is illustrated in Table 7-1.[6] Coconut oil and palm kernel oil are both lauric oils; their primary uses are in the manufacture of soap and in fillings and coatings for confectioneries (Nyberg, 1970, p. 97). Soybean, cottonseed, and peanut oils, for instance, are not good substitutes for the lauric oils in these special uses. Thus, the prices of coconut and palm kernel oils are closely related, but the relationship of lauric oil prices to other oil prices is small.

---

[6] The correlation coefficients used in Table 7-1 are measures of the linear association between two variables. A coefficient of one indicates a perfect linear association, and of course the coefficients of one on the diagonal of the table indicate that a price series is perfectly correlated with itself. Coefficients near one show high degrees of association; coefficients near zero imply a small degree of association; negative coefficients suggest an inverse relationship.

Table 7-1. Correlation coefficients between prices of selected oils, United States, 1952–1967

	Coconut	Soybean	Cottonseed	Peanut	Palm kernel
Coconut	1.0	0.30	0.21	0.34	0.94
Soybean		1.0	0.89	0.58	0.10
Cottonseed			1.0	0.60	0.25
Peanut				1.0	−0.52
Palm kernel					1.0

Source: Adapted from Albert J. Nyberg, "The Demand for Lauric Oils in the United States," *Am. J. Ag. Econ.,* 52 (1970):98, table 1.

Certain attributes of the lauric oils mean that no close substitutes exist for particular uses with current technology. However, if the supplies of lauric oils were to exceed the demand for oils in the special uses, then the prices of lauric oils would decline, and these oils would become more competitive with other oils in other uses, such as making margarine. Consequently, the demand function for lauric oils would become more price elastic (less inelastic) at lower prices. This is consistent with the point made previously, that the demand for one grade may be quite inelastic at high prices when that grade is a "required" component of a particular product but that, if the special demand is filled, the additional supply of that grade would cause price to move into a more elastic range of the demand function.

Imperfect Competition and Price Differences

Price differences between grades or qualities of products are often determined administratively by sellers of industrial products (e.g., prices for a line of refrigerators) or by those marketing "branded" commodities. This situation usually occurs where the number of sellers is limited and/or firms have successfully differentiated their product from other products. Premiums or discounts in such cases may be based on quality or cost differences, but they also may simply reflect the ability of the seller to exploit consumer ignorance.

Premiums or discounts for "quality" are not always determined on the basis of competitive supply-demand relationships as outlined earlier. A meat packer, for example, may sell his brand-name bacon at a price premium over a "standard" brand which more than covers the additional cost of the brand-name item. The seller conveys the impression that his product is superior in quality; on the basis of its physical attributes, it may not be superior. However, the seller in such cases is able to exercise some degree of market power in pricing.

The ability of producers or sellers of farm products to extract more money from consumers by such pricing practices depends on their ability to differentiate their product and to create a favorable "image" (including quality) with consumers. For many food products, it is difficult to do this because of the high degree of substitutability among different grades or brands. The demand, even for a branded agricultural product, is likely to be quite price elastic. In such cases, an attempt to increase the price premium for a particular commodity or brand would result in a substantial loss in sales.

Differences in demand among grades may provide the basis for a price discrimination scheme. This assumes, of course, that the seller or sellers have the monopoly power to make price discrimination work. Agricultural cooperatives have occasionally been able to do this. For instance, marketings to the higher-priced fresh fruit sector may be restricted with the remaining fruit going to a processing sector (presumably with a more elastic demand). Marketing orders permit the culling of low-quality fruit. David Price (1967) points out that total returns may be increased by culling out low-quality produce even though the demand for it is elastic. The price increase from the higher quality sold may be large enough to offset the effect of the reduced quantity sold, even after the costs of culling are covered. Mr. Price considers in detail the question of optimum (profit-maximizing) culling rates. Of course, returns are not automatically increased by culling low-quality produce (Waugh, 1971). Correct allocations under a price discrimination program depend on the demand functions for the different grades.

Price differentials serve an important function provided that they reflect the relative demands of buyers for different grades or qualities. Premiums or discounts for certain grades do not perform this function effectively if they are arbitrarily maintained on the basis of historical relationships such as may occur under government price-support programs. Thus, price-support programs are another type of "imperfection" for some agricultural commodities. At times, lower grades of tobacco, cotton, and wheat have been overpriced relative to higher grades (i.e., the discount on such grades has not been sufficiently wide). As a result, the lower grades have ended up in government warehouses while the higher grades have moved into consumption. By overpricing lower grades, the government also provides an incentive for farmers to continue producing excess quantities of the inferior grades of the product.

References

Burt, Oscar R. 1965. "Optimal Replacement under Risk," *J. Farm Econ.,* 47:324–346.

Colman, David R. 1966. "Elasticities of Demand for Two Grades of Beef," *Illinois Ag. Econ.,* pp. 11–18.

Dalrymple, Dana G. 1968. "On the Economics of Produce Grading," *Am. J. Ag. Econ.,* 50:157–159.

Dalrymple, Douglas J. 1961. "A Study of Consumer Preference for Applesauce Using the Two-Visit Interview Technique," *J. Farm Econ.,* 43:690–697.

Mehren, G. L. 1961. "The Functions of Grades in an Affluent, Standardized-Quality Economy," *J. Farm Econ.,* 43:1371–1383.

Nyberg, Albert J. 1970. "The Demand for Lauric Oils in the United States," *Am. J. Ag. Econ.,* 52:97–102.

Price, David W. 1967. "Discarding Low Quality Produce with an Elastic Demand," *J. Farm Econ.,* 49:622–632.

Taplin, John H. E. 1969. *Demand in the World Wheat Market and the Export Policies of the United States, Canada, and Australia.* Cornell Univ. Ph.D. thesis.

Waite, Warren C., and Harry C. Trelogan. 1951. *Agricultural Market Prices.* 2d ed. New York: John Wiley and Sons. Chapter 12.

Waugh, Frederick V. 1971. "Withholding by Grade," *Am. J. Ag. Econ.,* 53:500–501.

Zusman, Pinhas. 1967. "A Theoretical Basis for Determination of Grading and Sorting Schemes," *J. Farm Econ.,* 49:89–106.

CHAPTER 8

Spatial Price
Relationships

This chapter deals with factors which cause prices to differ between regions and particularly with the economic forces that are likely to cause prices in one region to change in relation to those in another. A simple model is presented to illustrate the impact of shifts in demand or supply or changes in transfer costs on price differentials between regions. The spatial price equilibrium model also provides a convenient analytical framework which may be used to determine the indirect as well as the direct effects of changes in production in one or more regions on the volume and direction of trade. In addition, such an analytical model may be used to ascertain the price effects of relaxing or increasing trade barriers between countries or regions.

Spatial price relationships are determined largely by transfer costs between regions provided competitive conditions prevail. Transfer costs, which include loading or handling as well as transportation charges, are often high in relation to the farm value of agricultural commodities, especially perishable products. Hence, farm prices may differ greatly by region, depending on whether the production area is near or far from the principal market areas. Farmers in more distant areas frequently refer to themselves as being "out on the end of a whip." Even modest changes in central market prices when combined with high and fixed transportation costs can result in wide swings in producer prices.

The principles that determine spatial price differences within a country apply equally well to international prices, provided no barriers exist to the movement of commodities between countries. For many agricultural commodities, of course, the conditions nec-

143

essary for free trade do not exist. There is no longer a single world market for grains, sugar, or dairy products. On the other hand, prices for cocoa, bananas, rubber, soybeans, palm oil, and tea are still determined under relatively competitive conditions.

The principles which underlie price differences between regions (assuming a competitive market structure including homogeneous commodities, perfect knowledge, and no barriers inhibiting trade) can be summarized as follows:

(1) price differences between any two regions (or markets) that trade with each other will just equal transfer costs;

(2) price differences between any two regions (or markets) that do not engage in trade with each other will be less than or equal to transfer costs.

Price differences between regions cannot exceed transfer costs. The reason for this should be obvious: any time the price difference is greater than transfer costs, buyers will purchase commodities from the low-priced market and ship them to the higher-priced market, thereby raising prices in the former and reducing them in the latter. This form of arbitrage will continue until it is no longer profitable to ship commodities between markets—that is, until the price difference between them no longer exceeds transfer costs.

Using these principles, theoretical spatial price relationships can be determined. One needs to know the pattern of trade (i.e., which areas ship to which markets) and transfer costs per unit of product. Where there are only one or few markets to which most of a given commodity is shipped, it is relatively easy to determine the pattern of trade and hence spatial price relationships. But where there are many possible points of production and consumption, it is much more difficult to determine the pattern of trade and hence the structure of prices. When no trade between regions or countries exists (i.e., when each is self-sufficient), price differences can be determined within limits, but not precisely. In such cases, regional price differences can vary so long as they do not exceed transfer costs (in the absence of trade barriers).

Determining Transfer Costs

Transfer costs are the most important single variable determining spatial price relationships. The transfer cost between any two points cannot be determined simply on the basis of an average transportation rate. It normally includes a fixed charge which is independent of the distance traveled (usually associated with loading or unloading) and a variable charge related to the distance over which the commodity is moved. Transportation costs *per mile* often decline as the distance traveled increases; thus, the cost of moving commodities between two points is not necessarily a linear function of the mileage. In most cases, however, the transfer cost *per unit of product* rises as distance increases, but less than proportionately.[1] Calculation of total transfer costs is further complicated by the fact that transportation rates are frequently regulated by public authorities. In the United States, rail and truck rates (with certain exceptions for agricultural commodities) are established by the Interstate Commerce Commission. The rate structure established for different commodities and methods of transportation becomes extremely complex as amendments and exceptions are granted in response to petitions submitted by railroads and truckers. As a result, transfer costs between any two points often are not identical for different forms of the same product, nor do these costs necessarily bear a close relationship to the distance separating markets.

Interregional price differences presumably are based on the least-cost method of moving commodities between points. But it may not be possible for every handler or shipper to use the least-cost system, especially where new handling methods are being introduced. Considerable time may elapse before firms are reorganized or sufficient equipment becomes available to take advantage of the more efficient system. For example, in the early 1960's, differences in butter prices between markets in the United States exceeded transfer costs using the most efficient method of transporting butter. It cost less per pound to ship butter in large, mechanically refrigerated railroad cars than in smaller, traditional iced cars; however, some shippers did not have sufficient production at any one time to make effective use of the larger cars or were not able to obtain them at the time they were ready to make

[1] The total transfer cost increases with distance, and consequently the cost per unit of product moved increases. Since the transfer cost contains a fixed component regardless of volume and distance traveled, the cost increase is not proportionate to distance.

a shipment. For this reason they were forced to use the more expensive transfer system, and price differences did not fully reflect the potential economies which existed at that time.

Geographical Price Relationships for Commodities
Originating in Many Areas and Sold in
One or a Few Central Markets

If all producers ship homogeneous units of the same commodity to a single central market, the price each producer receives under perfectly competitive conditions is the central market price less the cost of transferring a unit of that commodity to the central market. This is based on the reasonable assumption that buyers are indifferent as to the source of supply of a homogeneous product and would not therefore pay more for a unit of product from one area than from another. If producers in a particular region offered their product for less, this would cause prices for the same commodity produced in other regions to fall by an equal amount. Such price adjustments would be necessary for producers to remain competitive.

The impetus for price changes can come either from producing regions or from central markets. For many agricultural commodities, forces of demand and supply are brought together in central markets. Prices at the farm are usually closely linked to central-market price quotations. For example, the price which a country elevator offers farmers for grain is normally based on price quotations at a central market such as Kansas City or Minneapolis less total transfer and handling costs. Butter and egg prices in producing regions, likewise, have customarily been tied to prices established at Chicago or New York less the cost of moving commodities to these markets.

Central markets play a relatively less important role in pricing some commodities, such as fruits and vegetables sold to processors, than in pricing grains. But even where price-making forces are dispersed, prices in different regions are closely interrelated. Interregional price differences cannot, except for very brief periods, exceed the cost of moving commodities between regions.

Observed vs. Theoretical Price Differentials

Observed price differences between regions within the United States for such commodities as wheat, corn, and soybeans are generally consistent with those suggested by theory. Producer prices for grains decline in line with transfer costs as one moves inland from grain-deficit areas or from major ports through which the commodity is exported. Average prices received by farmers for corn and oats, for example, tend to be highest in the New England and South Atlantic states and lowest in the Great Plains (Waite and Trelogan, 1951, pp. 173–175). Quoted prices for flour and wheat in Buffalo differ from those in Chicago or Minneapolis by an amount that is approximately equal to the cost of transferring these commodities from one area to the other. Similar relationships prevail between wholesale prices paid for butter in New York and Chicago. Even in the case of milk, average prices paid to producers in different regions are highly correlated with the manufacturing price in the Midwest plus transfer costs to each region (Lasley, 1965). The degree of correlation is surprising in view of the presence of many separate marketing orders and attempts on the part of producer groups, or, in some instances, state or local officials to restrict the movement of milk between markets.

For a number of commodities, however, observed price differences between regions exceed transfer costs. There are a number of reasons why this may occur, including incomplete or inaccurate information concerning prices in other markets, nonhomogeneity of products, irrational preferences for products from certain areas, and institutional or legal barriers to the movement of commodities between regions.

Preferences of buyers are important in determining spatial price relationships. Products which appear to be homogeneous may not, in fact, be substitutable in the minds of buyers. Trading patterns are often dictated by traditional arrangements or personal contacts among sellers and buyers. This may lead a firm to continue purchasing commodities from a certain region or particular producers even though it might be able to obtain supplies of the same quality at a lower price from a different area.

Institutional and legal barriers to the movement of commodities between regions also contribute to distortions in spatial price relationships. Inspection requirements, sanitary codes, tolerance limits for chemical residues, tariffs, import quotas, and licensing requirements are typical of the devices used to restrict interregional or international trade.

Government price-support activities, likewise, can cause price differences between markets to exceed or fall short of those that would prevail if transfer costs alone were the major determinant of spatial price relationships. At times, prices of grain have been depressed in certain areas of the United States as a result of the government's decision to unload surplus stocks at a particular location. In addition, regional differences in price-support purchase and loan rates have, in some cases, exceeded transfer costs. For example, the price at which the government offered to buy butter was higher in New York at one time than in Chicago or at country shipping points in Wisconsin by more than the cost of moving butter to New York. This distortion of price relationships led to excessive movement of butter from the Midwest to New York and consequently higher government acquisition costs.

Market Boundaries

If producers have the option of shipping to different markets, the boundary between supply areas is determined by the price in each market and the cost of transferring the product from each point of origin to each destination. Natural barriers such as rivers or mountain ranges, man-made barriers such as a major highway, or political boundaries frequently determine the dividing line between supply areas for different markets; but where such barriers do not exist and prices paid to producers decline continuously as the distance from each market increases, the boundary between supply areas can be determined by drawing concentric circles around each market and noting the points at which producer prices (net of transfer costs) are the same. Given free choice, producers will always ship to the market offering the highest net price. But some producers may be located at points where the price is the same whether they shipped to one market or another. The locus of these points determines the market boundary.

The boundary between two markets will shift if the price rises in one market relative to the other or if transfer costs change. Differential rates of growth in population or income or the introduction of a more efficient processing system, for instance, may cause producer prices to rise in one market relative to another. This will tend to widen the market area serving the higher-priced market and reduce the area serving the other market.

The effect of changes in relative market prices and transfer costs on the location of a boundary point between hypothetical markets is illustrated in Figure 8-1. The downward sloping lines originating at each vertical axis show the net price that would be paid to a producer located at varying distances from markets A and B. At the initial price of $6 per unit in Market A and $5 per unit in Market B, and with transfer costs equal to 50 cents for each 100 miles in both markets, the boundary point would be located 400 miles from Market A and 200 miles from Market B. The price at this location would be $4 per unit.

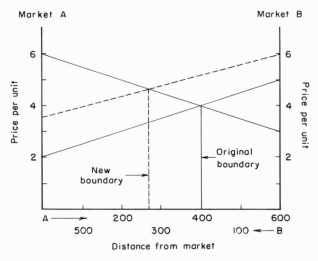

Figure 8-1. Effect of changes in market prices and transfer costs on the boundary between markets

If the price in Market B rises to $6 per unit, and if at the same time a more efficient transfer system is introduced in that market but not in the other, thereby reducing transportation costs to Market B by 20 per cent (i.e., to 40 cents per 100 miles), the new net price line for Market B would be shifted upward and would be less steeply inclined. The new position is indicated by the dashed line in Figure 8-1. Some producers located along the axis joining the two markets would shift from Market A to Market B; hence, the new boundary point would be located to the left of the old boundary.

The preceding illustration shows how *one point* on a boundary line between markets may be established. Prices, of course, will vary along the boundary line, depending on the distance from each market. Boundary lines between markets may be straight under some conditions and curved under others. When more than two markets are involved, the location of boundaries becomes very complex.

Any boundary line is the locus of points where net prices to producers are equal whether they ship to one market or another.[2] The manner in which theoretical boundary lines are established between adjacent markets is illustrated in Figure 8-2. In this illustration, the price at Market A is $6 per unit and at Market B, $5. Prices paid to farmers shipping to these two markets are assumed to decline uniformly in direct relation to the distances from each market; that is, the transfer cost is a linear function of distance, increasing 50 cents each unit of distance. Under these assumed conditions, the boundary is represented by a curved line passing through the points $m\ n\ o\ p$. These are points at which producers are indifferent as to which market they supply.

Returns from shipping to alternative markets are the same at each point on the boundary but the net price varies along the boundary. Farmers located at points m and p receive $3.50 per unit regardless of where they send their product, while producers at points n and o receive $4. In this example, the boundary is a

[2] This statement can be formalized algebraically. Let P_A = price at Market Center A, P_B = price at Market Center B, T_A = transfer cost from farm to Market A, and T_B = transfer cost from farm to Market B; then the boundary is defined by the points where $P_A - T_A = P_B - T_B$.

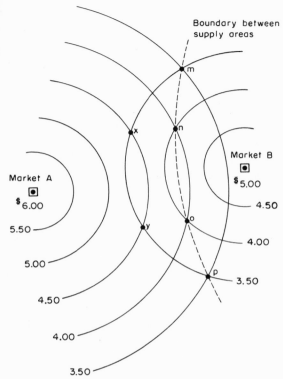

Figure 8-2. Location of boundary between areas supplying alternative markets

curve because the price is higher in one market center than in the other.[3] The boundary, of course, is closer to the lower-priced market center.

If the price in Market B equaled the price in A (i.e., $6 per unit), the boundary would be a straight line bisecting and perpendicular to a line joining the two market centers. Such a boundary would go through points x and y in Figure 8-2. Since the same cost-distance relation is assumed to hold for shipments in either

[3] Given the assumption that transfer costs are a linear function of distance, the curve is a hyperbola. Bressler and King (1970, pp. 126–129, 189–195) provide a much more complete discussion of the theory and practice of establishing boundaries between markets under various conditions including those associated with differences in product forms.

direction—a not unreasonable assumption—the straight-line boundary joins points which are equidistant from the two markets.

Spatial Equilibrium Models

Geographical price relationships can be analyzed in a formal way by using spatial price equilibrium models. These models make it possible to estimate (under very rigid assumptions) the net price that will prevail in each region and the quantity of a given commodity that any one region will sell or purchase from every other region. Such models enable one to determine the optimum or "least-cost" trading pattern, given supply and demand conditions within each region. From this optimum trading pattern an appropriate set of prices can be obtained, based on the principles outlined earlier: namely, that the difference in price between any two regions which trade with each other will just equal the transfer cost between these two regions, while price differences between regions not engaging in trade will be equal to or less than transfer costs.

Spatial equilibrium models are most useful in analyzing interregional price relationships and trading patterns where there are numerous consuming and producing regions. As pointed out in a previous section, if all regions except one produce surpluses and ship to a single deficit region, the structure of producer prices can be determined very simply by subtracting transfer costs from the central market price. But if each region produces as well as consumes a given commodity, one cannot always determine by inspection just which areas will have excess supplies available for sale to deficit regions and which will require imports. Nor is it always obvious which surplus regions will supply a particular deficit area.

The general principles involved in developing interregional trade models can be illustrated with the aid of diagrams showing supply and demand functions for each of two regions (Heady, 1961, pp. 231–233). Such functions are shown for a potential surplus region (A) and a potential deficit region (B) in the upper part of Figure 8-3. In the absence of trade, demand and supply would be equated at a price of $30 in Region A and $50 in Region B. At a price above $30 in Region A, some product would become avail-

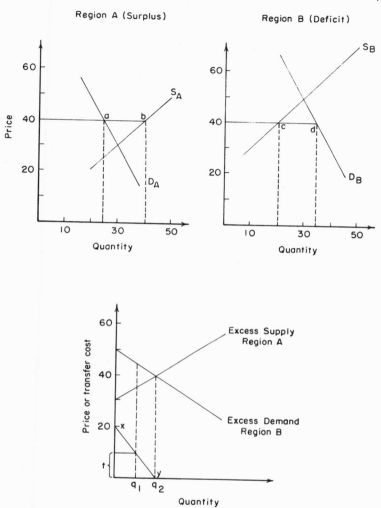

Figure 8-3. Two-region spatial equilibrium model

able for shipment to another area. Imports would be required to satisfy demands in Region B if the price were below $50.

The information obtained from these diagrams can be used to construct excess supply and demand curves as shown in the lower half of Figure 8-3. The excess supply curve is based on the horizontal distance between the supply and demand curves in Region

A at prices above the point of equilibrium (e.g., point *b* minus point *a* in the upper left-hand diagram). Excess supply is zero at the equilibrium price of $30. The excess supply curve is positively sloped like conventional supply schedules since the gap between supply and demand widens as the price increases.

The horizontal distance between the demand and supply curves below the point of equilibrium in Region B (e.g., point *d* minus point *c* in the upper right-hand diagram) provides the information needed to construct the excess demand curve shown in the lower half of Figure 8-3. The excess demand schedule is negatively sloped since the gap between the demand and supply curves widens as the price declines. The excess demand schedule intersects the vertical axis at the equilibrium price of $50 per unit, since there would be no unfilled demand at this price.

The excess demand and supply schedules shown in Figure 8-3 intersect at a price of $40 per unit. If no transfer costs exist between these two regions, a total of 15 units of the commodity would be shipped from Region A to Region B ($ab=cd=15$ units). The price in both regions would then be the same, $40 per unit. The volume traded between these two regions declines with the introduction of transfer costs. No trade would occur if it cost more than $20 to transfer a unit of product from Region A to Region B. In that case, demand and supply would be equated within each region and the price difference ($20) would be less than the transfer cost.

The effect of changes in transfer costs on the amount shipped between regions can be illustrated by constructing a "volume of trade" line which is shown as the diagonal line, *xy*, in Figure 8-3. The vertical intercept for this line (which indicates the transfer cost at which no trade would occur) is determined by subtracting the price at which the excess supply curve intercepts the vertical axis from the price at which the excess demand curve intercepts the same axis. As shown in Figure 8-3, no trade will occur if the transfer cost equals or exceeds $20 per unit. The horizontal intercept of the "volume of trade" line (which shows the maximum trade that can occur when transfer costs are zero) is located directly under the point of intersection of the excess demand and supply schedules. In the example, this point is q_2 or 15 units.

The volume that would be exported from one region to the other at any given transfer cost can be determined by drawing a horizontal line intersecting the vertical axis at the value which represents the transfer cost per unit. The number of units which will be transferred is indicated by the point at which the line representing transfer costs (t in Figure 8-3) intersects the volume-of-trade line. For example, at a transfer cost of $10 per unit, the total amount transferred would be q_1 (about 7.5) units. Given this information, the prices that could be expected to prevail in each region can then be determined. In this case, since the slopes of the demand and supply schedules in both regions are approximately equal, the effect of introducing a transfer cost of $10 per unit would be to reduce the price from $50 to about $45 in Region B and to raise the price from $30 to about $35 in Region A. If the slopes of the demand and supply schedules in the two regions had been different, price changes would not have been equal.

It should be apparent from the foregoing geometric analysis that a change in the volume of trade or in price relationships between regions may occur if either (1) any regional demand or regional supply curve shifts; or (2) transfer costs change. These are the critical variables which must be considered in attempting to predict spatial price relationships.

When more than two regions are involved, it is difficult to determine the pattern of trade or the structure of prices without the aid of mathematics. In order to obtain a solution where many regions have been defined, one must know the supply and demand relationships in each region (expressed in an algebraic form) and transfer costs from every region to every other region. One can then sum the regional supply and demand schedules mathematically and solve for the price at which aggregate demand and supply will be equated (see appendix to this chapter and Judge and Wallace, 1958). Once the equilibrium price is known, the price in every region can be estimated by adding or subtracting an appropriate differential. This may be based initially on normal or historical relationships that have prevailed between prices in different regions in the past. The price differentials initially assumed may not be consistent with the optimum solution, but eventually the two must be brought together to obtain the final solution (see below).

The estimated net price in each region derived from the equilibrium price for all regions can be substituted back into the regional demand and supply relationships in order to determine which regions will have a surplus or deficit and the amount that they will have available for export or will need to import from other regions. The total of excess supplies available from all surplus regions will just equal the import requirements of all deficit regions since the equilibrium price used in the analysis is calculated under this assumption. Linear programming techniques are used to determine the optimum or least-cost routing system (Heady and Candler, 1958, pp. 332–377). The linear programming solution insures that all the requirements of deficit areas are met and also indicates precisely how much will be shipped from each surplus region to each deficit region. The computing procedure is an iterative one, which simply means that successive solutions are obtained, each one satisfying the requirements at a lower total cost than the preceding one. In the final solution, the sum of all transfer costs is minimized and producer prices are maximized, given the supplies available and demand relationships as specified.

The elements of the final solution can be used to determine the geographical structure of prices that would be consistent with balancing demand and net supply (including imports or deducting exports) in each region. The price in each surplus region will be the price in the region to which it exports commodities, less the transfer cost. Price differences between regions also can be calculated directly based on the "dual" solution of the linear programming problem (Judge and Wallace, 1958).

If the regional price differentials initially assumed are inconsistent with those determined in the final solution, then it is necessary to recompute the aggregate demand relationship and the corresponding equilibrium price using the differentials derived from the final linear programming solution. The entire process is repeated until the differentials used in calculating the equilibrium price are approximately equal to those obtained in the final linear programming solution.

With modern computers, it is relatively easy to obtain answers to very complex problems of this kind even when many regions are involved, provided the necessary data are available. In order to obtain solutions, one needs to know the coefficients of demand equations for each region and either the actual supply available or the coefficients of supply equations appropriate to each region. In addition, one must be able to calculate unit transfer costs between each region and every other region. This is sometimes referred to as the matrix of transfer costs.

The final solution rests upon a number of assumptions, not all of which may be fulfilled in practice. These are as follows:

(1) All units of the product available in each region must be homogeneous with respect to quality and appearance; consumers are assumed to be indifferent as to the source of supply.

(2) Production and consumption within each region are presumed to occur at precisely the same point. Transfer costs within regions are ignored.

(3) No physical or institutional barriers exist to prevent the movement of goods between regions.

(4) Transfer costs are assumed to be uniform per unit of product, and to remain constant regardless of volume or direction of movement; however, they need not be proportional to distance.

The solutions obtained from models based on these assumptions are useful mainly as a standard against which existing price differences between regions can be compared. The optimum solution is based on the concept of a perfectly competitive market. Such models are of no help in explaining why actual prices deviate from calculated results, but the solutions obtained from the model can be used to identify situations in which marketing inefficiencies may exist. They also have been used experimentally to determine whether regional differences in support prices for grains are consistent with those that might be expected to prevail under perfectly competitive conditions (Leath and Blakley, 1971). In theory, spatial equilibrium models could be used by administrators to calculate location differentials for support prices.

Actual prices frequently deviate quite substantially from those calculated for a given year from spatial equilibrium models. The correlation between existing prices and those obtained from least-cost solutions are frequently no higher than 0.5 and in some cases are as low as 0.2 (see King, 1963, p. 16, for a summary of the results of empirical studies). The differences between actual and calculated prices may be due to any one or a combination of the following: (1) market imperfections, including inefficiencies in marketing, institutional barriers to trade between regions, lack of knowledge, or irrational economic behavior; (2) weaknesses in the model, such as the assumption that all supplies originate or are consumed at a single point in each region; (3) inadequate or inaccurate data concerning supply and demand coefficients, estimates of population in each region, transfer costs, and so forth.

Some of the weaknesses inherent in the model may be overcome at the cost of increasing complexity. For example, the errors associated with the assumption that there are no intraregional transfer costs can be reduced simply by increasing the number of origins or destinations and hence decreasing the size of each region. One could go so far as to define each farm or each household as a region, but the problems of determining regional supply and demand relationships would increase correspondingly. Even with modern computing facilities, there are limits to how many regions can be accommodated.

One-commodity spatial equilibrium models also ignore the important interrelationships that exist among commodities (King, 1963, pp. 193–198). While theoretical models have been constructed to take account of such relationships, it is difficult to obtain realistic solutions from them because of the enormous data requirements. Where several commodities are to be considered, one must have information on own and cross elasticities of demand and supply for each commodity in every region. Some models assume only that the supply of certain factors such as land is fixed in each region and then proceed to determine the optimum pattern of production as well as the volume and direction of trade between regions. These more complex models have limited usefulness in solving practical problems related to the location of production, but they serve to emphasize an important point: namely, that spatial price relationships must be viewed as a part of a general equilibrium solution in which formal account is taken of the interdependence that exists among commodities and regions.

Once a spatial equilibrium model has been constructed, it is relatively easy to alter one or more of the variables relating to demand or supply or to change transfer costs and then trace through the effects of such a change on the pattern of trade and the structure of prices. For example, if demand increases in a particular region due to a shift in population, this influences the amount of surplus or deficit in that region. This, in turn, can affect prices in all other regions. By working through a spatial equilibrium model, both the direct and indirect effects of a change in one or a combination of variables can be anticipated. This cannot be done without the aid of a model which explicitly recognizes the high degree of interrelationship that exists among prices in different regions.

Spatial equilibrium models have been employed by a number of economists to identify optimum international trading patterns and spatial price relationships that might be expected to prevail in the absence of trade barriers. In most cases, individual countries are identified as regions. The effects of tariffs or import quotas can be appraised by incorporating these in the model. One of the important uses of such models has been to determine which countries would gain and how much producer and consumer prices would change if present trade barriers, including domestic subsidies on production, import controls, tariffs, or variable levies, were to be relaxed. Bates (1968), for example, employed a spatial equilibrium model to estimate the long-run structure of world sugar prices and the trading patterns that would emerge if present U.S. sugar policies were modified. A somewhat similar procedure was used by Dean and Collins (1966) to measure the welfare and trade effects of changes in tariff policies applied to oranges in the European Common Market.

Conclusions

In the absence of barriers to the free movement of commodities, interregional price relationships respond to changes in supply and demand in different regions and to changes in transfer costs. A change in demand or supply in one region can have far-reaching effects even on regions not directly involved in trading with that region. Changes in transfer costs can likewise alter the relative advantage of producers in different areas. In general, a decrease in shipping costs will benefit more distant as compared with nearby producing areas. Thus, it is important to know something about the factors which influence spatial price relationships in attempting to predict changes in the competitive position of different regions.

An understanding of spatial price relationships is also essential to those with the responsibility of establishing regional differences in support prices. Price differentials that are inconsistent with optimum trading patterns and existing transfer costs can lead to uneconomic expansion of production in some areas and to irrational movement of commodities between regions, thereby resulting in higher government costs or a sacrifice in consumer welfare.

APPENDIX: A SIMPLE SPATIAL EQUILIBRIUM MODEL

This appendix illustrates a formal spatial price equilibrium model involving just two regions, assuming linear regional demands, fixed regional production, and known transfer costs. Other models might involve, for instance, regional supply relations rather than given fixed production. Of course, a "realistic" model would involve more than two regions.

Notation:

Q_1^* and Q_2^* = quantities produced in respective regions, which are indicated by subscript.

Q_1' and Q_2' = quantities demanded, including imports.

P_1 = equilibrium price in Region 1 with trade.

We assume Region 1 is the area with potential excess supply.

R = transfer cost per unit.

$P_1 + R$ = equilibrium price in Region 2 with trade.

For simplicity, we assume the same linear demand relation for each region and do not include "demand shifters."

Model: with trade, the equilibrium situation is

(1) $Q_1' = \alpha + \beta P_1;$

(2) $Q_2' = \alpha + \beta (P_1 + R);$

and, since total production is fixed,

(3) $Q_1^* + Q_2^* = Q_1' + Q_2'.$

In these equations, α, β, R, Q_1^*, and Q_2^* are assumed to be known. The unknowns are the equilibrium values P_1, Q_1' and Q_2'. This is a system of 3 equations with 3 unknowns.

Solution:

(a)   add equations (1) and (2)

$$Q_1' + Q_2' = 2\alpha + \beta R + 2\beta P_1.$$

(b)   From equation (3), we can write

$$Q_1^* + Q_2^* = 2\alpha + \beta R + 2\beta P_1.$$

We are, in effect, finding the equilibrium price by equating supply and demand.

(c)   Solving for the equilibrium price,

$$P_1 = \frac{1}{2\beta} \left(Q_1^* + Q_2^* - 2\alpha - \beta R \right).$$

(d)   Having obtained P_1, equations (1) and (2) are used to solve for Q_1' and Q_2'.

References

Bates, Thomas H. 1968. "The Long-Run Efficiency of United States Sugar Policy," *Am. J. Ag. Econ.*, 50:521–535.

Bressler, Raymond G., Jr., and Richard A. King. 1970. *Markets, Prices, and Interregional Trade.* New York: John Wiley and Sons.

Dean, Gerald W., and Norman R. Collins. 1966. "Trade and Welfare Effects of EEC Tariff Policy: A Case Study of Oranges," *J. Farm Econ.*, 48 (Part I):826–846.

Heady, Earl O., et al., eds. 1961. *Agricultural Supply Functions— Estimating Techniques and Interpretations.* Ames, Iowa: Iowa State Univ. Press.

Heady, Earl O., and Wilfred Candler. 1958. *Linear Programming Methods.* Ames, Iowa: Iowa State Univ. Press.

Judge, George G., and T. D. Wallace. 1958. "Estimation of Spatial Price Equilibrium Models," *J. Farm Econ.*, 40:801–820.

King, Richard, ed. 1963. *Interregional Competition Research Methods.* Raleigh, N.C.: Agricultural Policy Institute, North Carolina State Univ.

Lasley, Floyd A. 1965. *The Geographic Structure of Milk Prices, 1964–65.* Econ. Res. Ser., USDA, ERS-258.

Leath, Mack N., and Leo V. Blakley. 1971. *An Interregional Analysis of the U.S. Grain-Marketing Industry, 1966–67*. Econ. Res. Ser., USDA Tech. Bul. 1444.

Waite, Warren C., and Harry C. Trelogan. 1951. *Agricultural Market Prices*. 2d ed. New York: John Wiley and Sons. Chapter 7.

CHAPTER 9

Price Variation
through Time

This chapter emphasizes models of price determination which seek to explain persistent patterns of price behavior through time. Such behavior includes seasonal patterns of change, year-to-year fluctuations, trends, and cycles. An objective is to provide an understanding of why temporal changes occur and to help identify regularities in price behavior.

Prices observed through time are the result of a complex mixture of changes associated with seasonal, cyclical, trend, and irregular factors. The most common regularity observed in agricultural prices is a seasonal pattern of change. Normally, prices of storable commodities are lowest at harvest time and then rise as the season progresses, reaching a peak prior to the next harvest.

Some commodities such as hogs, beef cattle, eggs, and certain vegetables exhibit cyclical behavior. Price cycles for agricultural commodities tend to vary in length and in amplitude of fluctuations, but a clear tendency does exist within agriculture for production to expand in response to favorable prices, which in turn leads to lower prices in a subsequent period.

Seasonal and cyclical price changes may be superimposed on long-term trends that persist for years. For example, the price of beef in the fall of any year reflects seasonally large supplies, whether production is currently in the rising or declining phase of a cycle and whether the general trend of price is up or down. A knowledge of all of these relationships is useful in understanding price behavior.

Economists have devoted substantial effort to an attempt to identify empirical regularities in price behavior. Mathematical techniques are available to describe the seasonal, cyclical, trend, and irregular components of an economic time series. The techniques attempt to decompose the observed series into its constituent parts; these techniques are described in detail in numerous sources (such as Yamane, 1967). Unfortunately, a variety of factors reduce the usefulness of such analyses. Reliable estimates of the future can be made only insofar as seasonal patterns, trends, or cycles persist in a uniform manner. Cycles may be lengthened or shortened by external events. Changes in government programs, a severe drought, or a new international crisis obviously can create irregular price movements which are impossible to forecast.

Short-Time Price Variation

When agricultural prices are arrived at in the framework of marketplaces, an opportunity exists for a more or less continuous process of evaluation of factors influencing price. As negotiation and trades take place among buyers and sellers, specific prices are obtained. Hence, prices may change from week to week, from day to day, and even within the trading day.

Prices respond, in part, to current, actual changes in economic variables. Thus, a major factor in day-to-day price changes for livestock is day-to-day changes in market receipts. The quantity of a product available on a particular day is the result of many individual decisions by sellers. Day-to-day variation in demand is usually less volatile than in supply; changes in demand can be due to strikes, health scares, previously unexpected change in exports, and so forth.

Current cash prices also may respond to expected (future) changes in factors influencing price (Working, 1958). Thus, the current price of wheat may decline in anticipation of a dock strike, which would reduce exports. Or, expected changes in government price-support or export programs may influence current price. The precise mechanism for this phenomenon for grains prices is discussed in Chapter 12. In sum, short-term price changes arise from a process of continual evaluation of current and expected changes in factors influencing price.

Prices for some agricultural products are arrived at in institutional frameworks which tend to reduce or eliminate daily price changes. Contracts are in some cases negotiated between sellers and buyers with price fixed by a formula or by prior agreement. In addition, producers are becoming larger and more specialized, at least in the United States, which implies more stable production and marketing. Thus, one may hypothesize that the changing structure of agriculture and in marketing arrangements is resulting in less frequent price changes today than in past years.

Seasonal Variation in Prices

Sources of Seasonality

Seasonal price behavior is a regularly repeating price pattern that is completed once every twelve months. Such a regular pattern might arise from seasonality in demand, seasonality in supply and marketing, or a combination of the two. For instance, one might visualize a continuous, constant supply over a year with regular seasonal shifts in demand resulting in a seasonal price pattern.

Most agricultural products are characterized by some seasonality in production and marketing patterns. For crops, seasonality arises from climatic factors and the biological growth process of the plants. Many crops are harvested once a year and, depending on perishability, may be stored for sale through a marketing season. For livestock and livestock products, seasonality of production arises for diverse reasons including seasonal variation in climatic conditions, seasonality of feed supplies, and the biological character of the production process. However, seasonality in production is being reduced for livestock products (e.g., broilers and eggs).

Seasonality in demand also exists for agricultural products and is related to factors like climate and holidays. Thus, the demand for turkeys in the United States is greatest just prior to the Thanksgiving and Christmas holidays while the demand for ice cream rises in the summer and declines in the winter months; changes in the demand for cut flowers are closely associated with certain holidays. Seasonal differences in demand may not always be as obvious as these examples; however, some empirical research has been devoted to estimating demand relations by seasons (e.g., Stanton, 1961).

One model of seasonal price behavior is illustrated in Figure 9-1. In this model, seasonal price behavior arises from the seasonality of supply. We assume for simplicity that the year consists of three seasons and that the demand function (D) is the same for each season.

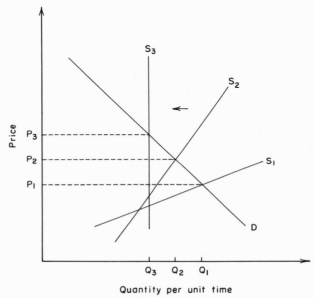

Figure 9-1. A model of seasonal supply and seasonal price change

The crop is assumed to be harvested in Season 1. Sellers then have the option of selling in any of the three seasons. Since producer–inventory holders have a choice of holding inventory or of selling at harvest, the supply curves (S_1 and S_2) for Seasons 1 and 2 have a positive slope. The slopes become progressively steeper for the successive seasonal supplies. Higher prices are required in the successive seasons to induce inventory holders to carry inventories. The seasonal price rise must cover (on the average) the costs of storage. Also, as time passes, the range of alternatives open to the inventory holder decreases.

In the model illustrated, it is assumed that the inventory carried into Season 3 must be sold in that season and cannot be carried over into the new crop year. Hence, the supply function for Season 3 is perfectly inelastic. Apples for fresh use, late summer onions, and fall potatoes are seasonal crops that cannot be carried into the next crop year. Thus, the model depicted in Figure 9-1 is a simplified version of a seasonally produced crop for which no inventories are carried from one year to the next. We turn, then, to what might be termed a "normal" seasonal price pattern.

The "Normal" Seasonal Pattern

The usual price pattern for a seasonal crop—harvested within a brief period but then sold throughout the year—is for the price to rise through the year as a function of the cost of storing the commodity. If grain merchants correctly anticipate future demands relative to supplies and hence store the "correct" quantity, the price will rise from a low point at harvest by just enough to cover storage costs from the time of harvest to subsequent points in the year (Figure 9-2). These price changes must be sufficient to induce some to sell and others to continue holding the commodity. Thus, the seasonal product is allocated through the year by the relationship of current price and expected prices to storage costs. As the next crop year approaches, price declines rather abruptly to the next seasonal low (Figure 9-2).

In essence, a merchant stores a commodity if he expects the benefits from storage to equal or exceed the costs of storage. If P_f is the expected future price, P_c the current cash price, and M the cost of storage between the two time periods, then storage takes place if

$$P_f - P_c \geqq M.$$

In this context, costs are broadly defined. They include the direct costs of warehouse space, fire insurance, interest on investment in facilities and inventory, and so forth. In addition, costs may be defined to include a risk premium for a possible adverse price movement while the commodity is in storage. The risk of a price decline while the merchant is holding the commodity is not a direct cost, but presumably a risk-adverse warehouseman would pay, if possi-

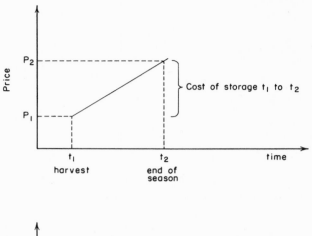

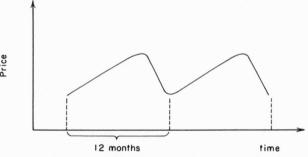

Figure 9-2.   Illustrations of theoretical seasonal price behavior

ble, to avoid the price risk, just as he buys fire insurance. Various authors (e.g., Cootner, 1967, p. 69) also have emphasized the "convenience yield" of holding inventories. This yield may be viewed as a benefit from holding inventories. Processors and probably grain merchants as well find some minimum inventory necessary or convenient. Thus, some inventories are held even when the expected price difference $P_f - P_c$ does not cover the direct costs of storage.[1]

For a number of reasons, the "normal" seasonal price pattern often does not prevail within any given year. Those storing the commodity may act on imperfect information—holding excess stocks, selling too much too soon, and so forth. Hence, prices may rise by more or by less than the cost of storage in a particular year.

[1] The nature of costs and the idea of a supply-of-storage function are further explored in Chapter 12.

On the average, over a period of years, seasonal price rises must cover costs; otherwise in the long run there would be no storage. Thus, the seasonal patterns depicted in Figure 9-2 are atypical, although the essence of the idea of seasonal price variability is shown.

The degree of storability of current inventories or the timing and size of the new crop also may influence the seasonal price pattern. End-of-season supplies of semiperishable commodities, such as apples or potatoes, are often uncertain. First, storage quality can vary from year to year. A poor quality would necessitate quick sales out of storage with a resulting small end-of-season supply. Second, storage supplies are often augmented by new crop production. Storage potatoes, for example, compete with new spring potatoes. Thus, the timing of harvest and the size of the spring potato crop influence the price of storage potatoes. If supplies toward the end of the storage season are short, prices rise dramatically; if supplies are large, seasonal prices will rise less than normal or even decline. Selected seasonal price patterns for potatoes in New York State are shown in Figure 9-3. The months from September to May cover the major harvest and storage period; spring and early summer potatoes are the major source of supply in the other months.

A "nonperishable" commodity is defined as one which can be stored from one crop year to the next (e.g., wheat). The previously developed model is appropriate for this type of commodity with one modification: Future expectations must explicitly consider the next crop year; the "optimal" carryover into the new crop year must be determined. Typically, new crop supplies would reduce prices sufficiently so that the carryover is small and related to the convenience of having some inventory at all times. However, a very small crop could result in an expected price difference $(P_f - P_e)$ which would cover the direct costs of storage and hence induce a substantial carryover into the new crop year. Storage policies and seasonal price patterns clearly are influenced by price expectations for the subsequent crop year.

Changing Seasonal Price Patterns

A particular price pattern, as we have seen, depends on intraseasonal supplies and demands and on storage costs over the season. Thus, price differences between months depend on these given

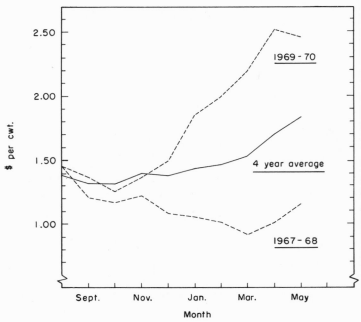

Figure 9-3. Potatoes: Monthly average prices received by New York State farmers, selected seasons and four-season (1967–1968 to 1970–1971) average. Data from Statistical Reporting Service, *Agricultural Prices,* USDA, Annual Summaries for 1968, 1969, and 1970, and subsequent monthly issues for 1971.

conditions and are assumed to equal storage costs for a seasonally produced crop. It follows that changing conditions should change the seasonal pattern. In a dynamic economy, the basic factors underlying a particular seasonal pattern are likely to change. For example, a decline in the seasonality of production, as has occurred for eggs (Larson, 1967A), reduces seasonal price movements. A change in storage costs, likewise, would change the seasonal price pattern.

A seasonal pattern has a fixed period of twelve months. An implication of the foregoing discussion is that the amplitude of the periodic fluctuations need not be fixed but may change systematically over the years. This potential for systematic changes plus the usual irregularities in a particular year make the use of historical seasonal price patterns for forecasting the future a very risky business.

Methods of Analysis

Various techniques, mostly descriptive, have been developed to analyze seasonality. One may begin simply by constructing a graph with, say, monthly prices on the vertical axis and time units on the horizontal axis. This helps to identify the uniformities or irregularities in the seasonal price pattern, and the observations may suggest that the seasonal pattern is changing in some systematic way. A second, common technique is to construct an index of seasonal prices. The base period is either a particular twelve months or an average of several twelve-month periods. The index for the base period is, of course, 100, and the weekly or monthly index numbers vary around the base. An index of 90 for June indicates that June prices for the period described were 10 per cent below the twelve-month average. In other words, each monthly price is expressed as a percentage of a twelve-month average. Monthly index numbers can be constructed for a period of years, and these can then be used to see if any systematic changes have occurred in the pattern. Many textbooks provide explicit details for the construction of seasonal indexes (e.g., Yamane, 1967, chapter 13).

Regression techniques also may be used to estimate the time-series components of price (or other variable). Jorgenson (1964) presents linear statistical models which are appropriate for analyzing time series with a seasonal component. Within the regression framework, it is also possible to fit a harmonic function to the data (e.g., Abel, 1962). The seasonal "cycle" has a fixed period of twelve months and, in some cases, may be represented quite accurately by sine or cosine functions. This provides an estimate of a smooth curve. Functions can be developed which allow for changes in the amplitude of the seasonal pattern with the passage of time. However, irregularities still may make for a poor fit, and semiperishable products may not have continuous observations over a twelve-month period, making the use of harmonic functions difficult. The multiple regression technique does have the advantage of estimating the "net" values of all the time-series components in one equation.

By analogy with spatial price equilibrium models, it is possible to develop intertemporal price equilibrium models. The "markets" are separated by time and storage costs, rather than by space and transport costs. This approach requires that demand and supply relations be estimated for each time period (e.g., a month) within the season and that storage costs be known. With this information, optimal quantity allocations and prices for a season could be determined. It would also be possible, in principle, to analyze the effects of changing storage costs, demands, or supplies on prices and on the optimum seasonal allocation of supplies (Takayama and Judge, 1964).

Annual Price Variation

Models of price determination under pure competition (Chapter 5) can be applied directly to explain year-to-year product price variation. The demand and supply functions may be viewed as representing annual averages with annual price changes arising from shifts in these functions.

In agriculture, a principal factor in yearly price variability is changes in supply. The supply available in any one year is based mainly on current production and perhaps to some extent on imports and on carryover from the previous crop year. Annual fluctuations in the production of farm products, as we have seen, are sensitive to many economic and noneconomic factors. Demand also may change, owing to fluctuations in export demands, variations in prices of substitutes, and systematic increases (at least in the United States) in population and income.

Year-to-year variation in prices is typically greater for crops, at least for those not under price support, than for livestock items; that is, the coefficient of variation (see Yamane, 1967, pp. 75 f., for a definition) is larger. Crops tend to have greater swings in annual production because (a) yields are sensitive to weather conditions and pests and (b) acreage planted and harvested often can be changed from year to year. Conversely, except for poultry, animal units require longer time periods to change, and yields are somewhat less sensitive to factors like weather. The demand for many crops is highly price inelastic. Hence, when substantial year-to-year shifts in supply are combined with an inelastic demand, price fluctuations are likely to be very great. This situation prevails for potatoes (Figure 9-4). Total production in the United States has

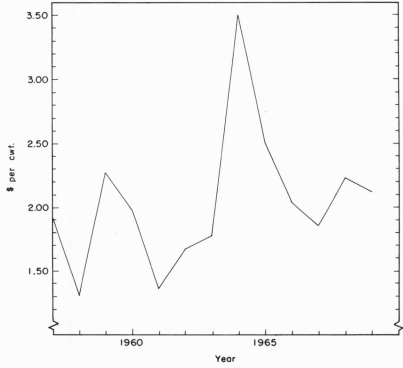

Figure 9-4. Potatoes: Season average price received by farmers, United States, 1957–1969. Data from U.S. Dept. of Agriculture, *Agricultural Statistics 1970,* p. 182.

varied from 241 to 325 million hundredweight in just the seven-year period 1964–1970. The average farm-level price elasticity of demand is thought to be about -0.2. The median farm price for the 1957–1969 time period was $2.00, and the range was from $1.36 to $3.50 per hundredweight.

Trends

Trends in agricultural prices are associated with general inflation and deflation in the economy and with factors specific to agricultural products, including changes in the tastes and preferences of consumers, increases in population and income, and technological changes in production. The prices of poultry and eggs declined during the 1950's and 1960's mainly because technological changes lowered costs of production and increased supplies. For example, broiler chicken production increased from about 3.5 billion pounds in the early 1950's to over 10 billion pounds in 1970. This increase was not completely offset by increases in demand, and farm-level prices trended downward from approximately 28 cents per pound to about 14 cents per pound in the twenty-year period. Thus, upward or downward trends in prices can be generated by persistent changes in either supply or demand.

Distributed lag responses also may be a factor in longer-term changes in economic variables. As previously discussed, economic responses are not instantaneous. Given a change in price, the change in quantity supplied is lagged and perhaps distributed through time. Thus, a one-time increase in price could result in observed increases in quantity supplied over two, three, or more years.

Cyclical Behavior

A cycle is a pattern that repeats itself regularly over a period of years. A true cycle is self-energizing and not the result of chance factors. The length of a cycle is the time from one peak to the next or from one trough to the next and is usually related to the time required to produce a new generation, such as hogs or chickens, or to wear out and replace a product. The latter applies primarily to industrial goods. If a high proportion of families were to purchase automobiles in a particular year, and the average useful life of a car is assumed to be seven years, the replacement demand for autos would increase at the end of each seven-year period, thus generating a cycle which might be repeated indefinitely. Agricultural cycles are more likely to be initiated by some external event, but once a cycle begins, it may be continued as producers respond to changes in prices (Figure 9-5).[2] A high price, which may be due to a poor growing season, can lead growers to increase production

[2] The most frequently used example is the "hog cycle" which is approximately four years in length. For instance, local maximums in annual price occur in 1951, 1954, 1958, 1961, 1966, and 1969—that is, price peaked every three to five years.

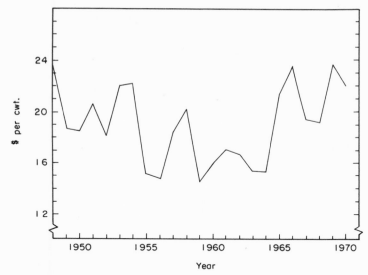

Figure 9-5. Price of barrows and gilts, eight-market average, 1948–1970. Data from Statistical Reporting Service, *Livestock and Meat Statistics,* USDA Stat. Bul. No. 333 (1963), p. 255, tables 169–171, and subsequent annual supplements.

in a subsequent period. This, in turn, will result in lower prices, followed by a cutback in production, thereby resulting in higher prices in some future period and the beginning of another period in the cycle.

Opinions differ as to whether cycles in agriculture are of the self-generating type or are caused by external events. Conflicting views as they apply to the "cattle cycle" are reviewed by Breimyer (1955, pp. 2f.). Cattle and hog cycles are thought by some to be the result mainly of changes in feed supplies, especially the amount of grass (pasture conditions) available to support the cattle population, and the size of the corn crop which affects hog production. Presumably, the number of animals retained for breeding will be increased when feed supplies are large and reduced when pasture conditions are poor or the corn crop is short. While changes in feed supplies may generate a cycle, the amplitude and length of such cycles is likely to be irregular.

There is considerable evidence of cyclical behavior in agriculture, especially in the number of beef cattle, hogs, and chickens on farms, although the amplitude and duration of livestock production cycles is by no means uniform. The identification of cycles is often complicated by the presence of strong trends or irregular movements, especially in prices. For this reason, forecasts made by mechanically projecting past cycles may be inaccurate. But an understanding of what lies behind cycles is important. Cycles are generated by lagged responses to changes in prices or other external events. Formal models incorporating such variables, especially lagged prices, have been developed which help to explain cyclical behavior (Gruber and Heady, 1968; Meadows, 1970). The simplest of these is the cobweb model to which we now turn.

The Cobweb Model [3]

A Description

The cobweb model provides a theoretical explanation of the cyclical component of certain price-quantity paths through time. Prices and quantities are viewed as being linked recursively in a causal chain. A high price leads to large production; the large supply results in low prices, which in turn result in smaller production, and so forth. More explicitly, the cobweb model arises from three factors which, if present, would result in cyclical behavior of price and quantity. First, a time lag must exist between the decision to produce and the actual realization of production. Second, producers base production plans on current or recent past prices. Hence, realized production, because of the time lag, is a function of past prices. Third, current prices are mainly a function of current supply, which, in turn, is mainly determined by current production.[4]

Consequently, the following chain of events occurs. Current quantity supplied is a function of past prices; i.e.,

$$Q_t^{(s)} = f_1(P_{t-1}).$$

[3] Ezekiel (1938) wrote one of the basic papers on the cobweb model. Waugh (1964) provides a more recent summary and bibliography. A paper by Larson (1967B) provides a critique and references emphasizing criticisms of the cobweb model.

[4] The supply schedule can be adjusted for carryover, but this does not change the fundamental argument.

The quantity produced in time t is sold in time t.

$$Q_t^{(s)} = Q_t^{(d)}.$$

The market clearing price for Q_t is determined by the demand relation.

$$P_t = f_2(Q_t^{(d)}).$$

Thus, the basic causal chain may be written

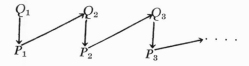

Two supply relations are implicit in the cobweb model. One is a "conventional" short-run function. However, because of the time lag in the production process, current supply is a function of lagged prices (as indicated above). More precisely, planned production is a function of current prices. Assuming plans are realized, current production is a function of past prices. An alternate statement is that production plans are based on expected prices, and expected prices are a function of current and past prices.[5]

The second supply relation is the very-short-run curve. Once production is realized, the model assumes that this quantity is sold. Current price is determined by current supply. (In other words, price is determined as illustrated in Figure 5-1, Chapter 5.) This assumption suggests that the model is most applicable to perishable or semiperishable farm products.

The name "cobweb" arises from the pattern formed by joining the successive price-quantity observations on a conventional supply-demand diagram (Figure 9-6). For convenience, we assume that poor weather resulted in a small supply and hence a relatively high price (P_0) in time t_0. The static short-run supply curve for

[5] In empirical supply analysis, various alternate measures of "planned production" and "expected price" have been suggested. These are discussed in Chapter 15.

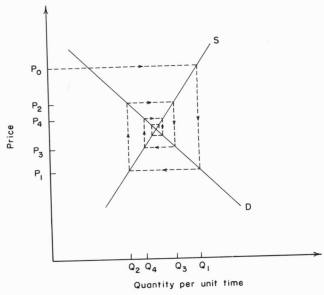

Figure 9-6. A cobweb model with a convergent cycle

"normal" weather, however, is shown as S. Hence, on the basis of
the P_0, producers plan to produce Q_1, which will be realized in t_1
because of the time lag required for the production process. Once
produced, the quantity Q_1 is sold in t_1, and the market clearing
price P_1 is determined by the market demand relation D. Price P_1
is the basis for production, which is realized as Q_2, which in turn
determines P_2. As the process continues, the cobweb develops.

The assumptions of the model may be summarized as follows.
(1) Price is determined in a competitive market structure; producers are "price takers." (2) Price is mainly determined by shifting
levels of very-short-run supply (a perfectly price inelastic relation
within each time period). (3) Production *plans* are based mainly
on current price. (4) An observable lag of at least one time period
is required for production response. Thus, there is a clear lag between a price change and a production change. (5) A cycle depends on actual production equaling planned production. (6) For
a clear cobweb, demand and supply relations must be static.

The importance of these assumptions and the reality of the

model are discussed in a subsequent section. We turn first to an exposition of the cycles that would result if the model is appropriate.

The cobweb model may lead, in principle, to divergent, convergent, or constant-amplitude (continuous) cycles in price and quantity. Typically, linear supply and demand relations are assumed. The convergent cycle is illustrated in Figure 9-6. The supply function has a steeper slope than the demand relation. The price-quantity cycles, under static conditions, would converge to equilibrium. If the demand function has a steeper slope than the supply function, then the cycle diverges. If the slopes are equal, then a continuous, constant amplitude cycle results. The appendix at the end of this chapter provides a more explicit mathematical statement.

A one-unit time lag in the production process is assumed in the foregoing discussion. The resulting cycle is two units in length. If the lag had covered two time periods, then the cycle would have been four units in length. Specifically, if monthly data were used and if twelve months elapsed between harvests, then the cycle presumably would be twenty-four months long. Thus, the model implies that the cycle will be twice the length of the production lag, where the model assumes current production is a function of the previous period's price.

Limitations

The general assumption of a lag between the planning of production and its realization, as embodied in the cobweb model, is realistic for most agricultural commodities, but the explicit assumption that current production is mechanically dictated by last season's price is weak. Expected price may not be closely tied to immediate past prices, though in some instances it is.

Current price typically is strongly influenced by current production, especially for perishable and semiperishable commodities that must be sold shortly after harvest. We also know, however, that price levels are influenced by other variables, which must be considered in a "realistic" model.

Prices of some farm products, such as livestock and livestock products, are determined in a more or less competitive market. But for commodities like the grains, cotton, and milk, prices are strongly influenced by government programs. In these cases, the simple cobweb model is not appropriate.

Realized production obviously does not always equal planned production. As we have seen, a variety of "random," noneconomic factors can influence yields. Thus, even if all other assumptions were met, it is unrealistic to expect a clear cycle with a constant period.

Nonetheless, the price and quantity paths of some farm products seem to have cyclical components, but two empirical "facts" about these cycles seem inconsistent with the cobweb model, at least in its simplest form. First, cycles usually do not converge or diverge; they tend to be continuous through time. On the other hand, the elementary model implies that the continuous cycle is a special case. Second, some cycles are twice the length suggested by the theory. For instance, a market-weight hog can be produced in twelve months from the time breeding decisions are made. The cobweb model would thus suggest a twenty-four-month cycle. However, the hog cycle has typically been about four years long.

At least four explanations are available for the continuity of agricultural price cycles in the context of the cobweb model. The first, most obvious, and least plausible explanation is that the elementary cobweb model is appropriate and that the slopes of the demand and supply relations are such that the special case of a continuous cycle results.

A second explanation is that the assumption that realized production equals intended production is often unrealistic. As a consequence, before a cycle can converge or diverge, a "random" shift in supply starts a new cycle. For instance, unusually favorable weather conditions could result in an unintentionally large supply and a low price. The low price would influence production plans for the next period, and consequently a new cycle would begin. The argument is plausible. However, systematic shifts in supply and demand also have the potential to speed convergence rather than prolong the cycle. The influence of a shift in demand is illustrated in Figure 9-7 and an appropriate, concurrent shift in supply (not illustrated) could result in even quicker convergence. Thus, an argument based on the invalidity of underlying assumptions would appear to be a two-edged sword.

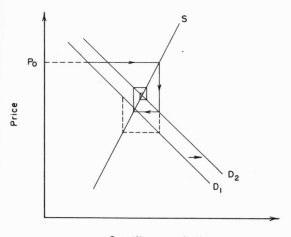

Figure 9-7. Cobweb model with changing demand

A third explanation (Waugh, 1964, pp. 739f.) is based on the linearity usually depicted in the cobweb model. Continuous oscillation is permitted by nonlinear functions (see Figure 9-8); that is, price could move to a stable platform and vary continuously at a constant level. However, such oscillations also may be unstable, where "stable" means that small deviations from the continuous

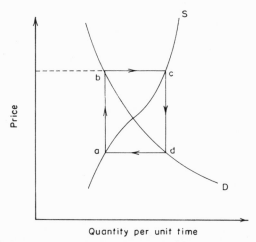

Figure 9-8. Cobweb model with curvilinear functions

(constant-amplitude) cycle will converge back to the original cycle.[6] Hence, one might hypothesize that the cobweb is characterized by a nonlinear, but stable, system. An alternate hypothesis is that the cobweb is best depicted by nonlinear equations and the recognition that these functions are not static.

A fourth argument is that the cobweb is an inappropriate model for explaining agricultural cycles. Larson (1967B), among others, takes this viewpoint and considers an alternate model; it permits cycles four times the length of the apparent lag, but it does not easily account for the continuity of the cycles.

Modifications and Applications

The cobweb model as depicted above is clearly too elementary for application to most real-world situations. More detailed econometric models are usually necessary for significant applied analyses; however, simplicity has the pedagogic virtue of isolating the key features of the model. The cobweb is a simple example of the recursive-type model, which views economic activity as a chain of events.

The commodity watermelons does provide a rough two-dimensional illustration of the cobweb model. Watermelons, once produced, cannot be stored, and price is determined largely by current production (Figure 9-9). The production plans of growers are approximated by relating changes in acres harvested to changes in prices lagged one year (Figure 9-10). Acreage is used in constructing the supply relation because it probably more clearly indicates growers' response to price. However, the slopes of the relationships (as implied in Figures 9-9 and 9-10) cannot be directly compared because different variables are involved. Suits (1955) provides a quantitative study of watermelons. In sum, changes in lagged prices result in changes in acres harvested. Acres harvested times yield gives production, and total production is an important determinant of price.

In constructing more "realistic" models, the supply and demand equations would be modified to allow for shifts in the functions. More than two equations also might be required to describe the

[6] If the product of the slopes at points a, b, c, d (Figure 9-8) is less than one, i.e., if $(abcd) < 1$, then the oscillations would be stable.

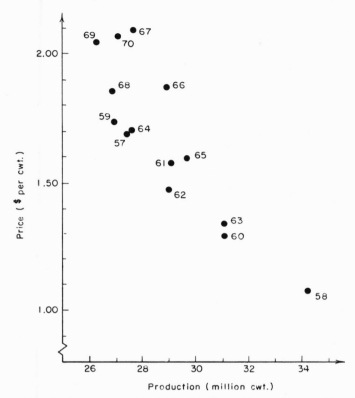

Figure 9-9. Watermelons: Relationship between farm price and total production, 1957–1970. Data from U.S. Dept. of Agriculture, *Agricultural Statistics 1971*, p. 197.

supply-marketing-price formation-demand process. For instance, Harlow (1962), in a model of the pork sector, considered equations for (1) number of sows farrowing, (2) number of pigs raised from these farrowings, (3) marketing weights of these pigs, and (4) storage supplies of pork. Thus, four "supply" equations were used instead of a single equation as implied in the elementary model. In addition, the price formation–demand aspects of the commodity must be considered.

Another difficult problem in model construction is defining the prices and costs to which farmers respond (i.e., the variables in the supply equations). In some cases, as implied previously, expected prices may indeed be a function of past prices, although using only

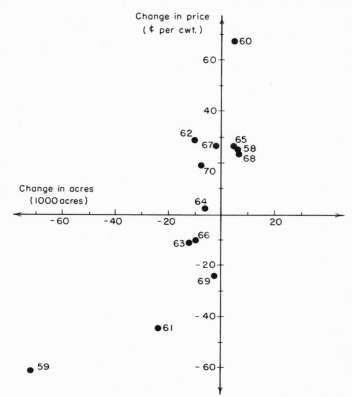

Figure 9-10. Watermelons: Relationship between changes in acres for harvest and lagged change in farm price, 1957–1970. Observations are first differences of annual data. For instance, change in acreage from 1965 to 1966 is related to the change in price from 1964 to 1965; this observation is labeled 1966. Data from U.S. Dept. of Agriculture, *Agricultural Statistics 1971*, p. 197.

last year's price is probably an oversimplification. In other cases, discussion of a forthcoming world food shortage in the press could lead to expectations of higher prices, or anticipated prices might be based on prices of contracts for the future delivery of the commodity or on announced changes in a government price-support program.

Producers typically cannot make instantaneous adjustments from one enterprise to another in response to an expected price change (as discussed in Chapter 4). Thus, production in the current period might be viewed as modified from last year's level in response to a price change. Current quantity supplied, then, is a function of last period's quantity supplied and expected price. Nerlove (1958) has developed such a model—a distributed lag supply equation, based on a somewhat different argument. He also has developed the implications of such a supply equation for the cycles of a cobweb model.[7]

The cobweb model may be modified, as we have seen, and still contain the essential features of the cobweb. However, at some point, modifications can result in a conceptually different model. Larson (1964) has presented a "harmonic motion" model which contains many of the features of the cobweb but which modifies the static short-run supply function and hence eliminates the cobweb. Thus, the principal difference in the two models lies in the approach to production response.

While the simple cobweb model depicts supply response as a change in level along a static short-run supply curve, Larson argues that supply response is best viewed as a *rate of change* in planned production through time. Producers' decisions are constrained by such factors as resource fixity, credit rationing, and uncertainty. It takes time to alter plans, and still more time for changes in plans to affect production. Thus, current production can remain relatively large even after prices decline. A lag exists in carrying through changes in production plans, and marginal changes from an existing level of output cannot be expected to bring down total production very markedly in a short period of time. For example, farmers respond to low pork prices by reducing the rate of breeding of sows, but both the number of pigs being fattened and the total number of sows bred (in gestation period) will remain large for some time. That is, the number of pigs in the "pipeline" of the production process, a number based on previous decisions, is large.

The time paths of price and quantity implied by the harmonic-motion model may be estimated as sine or cosine functions—hence the name of the model. Larson has applied the model to the hog cycle. He argues (1967B, pp. 171–173) that the model is applicable

----

[7] For certain values of the coefficients of the equations, there will be no cycle; in other cases, a cycle is possible.

to other commodities as well. This model does imply a cycle twice the length of the one implied by the cobweb; however, the harmonic-motion model seems most appropriate for commodities which have a more or less continuous production process or at least continuity in the decisions made by producers.

The time path solutions for price and quantity (Larson, 1964, p. 378) will be constant amplitude, cosine functions (180 degrees out of phase) only if "special" slope conditions prevail with respect to the relationships in the model. In this respect, the harmonic-motion model seems no more satisfactory than the cobweb model. Larson (pp. 380–383) discusses in detail the reasonableness of the assumptions underlying the model.

Another problem is that the period of the cycle is rigidly fixed by an assumption that planned production is realized after a fixed time interval. Producers often have some discretion in modifying production plans. Thus, the cycle may not follow a smooth and regular path, complicating the fit of a harmonic function.

Some Final Comments on Temporal Price Variability

We have seen that price changes may take many forms through time. This variability is not "good" or "bad"; it is the result of economic change. In a private-enterprise economy, price is one of the regulators of the economy. A technical improvement lowers the costs of production and hence makes production more profitable. A typical response to higher profits is larger production. The result is lower prices, which increase quantity demanded and also signal producers to lower production. In another example, we saw how price variability allocated a seasonally produced commodity over the marketing season. Changes in relative prices play a role in directing the economy.

However, our society has sometimes decided that extreme price variability is undesirable. Great price variability creates uncertainty for the producer. He may be handicapped in planning the future; he may be unwilling to make investments (internal credit rationing) because of price uncertainty; or lenders may be unwilling to provide capital because of price risk. Consumers with relatively constant demands for bacon may not be satisfied with wide swings in prices (due to production variability). They would prefer to base their consumption decisions on somewhat more stable prices.[8]

Price variability for agricultural commodities can be broadly attributed to two factors. One is the biological nature of the production process, which makes production partly dependent on uncertain noneconomic forces and leads to seasonal and cyclical variability; however, variability resulting from the biological character of agriculture may be reduced in the future. The time lag in the production process also is important. A second factor is the relative price-inelasticity of supply and demand functions. Thus, shifts in supply or demand can have a relatively large impact on prices.

APPENDIX: AN ELEMENTARY COBWEB MODEL

The simplest cobweb model can be written as three equations.

$$Q_t^{(s)} = \delta + \gamma P_{t-1} \text{ (supply).}$$
$$Q_t^{(s)} = Q_t^{(d)} \text{ (market clearing).}$$
$$P_t = \alpha - \beta Q_t^{(d)} \text{ (demand).}$$

With price on the vertical axis, the slopes are

$$\frac{dP}{dQ} = -\beta \text{ for the demand relation, and}$$

$$\frac{dP}{dQ} = \frac{1}{\gamma} = \gamma^{-1} \text{ for the supply relation.}$$

Thus, the slope conditions for the three types of cycles are

$$|-\beta| > |\gamma^{-1}| \text{ a divergent cycle,}$$
$$|-\beta| < |\gamma^{-1}| \text{ a convergent cycle, and}$$
$$|-\beta| = |\gamma^{-1}| \text{ a continuous cycle.}$$

[8] The consequences of price instability and of price stabilization programs are further discussed in Chapter 14.

One method of computing the *paths* of Q and P through time is by the "brute strength" technique of substitution. While not recommended for actual computations, it may help the reader to understand the conditions leading to various types of cycles.

Since $\quad P_t \quad = \alpha - \beta\,Q_t$ and
$$Q_{t+1} = \delta + \gamma\,P_t, \text{ it follows that}$$
$$Q_{t+1} = \delta + \gamma\,(\alpha - \beta\,Q_t)$$
$$= (\delta + \gamma\alpha) - \gamma\beta\,Q_t.$$
Also, $\quad Q_{t+2} = (\delta + \gamma\alpha) - \gamma\beta\,Q_{t+1}$, and
$$= (\delta + \gamma\alpha) - \gamma\,\beta\,[(\delta + \gamma\alpha) - \gamma\beta\,Q_t]$$
$$= (\delta + \gamma\alpha)\,(1 - \gamma\beta) + (\gamma\beta)^2\,Q_t.$$

Let $t = 0, 1, 2, 3, \ldots$ and the equations for computing Q in each period may be summarized as follows:

$$Q_1 = (\delta + \gamma\alpha) - \gamma\beta\,Q_0.$$
$$Q_2 = (\delta + \gamma\alpha)\,(1 - \gamma\beta) + (\gamma\beta)^2\,Q_0.$$
$$Q_3 = (\delta + \gamma\alpha)\,(1 - \gamma\beta) + (\gamma\beta)^2 - (\gamma\beta)^3\,Q_0.$$

.
.
.

Of course, to compute the sequence of Q's we must have estimates of $\alpha, \beta, \gamma,$ and δ and know the initial value of Q_0.

Since β is negative, the levels of Q are oscillating from period to period. The conditions for the three types of cycles also may be stated as

$(\gamma\beta)^2 > 1$ for a divergent cycle,
$(\gamma\beta)^2 < 1$ for a convergent cycle, and
$(\gamma\beta)^2 = 1$ for a continuous cycle.

For instance, if $(\gamma\beta)^2 = 1$, i.e., $|-\beta| = |\gamma^{-1}|$, then our sequence of Q's becomes

$$Q_1 = (\delta + \gamma\alpha) - (1)\,Q_0;$$
$$Q_2 = (\delta + \gamma\alpha)\,(0) + Q_0 = Q_0;$$

$$Q_3 = Q_1;$$
$$Q_4 = Q_0.$$

In other words, the Q's oscillate between

$$[(\delta + \gamma\alpha) - Q_0] = Q_1 = Q_3 = Q_5 = \text{etc.}$$
and $\quad Q_0 = Q_2 = Q_4 = \text{etc.}$

Readers with some mathematical background may have observed that

$Q_{t+1} = \gamma\beta \, Q_t$ and
$P_{t+1} = \gamma\beta \, P_t$ are first-order difference equations.

General solutions are available for such equations at various points t through time, but a development of this topic is beyond the scope of this chapter.

References

Abel, Martin. 1962. "Harmonic Analysis of Seasonal Variation with an Application to Hog Production," *J. Am. Stat. Assoc.*, 57:655–667.

Breimyer, Harold F. 1955. "Observations on the Cattle Cycle," *Ag. Econ. Res.*, 7:1–11.

Cootner, Paul H. 1967. "Speculation and Hedging," *Food Res. Inst. Studies*, 7:65–106 (Supplement).

Ezekiel, Mordecai. 1938. "The Cobweb Theorem," *Quart. J. Econ.*, 53:255–280.

Gruber, Josef, and Earl O. Heady. 1968. *Econometric Analysis of the Cattle Cycle in the United States.* Iowa State Univ. Res. Bul. 564.

Harlow, Arthur A. 1962. *Factors Affecting the Price and Supply of Hogs*, Econ. Res. Ser., USDA Tech. Bul. 1274.

Jorgenson, Dale W. 1964. "Minimum Variance, Linear, Unbiased Seasonal Adjustment of Economic Time Series," *J. Am. Stat. Assoc.*, 59:681–724.

Larson, Arnold B. 1964. "The Hog Cycle as Harmonic Motion," *J. Farm Econ.*, 46:375–386.

——. 1967A. "Price Prediction on the Egg Futures Market," *Food Res. Inst. Studies*, 7:49–64 (Supplement).

——. 1967B. "The Quiddity of the Cobweb Theorem," *Food Res. Inst. Studies*, 7:165–175.

Meadows, Dennis L. 1970. *Dynamics of Commodity Production Cycles*. Cambridge, Mass.: Wright-Allen Press.

Nerlove, Marc. 1958. "Adaptive Expectations and Cobweb Phenomena," *Quart. J. Econ.*, 73:227–240.

Stanton, B. F. 1961. "Seasonal Demand for Beef, Pork, and Broilers," *Ag. Econ. Res.*, 13:1–14.

Suits, Daniel B. 1955. "An Econometric Model of the Watermelon Market," *J. Farm Econ.*, 37:237–251.

Takayama, T., and G. G. Judge. 1964. "An Intertemporal Price Equilibrium Model," *J. Farm Econ.*, 46:477–484.

Waugh, Frederick V. 1964. "Cobweb Models," *J. Farm Econ.*, 46:732–750.

Working, Holbrook. 1958. "A Theory of Anticipatory Prices," *Am. Econ. Rev.*, 48:188–199.

Yamane, Taro. 1967. *Statistics: An Introductory Analysis*. 2d ed. New York: Harper and Row.

CHAPTER 10

Behavior of
Aggregate Farm Prices

Thus far, the discussion has focused mainly on the factors that determine the prices of individual commodities. In this chapter, we examine the causes and economic consequences of changes in the general level of farm prices and, more particularly, the relationship between average farm and nonfarm prices. Changes in the general level of farm prices affect the ability of farmers to repay debts, the profitability of investments in land, buildings, and equipment, and the competitive position of one country relative to another in selling farm products on world markets. Changes in relative prices are of even greater importance from a social and political point of view, since they affect the welfare of farm families and the level and distribution of income between the farm and nonfarm sectors of the economy.

Agricultural policies are strongly influenced by changes in the general level of farm prices. History has demonstrated that governments are much more likely to intervene in pricing farm products following periods of a general decline in commodity prices than when prices are rising. The depression of the early 1930's provides an excellent illustration of the profound effect falling prices can have on the willingness of farmers and their elected representatives to accept government intervention. Most of the programs which the U.S. government has maintained in an effort to raise or support farm prices over the past four decades were introduced as a result of the dramatic decline in prices that occurred in the late 1920's and early 1930's.

Historical Changes in the Average Level of Farm Prices

It is not easy to determine precisely how much the general level of farm prices has increased or decreased over a period of years for the simple reason that not all prices move up and down together or at the same rate. Prices at any one point in time can be likened to a swarm of insects, some of which are rising while others are descending. To obtain a measure of changes in the general level of prices, the average path, incorporating the diverse movements of individual commodity prices, must be defined. This is commonly done through the use of index numbers.[1]

An index number, like any average, reflects the sampling procedure and the weights attached to each component. One can give an upward or downward bias to an index by including or omitting certain commodities and by altering the weights assigned to the different commodities. For example, between 1960 and 1970, the prices of beef and milk rose much more than the prices of corn or broilers. An index giving more weight to the former items would be higher at the end of the decade than one based mainly on the latter commodities.

The absolute value of an index also is influenced by the year or years selected as a base. An index of farm prices for the current year using prices in 1910–1914 as a base will be more than twice as high as one using 1967 as a base. The average level of farm prices prior to World War I was less than half of what it was fifty-five years later.

In general, an index based on prices received by farmers exhibits greater amplitude of fluctuations than one based on the wholesale prices of farm commodities or on retail food prices. Farm-level prices tend to be more volatile than retail food prices for reasons that were discussed earlier. Thus, the character of the index will be influenced to some degree by the stage in the marketing process from which the price series are drawn to construct the index.

Historical changes in the wholesale prices of agricultural commodities between 1900 and 1970 are shown for the United States in Figure 10-1. Average wholesale prices of farm products tripled dur-

---

[1] See the appendix at the end of this chapter for a more complete discussion of index numbers and the manner in which they are constructed.

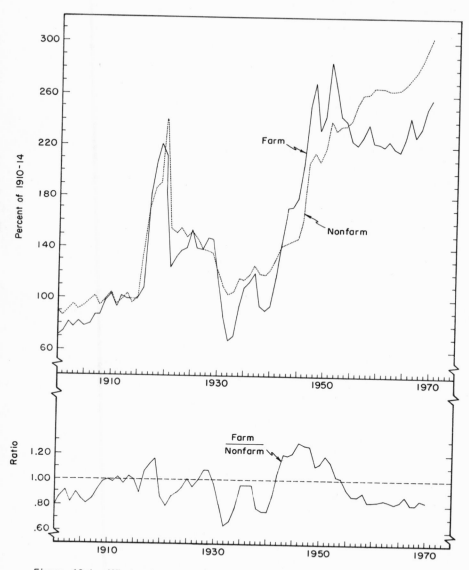

Figure 10-1. Wholesale prices of farm and nonfarm products, 1900–1970. From U.S. Dept. of Agriculture, *Handbook of Agricultural Charts,* 1965, pp. 12–13, and 1971, p. 8.

ing the first two decades of this century, giving rise to what has sometimes been referred to as the modern "golden age" of agriculture. But within slightly more than a decade after 1920, average farm product prices had sunk to the level prevailing in 1900. Many farmers, especially those who had paid high prices for land during the boom years of World War I and had financed their purchases by borrowing, found themselves in financial difficulties. More than three times as many bushels of corn or wheat were required to meet the same debt repayments in 1932 as in 1919. The mood of farmers changed drastically in the 1920's and early 1930's as thousands of them lost their farms and thousands more were threatened with the same fate because of their inability to meet their mortgage payments. Congress eventually responded to the demands for action by adopting a number of programs designed to help refinance existing debts and to support farm prices and incomes. As a result of this experience, government intervention in pricing farm products became widely accepted, not only in the United States, but in Canada, New Zealand, Australia, and most countries of Western Europe as well.

Farm prices rose again during and immediately after World War II much as they had thirty years earlier, but the rise was followed by a much less severe decline in the 1950's than had prevailed in the 1920's. In contrast to the experience following previous wars, the general level of nonfarm prices, after a brief pause, continued to rise. The persistent rise in nonfarm prices in the face of declining or stable farm product prices produced what became popularly known as the "cost-price" squeeze in American agriculture in the 1950's and early 1960's.

Changes in the Terms of Trade of Farm Products

The welfare of farmers, of course, is influenced much more by relative price movements than by the absolute level of farm product prices. The ratio between farm and nonfarm prices is sometimes referred to as the "terms of trade" of farm products.[2] An increase in

[2] This term as commonly used in economic literature refers to the ratio of the prices of goods and services exported to the prices of items imported. When one reads of an improvement in the terms of trade, this usually means

the average level of farm prices relative to the prices of other goods and services in the economy obviously leads to an improvement in the welfare of farmers, while the reverse, unless accompanied by offsetting gains in productivity, leads to a loss of real income.

One measure of the terms of trade of farm products is the ratio between the average wholesale prices of farm commodities and the average wholesale prices of nonfarm goods (mainly industrial products and raw materials). This ratio is shown in the lower half of Figure 10-1. Note that during both major wars the terms of trade moved in favor of farmers, while in the 1930's and again in the 1950's, they moved against farmers. In general, during periods of inflation generated by sharply rising demand, farm prices tend to climb faster and more than the prices of nonfarm commodities, while in periods of general deflation farm prices fall more rapidly and further than industrial prices. Given this experience, it is not surprising that farmers, at least until recently, have generally favored inflationary policies over those that might lead to deflation.

The ratio of the terms of trade of farm products most commonly referred to in the United States is the "parity ratio." As originally defined in legislation adopted in the 1930's, the ratio is the Index of Prices Received by Farmers divided by the Index of Prices Paid by Farmers for items used in production and family living, both on a 1910–1914 base. The ratio equals 100 whenever the prices-received index and the prices-paid index have increased relative to 1910–1914 by the same percentage. The last time the parity ratio equalled 100 was in 1952 when both indexes were approximately 2.9 times the level prevailing in 1910–1914. Throughout the decade of the 1960's, the ratio averaged between 70 and 80, which means that the relationship between the prices received and paid by farmers was between 20 and 30 per cent less favorable to farmers than in the 1910–1914 period.

Care must be exercised in drawing inferences from indicators of changes in the terms of trade of farm products such as the parity ratio. Merely changing the base year or years can make the terms of trade look more or less favorable to farmers. While the parity

that export prices have risen relative to import prices; however, the concept can be applied equally well to the ratio between farm and nonfarm prices.

ratio in 1970 was 72 on a 1910–1914 base, the ratio of the prices received to the prices paid by farmers for the same year on a 1967 base (the one now used for all government index numbers) was 96.[3]

A decline in the terms of trade of farm products, other things remaining the same, obviously will lead to lower incomes for farmers. But changes in efficiency can offset part or all of the decline in relative prices. For this reason, an index of the terms of trade which takes account solely of changes in relative prices and ignores changes in output per unit of input is not a reliable indicator of changes in the welfare or real income of farmers.

Gains in efficiency have helped to compensate for agriculture's adverse terms of trade in recent years. In 1970, for example, farmers in the United States were producing 75 per cent more output per unit of input than in 1910–1914. As a result, average real incomes were substantially higher in 1970 than in the period just preceding World War I, despite the fact that price relationships were 28 per cent less favorable to farmers at the end of this sixty-year period than at the beginning. Furthermore, the total farm income in 1970 was being shared by a much smaller number of farmers than in the earlier period.

Alternative Explanations of Aggregate Farm Price Behavior

Farm prices are notoriously unstable in comparison with the prices of many (but not all) nonfarm goods and services. Differences in price behavior between the farm and industrial sectors of the economy have been attributed by Hanau (1960) to a number of causes, including the following:

(1) the nature of the aggregate demand and supply curves which tend to be more price-inelastic for agricultural commodities than for many industrial products;

[3] Both ratios are based on actual market prices prevailing in 1970. The U.S. Department of Agriculture also computes an adjusted parity ratio which takes account of government price- and income-support payments made to farmers. These payments are converted into a price equivalent and added to the market prices of such commodities as wheat, corn, and cotton. The adjusted parity ratio for 1970 on a 1910–1914 base was 77.

(2) greater year-to-year fluctuations in the production of agricultural commodities combined with unequal rates of growth in
demand and supply, the latter due mainly to improvements
in technology;

(3) instability in international market prices, which are more important for a number of agricultural products than for many
nonfarm goods and services;

(4) differences in market organization and structure which make
it possible for many nonfarm firms to exercise some degree
of control over prices and to adjust production in response
to a change in demand rather than to accept lower prices.

The aggregate demand for farm products in most countries is
highly inelastic unless producers have access to export markets
that can absorb varying quantities with little effect on prices.[4] Empirical studies indicate that the aggregate farm-level price elasticity of demand for all food in the United States is less than -0.2
and probably closer to -0.1 (Cochrane, 1958, pp. 37–41, and
Tweeten, 1967). This means that a one per cent increase in the per
capita availability of food will depress average farm prices by any-
where from 5 to 10 per cent. The demand for exports and nonfood
crops such as fibers probably is slightly more elastic, and for this
reason the aggregate price elasticity of demand for all farm products in the United States may be closer to -0.25, but all evidence
points to the fact that it is substantially less than -1.0.

The aggregate short-run supply of farm products also is extremely inelastic. Tweeten and Quance (1969) estimate that the
short-run price elasticity of aggregate supply of farm products in
the United States falls somewhere between 0 and 0.2. Their analysis suggests that the elasticity of supply is slightly lower in response to falling prices than to rising prices although the differences
are not very great. Long-run elasticity, as one might expect, tends
to be somewhat higher.

For reasons that were discussed in Chapter 4, farmers usually

---

[4] The demand schedule facing a minor exporting country may be elastic
even though the aggregate demand for all farm products on world markets is
highly inelastic. This is analogous to the situation in which the demand schedule facing an individual farmer is infinitely elastic (horizontal demand schedule) despite the fact that total demand is inelastic.

find it unprofitable to reduce the use of inputs such as land, family labor, and machinery in the short run in response to lower farm prices. They can sometimes switch from the production of one commodity to another; however, aggregate production tends to remain the same, given normal weather. In contrast, manufacturing firms are more likely to reduce the length of the work week and to cut production if orders drop. Thus, the short-run effect of a general recession or depression is to bring about a sharp decline in agricultural prices but a reduction in output and employment in the industrial sector, often with little or no change in published prices.

Because of the biological nature of agricultural production, its widespread geographical dispersion, and the unpredictable rates of development of new production technologies, it is difficult to maintain equality between the rates of growth in aggregate supply and demand. During the 1940's, demand shifted to the right abruptly because of wartime needs. The adjustment in supply lagged behind changes in demand, with the result that prices rose very sharply. In contrast, during the 1950's, the aggregate supply curve moved to the right in what Cochrane (1958, p. 47) describes as a "hopping or skipping action" related to the advent of new technology. This occurred at a time when export demands for U.S. farm products were declining. Given the severe inelasticity of both the demand and supply functions, this combination of events led to a substantial drop in the theoretical equilibrium level of average farm prices. Actual market prices did not decline to the equilibrium level, however, because of government price-support programs. Surplus commodities were acquired by the government at support prices, and programs were introduced in an attempt to cut production. The experience illustrates one of the important characteristics of agriculture: namely, that modest shifts in aggregate supply relative to demand can lead to sharp changes in prices, in the absence of supply-management programs.

A part of the instability in agricultural commodity prices is attributable to fluctuations in export demands. A short cotton or grain crop in one or more of the major exporting or importing nations can lead to a sudden increase in demand for the remaining supplies. Residual market prices are particularly vulnerable to relatively modest shifts in supply, often caused by fluctuations in crop yields associated with favorable or unfavorable growing seasons. National support policies which have encouraged self-sufficiency in countries formerly importing farm products also have contributed to instability in the residual export market. Residual markets (excluding markets in which special trading arrangements or bilateral agreements are in effect and those protected by import quotas and tariffs) are now so limited for commodities like sugar and dairy products that small shifts in demand or supply often have a large impact on export prices.

Countries with a high degree of variability in yields are responsible for some of the fluctuations in export prices. For many years, world coffee prices rose or fell primarily in response to changes in production in Brazil, the major exporter and also the country with highest degree of variability in yields. More recently, the Soviet Union has contributed to instability in the prices of wheat and vegetable oils. Total agricultural production in the Soviet Union varies greatly from year to year because of its northern latitude (which limits the growing season in some years) and uncertain rainfall. A few bushels' difference in average wheat yields can shift the Soviet Union from a net exporter to a net importer of grain. Similar variations in sunflower yields can cause export prices of vegetable oils to drop substantially in years of large crops and to rise at other times when they have only limited quantities available to sell on European markets.

Attempts have been made to compensate for instability in export markets due to shifts in either demand or supply by negotiating international agreements among major exporting countries for such commodities as sugar and coffee. The objective of such agreements is to maintain prices within a certain range by adjusting exports to compensate for changes in demand or supply. This is done by assigning export quotas to each participating country. A similar stabilizing function has been performed by the Canadian Wheat Board and the U.S. Commodity Credit Corporation for wheat and other grains. By storing surpluses in years of large crops and releasing stocks in years of short crops or increased demand, they have helped to reduce short-term price fluctuations.

Agriculture's terms of trade may suffer from a rise in the prices of industrial products as well as a fall in the prices of commodities sold by farmers. Raul Prebisch (1964), an economist from Argentina with a special interest in the export problems of the less developed countries, attributes at least a part of the postwar decline in the terms of trade of agricultural exporting nations to the failure of the industrial countries to share the fruits of technical progress with those purchasing industrial goods. A large fraction of the gains from technical improvements in manufacturing, according to Prebisch and others, are passed on to workers in the form of higher wages rather than to consumers as lower prices. Strong unions demand wage increases that frequently exceed productivity gains. Firms operating in oligopolistic industries then pass on the higher costs to their customers, but agricultural producers, operating as they do under more competitive conditions, have no opportunity to do likewise and in fact may suffer from lower prices as a result of increasing supplies associated with changes in technology. Thus, differences in market structure and the actions of strong trade unions can lead to higher industrial prices at a time when agricultural commodity prices are falling.

The empirical evidence regarding the terms of trade between agricultural and industrial prices is not entirely consistent with the Prebisch hypothesis. While the prices of machinery generally have risen, the prices of a number of other nonfarm goods purchased by farmers declined between 1950 and the late 1960's, including such items as fertilizer, some types of insecticides and herbicides, appliances, and tires. This suggests that at least some of the benefits of technical improvements in the industrial sector may be passed on to consumers rather than retained by labor or capital. There is ample evidence of instability in the terms of trade, but a careful analysis of price changes over long periods of time reveals no clear tendency for the terms of trade between agricultural commodities and industrial products to move consistently against agriculture, nor for the prices of agricultural exports of less developed countries to pursue a persistent downward trend relative to the prices of imports. This conclusion is supported by Hanau (1960, pp. 135–137), McCrone (1962, pp. 111–117), Morgan (1963), and Hallett (1968, pp. 40–44).

Effects of Inflation and Deflation on Agriculture [5]

Farm and nonfarm prices tend to move in the same direction over a period of years, both being propelled by common inflationary or deflationary forces, although not necessarily at the same rate. During the worldwide deflation which occurred in the last quarter of the nineteenth century, both farm and nonfarm prices declined almost continuously. The great movements in farm prices during the present century also have been associated with general inflation and deflation. Both farm and nonfarm prices rose dramatically during the first two decades of this century and again during the 1940's (see Figure 10-1), but there have been brief periods when farm prices were stable or declining despite the presence of inflationary pressures in the economy. For example, between 1955 and 1965, the trend of average farm prices remained relatively flat while nonfarm prices continued to creep upward.

Historically, agriculture has benefited from inflation of the "demand pull" type. In this situation, the demand for farm products tends to outpace growth in supply, and the prices of farm commodities tend to be bid up faster than the prices of manufactured goods and services. Periods of rapid inflation have usually been accompanied by an improvement in the terms of trade of farm products and a rise in the real income of farmers. Those with large debts obtain an additional benefit since they can pay off their obligations with "cheap" dollars. In addition, older farmers who are ready to retire gain from the appreciation in land values.

The effects of moderate or creeping inflation, especially of the "cost-push" type, are much less favorable for agriculture. Farmers still benefit from the ability to pay off debts with fewer units of farm products, provided their prices rise. The value of their assets also tends to appreciate. But current real incomes may even decline as a result of rising costs, especially for labor and machinery. Interest rates and taxes also tend to rise. Brandow (1971) argues that cost-push inflation of the type experienced in the United

[5] See Bronfenbrenner, 1968, for an excellent review of the causes of inflation and deflation and their economic consequences.

States in the late 1960's adversely affects agriculture, and that inflation of this type is likely to persist.

Deflation, of course, is still more unfavorable for agriculture. The terms of trade tend to move against agriculture in periods of declining prices and debts become more difficult to pay. Only those with incomes fixed in dollars or units of some other currency gain from deflation, and these groups usually constitute only a small minority of any population.

One of the serious negative effects of inflation is that it may result in the loss of export markets if prices in the exporting nation rise relative to those in other countries. The adverse effects of rapid rates of inflation on exports can be averted by periodic devaluation of a country's currency relative to that of other nations. The effect of devaluation is to enable other countries to obtain more of the currency of the country which devalues. This gives the country devaluing its currency a competitive advantage, provided other countries do not do likewise, but it also raises the prices of goods imported into that country. Thus, it benefits export industries, but at the expense of those relying on imported goods.

The ultimate consequences of devaluation can be extremely complex, but the first-round effects are quite straightforward. Assume the dollar is devalued 10 per cent relative to the German mark. For simplicity, assume also that the exchange rate before devaluation is four marks to the dollar and that the price of U.S. hard wheat delivered to Hamburg, Germany, is $2.00 per bushel. With a 10 per cent devaluation of the dollar a German importer can now obtain $2.20 for the eight marks formerly required to purchase a bushel of wheat. Eight marks will buy 10 per cent more wheat than formerly, provided the U.S. price of wheat does not increase. German cars and other items imported into the United States, of course, will now cost 10 per cent more, again provided the prices quoted in marks remain unchanged.

Domestic prices of commodities which are exported, of course, will not necessarily remain stable following a revaluation of currencies. If the prices of such commodities continue to rise in the country devaluing its currency, the initial competitive advantage will be lost. Other countries, fearing they may lose export markets, also may devalue their currencies. Changes in import duties, likewise, may serve to neutralize or offset at least part of the effects of currency revaluation. For example, an increase of 10 per cent in the import duty (variable levy) on wheat in the European Common Market following a 10 per cent devaluation of the U.S. dollar would make U.S. wheat just as expensive to millers in Germany as it was before the change in relative currency values occurred.

A country that has a rate of inflation higher than in other countries and fails to devalue its currency by a compensating amount will either lose markets or the real incomes of those farmers producing export crops will decline. If other countries do not raise the prices of competing export commodities, a country in which costs are rising owing to general inflation will be unable to increase its own export prices in order to compensate for higher costs. Eventually, producers will shift to other commodities or seek employment outside of agriculture as returns from export crops decline. Argentina provides an excellent case study of the adverse effects of high rates of internal inflation, not fully compensated for by devaluation, on the returns to those producing export crops. During the 1940's and 1950's, the government devalued the currency periodically, but in some cases not frequently enough or by an amount sufficient to prevent the incomes of farmers producing export crops from being squeezed. The long-run effect of this was to reduce incentives to produce export commodities and potential export earnings.

Concluding Comments

Prices perform their function of allocating the use of resources and distributing income best when the general trend of prices is reasonably stable. High rates of inflation or deflation frequently distort price relationships and may lead to a serious misallocation of resources. Incomes also may be redistributed in a somewhat haphazard or irrational manner during periods of general inflation or deflation since the prices of some products inevitably rise or fall more than others.

Agriculture has experienced wide fluctuations in the terms of trade over the past sixty years as a result of two world wars and a major depression. The ratio of farm to nonfarm prices has been depressed recently by rapid changes in technology. It has proven very difficult to match the rate of growth of aggregate supply with demand so as to avoid either surpluses or deficits of agricultural commodities. U.S. agriculture will continue to be confronted with relatively unfavorable terms of trade as long as the problem of excess production capacity remains.

APPENDIX: PRICE INDEXES

Price level movements are measured by index numbers, including indexes of retail, wholesale, and farm prices. That is, index numbers are used to measure average changes in prices (or other variables) at some point in time relative to a base year or period of years. A specific index number series, such as the Consumer Price Index, provides an empirical measure of a general concept, such as the level of retail prices. Clearly, there is likely to be a problem in obtaining observations that represent the concept being measured. This appendix briefly reviews selected methods of constructing index numbers, some problems encountered in computing such numbers, and the interpretation and use of index numbers. This appendix, however, does not contain a complete discussion, and the reader should consult other references for greater detail (such as Yamane, 1967).

Constructing an Index

In its simplest form, an index number may be thought of as a ratio. The denominator of the ratio contains the "base period" observations and the numerator the "current" observations. The resulting ratio measures current observations as a percentage of the base period. The ratio of the current price of a particular product (or service) to a base period price is defined as the "price relative."

$$R = \frac{P_{1i}}{P_{0i}},$$

where P_{1i} = current price of the ith commodity and
$\quad\;\; P_{0i}$ = base period price of the commodity.

As time passes, current price changes, and we obtain a series of price relatives for a given base period.

An index number can be constructed as an average of price relatives. For example, the arithmetic mean for n commodities and services would be

$$I = \frac{\sum\limits_{i=1}^{n} \dfrac{P_{1i}}{P_{0i}}}{n}.$$

In 1967, the average price received by farmers for beef cattle was $22.30 per 100 pounds, for hogs $18.90, and for sheep $6.35. Selecting 1967 as the base year, the price relatives would be 1.0 in that year. In 1970, the prices of meat animals had risen; the respective prices for beef cattle, hogs, and sheep were $27.10, $22.70, and $7.64. An index of meat animal prices for 1970 may be constructed as an average of the three price relatives.

$$I_{70} = \frac{\dfrac{27.10}{22.30} + \dfrac{22.70}{18.90} + \dfrac{7.64}{6.35}}{3} = 1.206.$$

It is common practice to multiply the index by 100 and write 120.6.

Other averages such as the geometric or harmonic mean could be used. These generally give different numerical results. Perhaps a more important problem, however, is that simple averages give each item in the index equal weight. In the meat animal illustration, sheep received equal weight with beef cattle, but sheep marketings are clearly much smaller than beef cattle marketings in the United States. One weighting method is to use percentage weights based on the value of marketings of each commodity in the index relative to the total value of marketings.

Weights may be formulated as follows. For one commodity,

$$W_{0i} = \frac{V_{0i}}{\Sigma V_{0i}},$$

where $V_{0i} = P_{0i} Q_{0i} = $ value of marketings of commodity i in base period 0, and $\displaystyle\sum_{i=1}^{n} V_{0i} =$ total value of n items in index.

By definition, $\displaystyle\sum_{i=1}^{n} W_{0i} = 1.$

A weighted arithmetic mean gives the following index number definition:

$$I = \frac{\Sigma W_{0i} \dfrac{P_{1i}}{P_{0i}}}{\Sigma W_{0i}} = \Sigma W_{0i} \frac{P_{1i}}{P_{0i}}, \text{ since } \Sigma W_{0i} = 1.$$

This formula is one way of defining the *Laspeyres* index, which uses quantities (Q_{0i}) in a base period as weights. To see this, recall

$$W_{0i} = \frac{V_{0i}}{\Sigma V_{0i}} = \frac{P_{0i} Q_{0i}}{\Sigma P_{0i} Q_{0i}}.$$

Then substitute for W_{0i} in the definition of I.

$$I = \sum_{i=1}^{n} \frac{P_{0i} Q_{0i}}{\Sigma P_{0i} Q_{0i}} \frac{P_{1i}}{P_{0i}} = \frac{\Sigma Q_{0i} P_{1i}}{\Sigma Q_{0i} P_{0i}}.$$

In this equation, only P_{1i} changes with the passage of time. The preceding equation is also defined as a *weighted aggregative price index*.

There are a number of alternative weighting systems for index numbers. The *Paasche* index replaces the base period weights (Q_{0i}) in the Laspeyres formula with current year weights (Q_{1i}). It is difficult, however, to obtain and maintain current quantity weights. *Fisher's ideal index* is the square root of the product of the Laspeyres and Paasche formulations. Most price indexes in the United States use a Laspeyres or a modified Laspeyres formula.

Problems in Constructing Indexes

The difficulties of index number construction can be classified under three headings: (1) selecting components of the index, (2) choosing the base period, and (3) choosing the weights.

As mentioned previously, an index is constructed to represent a particular concept, but the cost of collecting data generally prohibits exhaustive coverage. The Consumer Price Index uses the prices of about 400 items, and these prices are collected in thirty-nine Standard Metropolitan Statistical Areas and seventeen smaller cities. The price index is based on a small sample of all possible retail prices. Thus, the analyst has the problem of selecting items to include in the index. The sampling problem is complicated by the numerous outlets selling the various items, by the possibility that posted or listed prices are not the actual sale prices, by price specials not coinciding with the day or days price information is collected, and so forth.

In the Consumer Price Index, prices are obtained for items that are precisely defined (in terms of quality specifications) and for which observations are readily available. Thus, this index attempts to preserve uniformity of quality through time. As new products become available or items change in quality and others become obsolete, the index must be modified to reflect these changes.

In obtaining information used to compute the Index of Prices Received by Farmers, the U.S. Department of Agriculture asks individuals to report the average price received for each commodity by farmers as of a particular day each month. No quality specifications are contained in the instructions. Hence, the index can change simply because the average quality of the product sold changes. This again emphasizes that indexes, by the selection of data, can measure quite different concepts (either intentionally or unintentionally).

Since index numbers are constructed for the purpose of making comparisons, the base period is often thought of as a time of "normal" prices. A common practice is to use an average of prices for several years as the "base price." The denominator P_{0i} then is not a single price but is an average of prices over, say, three years.

Currently, all U.S. government index numbers use the single year 1967 as the base. Because of the changing product mix and changing quality, the base period should not be too far removed from the current period.

The quantity weights need not come from the same time period as the price base, and indeed they often do not. The weight for each commodity in the Index of Prices Received by Farmers is a ratio, which is the commodity's proportion of total income for the years 1953–1957. While the current price base is 1967, the index also is available on a 1910–1914 base. Index numbers calculated by the Department of Agriculture, including both the Index of Prices Received by Farmers and the Index of Prices Paid by Farmers for items used in production and family living are modified from time to time to reflect changes in the relative importance of different commodities and services. When changes are made in weights and/or base periods, the new index can be chained or spliced to the old index (Yamane, 1967, pp. 281–294).

In computing a farm-prices-received index, the weights could be based on quantities produced or quantities marketed. Quantities marketed are typically used. In the United States, the quantity produced and the quantity marketed are nearly identical. In a developing country, a high proportion of the food produced is often consumed on farms and not sold. In this situation, quite different weights would be obtained from quantity produced as contrasted with quantity marketed.

The quality or accuracy of an index depends, in part, on the quality of the data going into the index and hence on the amount of resources devoted to obtaining accurate price and quantity information. Personal judgments inevitably enter into the decision-making process of index number construction, but this does not necessarily mean that index numbers are biased. Government agencies, including the U.S. Department of Agriculture, take great care in trying to make the index numbers as representative of the price or production series they are trying to measure as financial resources will permit.

Uses of Price Indexes

The major use of a price index is simply to describe the average price movement of a combination of goods and services with the passage of time relative to the base period (when $I = 100$). A current index number of 110.7 means that prices on the average are 10.7 per cent higher than in the base period. For a Laspeyres-type index, it also is valid to compare adjacent years, such as the values 110.7 and 112.5. The user should understand the concept being measured (and conversely what is not measured) by the index. For example, the Consumer Price Index uses prices paid by urban consumers; it is not an index of prices paid by farmers.

The principal problem encountered in using index numbers is to interpret them correctly. If carefully constructed, they provide a reasonably accurate measure of changes in relative prices over a period of years, but they are not a good indicator of well being or of relative income changes. The selection of alternative base periods for purposes of comparison can lead to widely different conclusions about relative price movements and the welfare of different groups. Between 1940 and 1950, average farm prices rose relative to the Consumer Price Index, but between 1950 and 1960, the situation was reversed. Thus, one would be tempted to conclude that farmers were relatively well off in the late 1960's if the comparison between farm and all retail prices was based on $1940 = 100$; he would conclude just the opposite if he were making the comparison based on index numbers of farm and retail prices using 1950 as a base.

Sometimes monthly price indexes are seasonally adjusted. Prices are assumed to have a "normal" seasonal pattern within the year; for this reason alone, a monthly index would move up and down. The seasonal adjustment attempts to remove the effect of the "normal" seasonal pattern. The appropriate comparison in a seasonally adjusted index is between different years for the same month. Comparisons between adjacent months within a year can be confusing. The *unadjusted* index, for example, may rise from one month to the next, but if the price rise is less than the normal seasonal rise, then the seasonally *adjusted* index would decline.

In addition to their descriptive functions, price indexes are used to "deflate" various price and income series. The deflated series is obtained simply by dividing a price or income series by an appropriate index. The resulting price series indicates how the individual price has changed relative to the denominator which usually is selected to reflect general price movements. For instance, if the price of pork remains constant while the retail price index rises, the "real" or "deflated" price of pork falls. The same principles are involved in calculating prices or incomes in "constant dollars." For example, the per capita income of farmers in "1958 dollars" is the actual income in current dollars for each year divided by an appropriate index of prices for the same year with 1958 equal to 100. The resultant series shows changes in "real" or "deflated" income. Some of the advantages as well as problems associated with using deflated rather than actual data in empirical work are discussed in Chapter 15.

References

Brandow, George E. 1971. "The Distribution among Agricultural Producers, Commodities and Resources of Gains and Losses from Inflation in the Nation's Economy," *Am. J. Ag. Econ.*, 53:913.

Bronfenbrenner, M. 1968. "Inflation and Deflation," *International Encyclopedia of the Social Sciences*. New York: The Macmillan Co. and the Free Press. Vol. 7, pp. 289–300.

Cochrane, Willard W. 1958. *Farm Prices: Myth and Reality*. Minneapolis: Univ. of Minnesota Press.

Hallett, Graham. 1968. *The Economics of Agricultural Policy*. Oxford: Basil Blackwell.

Hanau, A. F. 1960. "The Disparate Stability of Farm and Nonfarm Prices," *Proceedings of the Tenth International Conference of Agricultural Economists, 1958*. London: Oxford Univ. Press. Pp. 124–156.

McCrone, Gavin. 1962. *The Economics of Subsidising Agriculture*. London: George Allen and Unwin, Ltd.

Morgan, Theodore. 1963. "Trends in Terms of Trade and Their Repercussions on Primary Producers," *International Trade Theory in a Developing World*. Ed. R. Harrod. London: Macmillan. Pp. 52–72.

Prebisch, Raul. 1964. "The Economic Development of Latin America and Its Principal Problems," as reprinted in *Leading Issues in Devel-*

opment Economics. Ed. Gerald M. Meier. New York: Oxford Univ. Press. Pp. 339–343.

Tweeten, Luther G. 1967. "The Demand for United States Farm Output," *Food Res. Inst. Studies,* 7:343–369.

—— and C. Leroy Quance. 1969. "Positivistic Measures of Aggregate Supply Elasticities: Some New Approaches," *Am. J. Ag. Econ.,* 51:342–352.

Yamane, Taro. 1967. *Statistics: An Introductory Analysis.* 2d ed. New York: Harper and Row. Chapter 11.

PRICING
INSTITUTIONS

Institutional arrangements related to agricultural product prices are considered in this section. In Chapter 11, alternate methods for discovering or establishing farm prices are described and appraised. The mechanics and performance of commodity futures markets—institutions that are somewhat unique—are discussed in greater detail in Chapters 12 and 13. Topics related to agricultural price policies are considered in Chapter 14, including the objectives of support programs and the economic consequences of alternative methods employed to support or stabilize farm prices.

CHAPTER 11

Mechanisms for Discovering
or Establishing Farm Prices

This chapter deals with alternative mechanisms for discovering or establishing farm prices.[1] The major methods used to arrive at a specific price for each lot or grade of an agricultural product are described briefly in the pages that follow. In addition, an attempt is made to appraise the performance of alternative pricing arrangements.

A distinction is sometimes made between price determination and price discovery. Price determination deals with the theory of pricing and the manner in which economic forces influence prices under various market structures and lengths of run (Chapter 5). The term "price discovery" is used to describe the process by which buyers and sellers arrive at specific prices. But not all agricultural commodity prices are "discovered" through the process of higgling between buyers and sellers or on the basis of bidding at auctions or on organized exchanges. Many prices are now established by a public agency or an administrator, negotiated by a producer organization, or calculated using some kind of pricing formula. We prefer to use the term "pricing arrangements" to denote the complex set of institutions and methods used to discover or fix farm prices.

Alternative Pricing Methods

The various methods used to arrive at prices for farm products have been classified in a number of ways (Rhodes, 1971 and Rog-

[1] The discussion is limited to methods employed in pricing farm products. For information on factors which influence marketing margins and retail food prices as well as the methods used to price industrial products and other non-farm goods and services see Caves, 1967; Kaplan *et al.*, 1958; and Preston, 1963.

ers, 1970). The following categories cover most of the pricing systems now employed in agriculture:

(1) individual negotiation,
(2) trading on organized exchanges or auctions,
(3) formula pricing,
(4) group bargaining conducted by producer associations or cooperatives, and
(5) administrative decisions, including those made in both the private and public sectors.

Individual bargaining or higgling between buyers and sellers is still the most common method of pricing farm products over much of the world. In the United States, the prices of hay and dairy heifers are still determined mainly through this process.

Organized markets, such as auctions or commodity exchanges, tend to replace individual buying and selling as the volume sold increases. Auctions, for example, are widely used to establish the prices of livestock although the proportion of animals marketed in this way has declined in the United States in recent years.

The experience of the United States suggests that still different pricing arrangements are likely to emerge at a later stage of development.[2] Direct selling to chain stores or to meat slaughtering plants has increased since World War II, while the volume sold through organized exchanges or central markets has declined. With direct buying, prices tend to be established on the basis of formulas, negotiated contracts, or collective bargaining procedures. Pricing has become more complicated as the role of central markets has declined, although such markets still serve as a basis for pricing since many of the formulas used to establish producer prices are tied to central market price quotations. A common procedure is to agree to deliver a product such as eggs at a price (with fixed premiums or discounts based on grade, size and other factors) which moves up or down in accordance with the price established on some particular market or a published price quotation. This has led to a system which Breimyer (1967, p. 99) describes as "trading on someone else's prices."

[2] Shepherd has suggested that pricing methods in agriculture progress from bargaining on each transaction to centralized markets, then to decentralized markets, and finally to a price committee system (quoted by Rogers, 1970, p. 6).

Thus far, collective bargaining procedures have had limited use in agriculture, but such procedures have been employed for a number of years to determine contract prices for vegetables sold to processors in certain areas and to negotiate premiums above the minimum prices established under federal marketing orders for milk. Considerable interest has developed from time to time in attempts to devise a committee system to establish a base price for eggs and to make appropriate changes when needed.

Prices paid to producers for milk sold for fluid use throughout the United States are now established mainly on the basis of formulas and administrative decisions made by public agencies. Price-support loan rates or purchase prices for supported commodities also are determined in this way, although actual market prices for many supported commodities are still established on the basis of transactions which occur on organized markets, particularly when supplies are small enough to force prices above the loan rate.

Criteria for Evaluating Alternative Pricing Arrangements

In attempting to evaluate the performance of alternative pricing mechanisms, one is faced with the problem of what criteria to use. First, it is important to decide which, if any, of the several functions that prices are expected to perform in an economy are to be given priority. Is the primary purpose of the pricing system to equate demand and supply in the short run (i.e., avoid surpluses), to guide future production, or to insure a level of prices that will achieve some specified welfare objective? Not everyone agrees that a price-discovery mechanism that simply "clears the market" (i.e., equates short-run supply and demand) is best under all circumstances. A particular pricing mechanism may do an excellent job of rationing the available supply, but it may yield prices which are too unstable to serve as reliable guides for production decisions or which do not yield a satisfactory level of income to producers. Severe price fluctuations, which sometimes occur on commodity markets, can provide misleading price signals, thereby leading to unstable production, as the cobweb model suggests, to incorrect storage decisions, or to inefficient use of marketing and processing facilities. On the other hand, a pricing mechanism that is designed to achieve certain welfare objectives, such as stable prices or a given level of farm income, may lead to surplus production and the loss of markets as consumers substitute lower priced alternatives for the price-supported product.

Another criteria that may be used to evaluate alternative pricing mechanisms is the speed and accuracy with which economic information is transmitted and interpreted. If the information is distorted, biased, or incomplete, it may lead to a serious upward or downward bias in pricing.

Finally, the cost of pricing under alternative arrangements needs to be considered. The cost of pricing includes the value of the time of participants in the pricing process as well as the cost of obtaining appropriate information. The concept may even be broadened to include the cost of resource misallocations resulting from inaccurate or biased pricing decisions. The cost of obtaining additional information, of course, must be considered in relation to the possible gains in accuracy and the economic effects of improving price-discovery mechanisms.

No one pricing mechanism is superior in all respects. Every pricing method has been subject to criticism at some time or other because it scores relatively low on one or more of the criteria that have been suggested. Since individuals can be expected to assign different weights or priorities to the various functions prices are expected to perform, inevitably some will prefer one type of pricing mechanism over another. Some, for example, will prefer to give greater weight to price stability or to minimizing the time and cost involved in making pricing decisions, while others will prefer a pricing system that promptly and fully reflects changes in supply and demand, even if it leads to widely fluctuating prices.

Producers frequently condemn a particular pricing arrangement, especially when it yields prices which they consider too low. This may or may not be the fault of the pricing mechanism itself. Low prices may simply reflect underlying supply and demand conditions. But it is also possible that imperfections in the pricing mechanism are partly at fault. For example, the incoming information may be incomplete or biased, or it may be inaccurately interpreted by potential buyers and sellers. The lack of a sufficient number of buyers or possible collusion among them also may depress prices. Psychological reactions, likewise, cannot be ignored. In a declining market, all news may be interpreted as unfavorable, while in a rising market, the opposite situation often prevails. Thus, traders may "overreact" to possible changes in demand or supply, at least over short periods of time, thereby producing prices which fluctuate excessively. But, in particular cases, it is often difficult to ascertain whether "unsatisfactory" prices are due to deficiencies in the pricing mechanism itself or to fundamental economic forces.

Individual Negotiations

Millions of pricing decisions are made each year on the basis of individual negotiations between buyers and farmers without benefit of a formal market. Prices established under such a decentralized system will approximate the equilibrium prices implicit in a competitive market only if reasonably accurate economic information is readily available to both buyers and sellers. Even with such information available, prices will vary with each transaction. A range of prices rather than a single equilibrium price is likely to prevail. This range may reflect "true" differences among the lots of the product based on quality and location, but it also probably reflects imperfections in the pricing method, including the relative bargaining power and trading skills of the participants. Price reporting where so much variability exists is time-consuming, expensive, and sometimes inaccurate.

A decentralized pricing system provides scope for individuals who like to capitalize on their trading skills or who enjoy participating in the bargaining process. However, it is a relatively expensive method of determining prices if a high value is placed on the time of those involved in the negotiations. In less developed countries, where alternative uses for family labor are limited, there may be little or no real cost to society and certainly no sacrifice in income to the individual if he spends half a day in a market or bazaar selling a few pounds of produce. But this system of pricing becomes progressively less satisfactory as the volume of production per farm increases and the opportunity cost of time spent in bargaining rises. For this reason, as agriculture becomes more commercialized, the price a farmer receives is less likely to be determined by individual negotiation.

Farmers frequently complain that prices received under a decentralized pricing system have a downward bias. This view is based on the belief that buyers have the upper hand because few buyers exist relative to the number of farmers offering produce for sale. With the rise of chain-store marketing and the accompanying disappearance of local wholesale buyers or itinerant truckers, the number of alternative outlets available to an individual grower unquestionably has declined. Potentially, at least, large buyers are in a position to play off farmers against each other by claiming to be able to obtain produce at lower prices from a neighbor or another area. A reduction in the number of buyers, however, need not result in a decline in competition, since chains require a large volume of produce and must actively bid against one another for the available supplies. But in selling to chain stores, small producers may be disadvantaged relative to large producers. Buyers cannot be expected to spend the time required to bargain individually with those who have only a small volume to sell.

It is very difficult to ascertain from empirical evidence whether changes in the degree of concentration on the buying side have had any adverse effect on farm prices. Many of those who are closely associated with the fruit and vegetable industry believe that chain stores have used their economic power to the disadvantage of small local processors who are mainly "buyer's label" packers (i.e., processors who do not have an established brand name but place the buyer's label on the can). The squeeze on the margins of local processors has in some cases made it difficult for them to pay very attractive prices to farmers. But again, one cannot be certain whether the weak competitive position of small local processors and producers in some regions is a function of chain-store buying or of more fundamental changes in the economics of production and marketing, including economies of scale. If, in fact, prices have been depressed as a result of the decline in the number of buyers, a structural change should be evident in the relationship between production per capita and price. A given volume of production would presumably be associated in the more recent period with a lower real price as compared with preceding periods when the number of buyers was greater. There is little or no empirical evidence to suggest this has occurred.

Organized Exchanges or Auctions

Organized commodity exchanges still play an important role in pricing grains and soybeans in the United States. A number of internationally traded commodities such as cocoa, sugar, and rubber also are priced in this way. These commodities are sufficiently homogeneous that reasonably accurate and consistent grade standards can be maintained.

Two types of trading occur on organized markets. One is the "spot" or cash market which involves trading in actual commodities, normally on the basis of samples. The other is in futures contracts which specify the minimum grade or particular grades of a commodity which must be delivered in fulfillment of the contract at some future date. In markets where both types of trading take place, the near futures price serves as the base for discovering the cash prices paid for specific lots of commodities; buyers and sellers negotiate cash prices as discounts or premiums from the near futures with these differences based on the grade, moisture content, etc. of a particular lot of grain. Even when cash transactions do not take place on a central market, the futures market is sometimes used as a reference for pricing. The mechanics of trading futures contracts and their function in pricing farm commodities are discussed in much greater detail in the two succeeding chapters.

The physical volume of trading in organized cash markets has declined in recent years. Trading in spot eggs on the New York Mercantile Exchange, for example, has disappeared. Direct buying of fresh fruits, vegetables, butter, and cheese has contributed to a corresponding decline in the organized markets for these commodities as well. On the other hand, futures trading has increased, especially with the introduction of new contracts in recent years for shell (fresh) eggs, pork bellies, live hogs, live cattle, and frozen orange juice.

Auction markets provide facilities for arriving at prices for those commodities which are more difficult to standardize, such as live animals and tobacco. Physical inspection of these items is important since quality varies greatly. Under the auction system, buyers are able to observe each animal or each lot of produce. Prices are then determined on the basis of competitive bids for each lot. Conventional auction markets make it possible to establish prices efficiently for a wide range of commodities, but they have the disadvantage of requiring the physical assembly of the commodities to be sold at a particular location. This can be time-consuming and more costly than direct buying and selling.

In order to avoid the costs of assembling products in one place, teletype or telephone auctions have been instituted for some commodities. The process of open bidding is the same, but buyers must rely on accurate descriptions of the specific lots submitted by teletype or over the phone rather than actual observation (Rhodes, 1971). Through the use of computers, the auction concept might be extended over a much broader area, enabling individuals in various parts of the country to bid on specific lots of commodities designated by grade (e.g., eggs) and to match bids and offers without requiring the physical assembly of products or the presence of buyers and sellers in one place.

The major advantage of organized commodity markets is that they provide an impersonal, low-cost method of pricing which typically is not subject to control by either buyers or sellers. They perform the important function of discovering prices that will equate short-run demand and supply. The prices established in such markets approximate equilibrium prices when the following conditions are met: (1) the volume of transactions is large; (2) the quality of the produce sold on the exchange is broadly representative of total production; (3) a sufficiently large number of buyers and sellers participate in trading so that manipulation of prices is difficult or impossible; (4) unbiased and complete information with respect to supplies of the commodity and factors affecting demand are available to traders; and (5) prices are above government support levels.

The major criticism directed against commodity markets (assuming the preceding conditions are met) is that prices tend to fluctuate "excessively," and at times, perhaps, irrationally, in response to rumors or mass psychology. Unfavorable weather, for example, can lead to buying in anticipation of a price increase. This may attract other buyers who want to capitalize on a rising market. The reverse may occur in a falling market. Such changes in speculative demand, as discussed in Chapter 2, can serve a useful purpose to the extent that the expectations are correct. Problems arise, however, when expectations are wrong or exaggerated. They unnecessarily reinforce or magnify price changes, thereby leading to greater amplitude of fluctuations than required simply to clear the market or to allocate inventories.

With the passage of time, markets tend to correct excessive changes in prices. Furthermore, recent empirical evidence indicates that futures markets with a large volume of trading do not have lengthy "runs" of prices in response to psychological buying and selling (see Chapter 12). Thus, while the actual price may deviate from the equilibrium level at any particular point in time, the average price is likely to be unbiased except where market imperfections exist (see Chapter 13).

For planning purposes, an estimate of the long-run equilibrium price obviously is most useful. Current market clearing prices frequently deviate substantially from the long-run equilibrium price and hence do not provide a very reliable guide for planning future production. Schultz (1949, p. 167) maintains that resource misallocation has been more serious for commodities with organized spot and futures markets than for commodities priced in other ways. But instability does not characterize all commodity markets. In addition, futures markets, by offering producers an opportunity to hedge, provide a means of reducing price risks.

The trend toward direct buying of livestock by packers and of eggs, fruits, and vegetables by national grocery chains has complicated the process of price discovery and price reporting. Buyers and sellers are no longer brought together in one or a few places. Meat packers, for example, have abandoned plants in central cities and erected new ones in areas closer to sources of supply. Terminal markets now handle a much smaller proportion of total production than formerly (National Commission on Food Marketing, 1966, p. 22). It obviously is more difficult to obtain a representative price quotation from a large number of decentralized markets than from a few central ones.

As the volume sold through central markets becomes smaller, the prices established on such markets are likely to fluctuate more and may reflect different qualities than the average of the entire output. For example, terminal markets for fresh fruits and vegetables tend to become residual markets, i.e., markets where shippers send products that could not be sold directly to buyers. If the residual supplies happen to be large on a particular day and the number of buyers seeking to augment normal supplies is small, prices will be depressed; on the other hand, prices will be high if chain stores find their usual sources of supply inadequate and seek to make up the deficits through purchases on terminal markets. A thin market (i.e., few buyers and sellers) combined with sudden and sometimes unpredictable shifts in demand and supply for particular days can lead to wide swings in prices; but this does not necessarily mean that the average level of prices is depressed below that of the same quality produce sold direct. If buyers thought they could consistently obtain better deals on terminal markets, they would shift their buying to such markets. This would then help to raise prices. Of course, if the average quality of produce sold on a terminal market differs from that of produce sold direct, the price quotation for that market would be lower. If the terminal market price is used as a basis for pricing commodities bought directly, differentials should be established to reflect such quality differences. Terminal quotations can be used as a basis for shipping point pricing as long as the average quality of products sold on such markets is approximately equal to that of products sold directly, or if quality differs in a consistent and recognized manner.

Formula Pricing

The use of formulas in pricing agricultural commodities is becoming more common. Formulas are being used to facilitate direct buying and to simplify or reduce the costs involved in making pricing decisions. Among the commodities priced in this way are eggs, wholesale meat, and milk.

Pricing formulas are usually based on some reported price, such as a quotation derived from a central market or the price paid to producers in a particular region or location. More complex pricing formulas for milk have been developed incorporating price movers, such as the percentage of deliveries sold as fluid milk, and index numbers reflecting changes in the general level of prices, costs, or demand.

Egg producers frequently are paid on the basis of a quoted price such as the one generated by Urner Barry or the U.S. Department of Agriculture Market News Service.[3] Wholesale prices for meat in many areas are based on prices quoted in the National Provisioner "Yellow Sheet," a commercial market report based on end-of-day prices in Chicago. For example, the price of meat shipped from Omaha to New York City in the early 1960's, as reported by the National Commission on Food Marketing (1966, p. 26), was the "Yellow Sheet" price for the day prior to shipment less 50 cents per hundredweight (transportation cost difference between Omaha and Chicago) plus 2 dollars per hundredweight (to cover transportation cost between Omaha and New York).

Producer prices for milk sold in federal order markets are determined on the basis of pooled returns from handlers who are compelled to pay minimum prices (usually based on formulas) for milk depending on use. Higher prices are maintained for milk put into bottles or cartons than for milk converted into ice cream, cheese, butter, and skim milk powder. Until the mid 1960's, so-called "economic formulas" were used in markets like Boston and New York to price fluid milk (often referred to as Class I milk). Minimum Class I prices were based on formulas which incorporated index numbers reflecting general price movements and changes in supply, demand, or costs (Manchester, 1971). More recently, federal order prices for fluid milk have been tied to the average price paid to dairymen for manufacturing milk in Minnesota and Wisconsin (plus differentials which vary by regions or markets). Class II or manufacturing prices usually are based on the same price series or a pricing formula which moves up and down in response to changes in market prices for manufactured dairy products.

A well-designed formula offers the advantages of providing an impersonal, prompt, and low-cost method of adjusting prices. Once adopted, a pricing formula makes it possible to change prices more or less automatically in response to changes in the designated base price or whatever movers are incorporated in the formula. For government administrators, this is a desirable feature, particularly if it

[3] Even this system of pricing is breaking down as regional cooperatives attempt to fix prices and chain stores contract with particular producers for delivery of eggs at a fixed price or purchase eggs on a bid basis.

becomes necessary to reduce prices. A formula can perform this function impersonally, thereby taking pressure off the administrator. Formulas also provide a relatively prompt method of adjusting prices. Prior to the introduction of formulas for pricing milk, fluid prices were changed only after a hearing and referendum conducted among producers. This procedure made it possible for all interested parties to express their views before a change was made, but it often required several months to complete the process. Prices are now adjusted automatically in response to changes in the movers incorporated in the formula; no hearings are required as long as the formula remains the same.

The two major weaknesses of pricing on the basis of formulas are, first, that the formula may get out of date and, second, that the base price to which the formula is tied may become unrepresentative. In the extreme case, if total volume marketed is priced on the basis of a formula, no market prices would exist to serve as the basis for the formula (Rhodes, 1971). Any formula, no matter how well designed, is likely to become unsatisfactory unless changed periodically. For this reason, it is desirable to provide a built-in mechanism for re-evaluation and revision from time to time. Producers may be reluctant, however, to modify a pricing formula if the modification were to result in a lower price. As with other pricing methods, a pricing formula which is designed to achieve welfare objectives may lead to excess production, while one designed simply to clear the market may not yield very attractive prices to producers. Thus, it is important in designing a formula to decide which objectives should be given priority.

Group Bargaining

Dissatisfaction with other pricing arrangements has led farmers, in some cases, to form bargaining associations (or cooperatives) in an attempt to negotiate more favorable prices with buyers. Through joint efforts, farmers hope to achieve results similar to those obtained by the more successful labor unions. There are important legal differences, however, between collective bargaining by farmers with regard to product prices and bargaining by labor unions over wages (Ladd, 1964, pp. 97–106). Under the National

Labor Relations Act, an employer is compelled to enter into negotiations with representatives of a union provided it has been certi-
fied as the appropriate bargaining agent. Thus far, Congress has
not provided farmers with corresponding legal authority, although
a number of bills have been introduced with this in mind. The
objective of such legislation would be to force processors and handlers to bargain in good faith over prices and other contract terms
once an organization of producers had been approved as a qualified association. To become qualified, an organization would have
to meet certain requirements, including representing a sufficient
number of producers to make bargaining feasible.

While interest in collective efforts to improve farm prices has increased in recent years, the concept of organizing farmers in an attempt to influence prices is by no means new. During the latter
part of the nineteenth century and again in the 1920's, numerous
attempts were made to organize large-scale cooperatives or associations of farmers with the objective of obtaining higher prices
from meat packers, milk distributors, and other buyers of farm
products (Galbraith, 1952, pp. 163–167). The most famous attempt
to organize farmers into national selling organizations occurred immediately following World War I. At that time, Aaron Sapiro, a
dynamic and convincing speaker, encouraged farmers to combine
and sell collectively through their own organizations rather than
individually. As a result of his efforts, several national cooperatives
were formed, including one for grain and another for livestock. But
within a few years, these organizations had collapsed. They failed
because they could not prevent their members from selling outside
the organization despite "iron-clad" contracts "compelling" members to market through the association. This occurred because
producers who were not members continued to sell and benefit
from the action of the cooperative in holding farm products off the
market, while members received little or nothing since their produce was not being sold.

The experience of the 1920's demonstrates the fundamental
weakness of voluntary associations formed in an attempt to raise
prices on a national scale. It is difficult to get everyone to join,
especially when the potential benefits of remaining outside of the
association are so great. Even if an organization is successful in

signing up a large number of producers initially, it is difficult to hold them if they find others gaining at their expense.

While most national organizations formed in an attempt to increase the bargaining power of farmers have failed to achieve their primary objective, a number of local or regional organizations have had at least a moderate degree of success in improving producer prices. Such regional or local associations have been formed mainly among farmers selling vegetables or fruit to processors and milk to city distributors.

The ability of bargaining associations of producers to negotiate more favorable prices depends first and foremost on their ability to control a substantial proportion of the total supply. If large numbers of producers who grow the same or competing crops refuse to join, a bargaining association can do very little to raise prices. Voluntary efforts to control supply generally have been unsuccessful for the reasons mentioned previously. To overcome this weakness, cooperatives or bargaining associations interested in raising prices have frequently made use of federal or state marketing orders to restrict marketings or to divert part of the supply to secondary markets. A marketing order cannot be put into effect, however, unless it is first approved by a two-thirds vote of producers and conforms to specifications set forth in the federal or state enabling legislation. Orders have been successful in enhancing prices, at least in the short run, for cling peaches in California, raisins, and several other specialty crops. Over the longer run, producers have been less successful in maintaining above-equilibrium prices through the use of marketing orders because it has not been possible to prevent growers from increasing production, either within the area covered by a marketing order or in competing areas.

The success of a bargaining organization depends not only on the degree of control they are able to exercise over supply but also on the characteristics of the firms to which they sell and the price elasticity of demand for their products. Labor unions have learned from experience that it is easier to obtain substantial wage increases from employers in industries in which a few firms are dominant, such as the rubber tire, automobile, or aluminum industries, than from those composed of many small firms scattered over a wide geographical area, like the textile industry. The profit position of firms also has a bearing on the success of wage negotiations, and presumably the same would be true of producer efforts to raise prices.

In general, the more inelastic the retail-level demand schedule for a commodity, the easier it will be for producers to negotiate a higher price, since middlemen can readily pass the increase on to consumers without any substantial loss of sales. On the other hand, if those to whom farmers sell must compete against lower priced imports from other countries or regions or substitute products, it is more difficult to raise prices. An implication of an elastic demand, of course, is that higher prices reduce total revenue.

A strong case can be made for collective action on the part of growers if the objective of bargaining is simply to provide a more equitable or stable pricing mechanism. Widely fluctuating prices for commodities such as red tart cherries or onions offer few advantages to consumers and certainly do not provide reasonable guides for future production. Where handlers or processors are few in number and highly organized, producers may find it necessary to form their own association in an attempt to prevent exploitation and develop what Galbraith (1952) calls "countervailing power." Producers would prefer to have at least some influence over the prices they receive rather than to remain passive "price takers." Bargaining associations also can play a constructive role in collecting information and in negotiating contract terms, including quality premiums and discounts or incentive payments. Producers are likely to become better organized and collective bargaining procedures developed more fully as vertical integration in agriculture increases and contracting for production becomes more common. (Additional information concerning the legal and economic problems involved in attempting to raise farm prices through collective action is contained in *Bargaining in Agriculture* [see Rhodes, 1971].)

Administrative Decisions

Few agricultural commodity prices are administratively determined in the United States except for price-support loan rates or the buying prices announced by the government for supported commodities such as wheat, corn, cotton, and manufactured dairy products. In this respect, agriculture differs substantially from the industrial sector of the economy. Administered pricing in agriculture is almost exclusively a government function, whereas in the nonfarm sector such decisions are often made by private firms. In addition, of course, the prices of electricity and other public services are regulated by public agencies.

Individual farmers, unlike many firms producing nonfarm goods, have little opportunity to control or administer prices. The opportunity to do so is limited to those firms which produce a unique or differentiated product or otherwise have some monopoly power (i.e., the firm must face a demand curve that is less than perfectly elastic). Firms producing a differentiated product do have some discretion in deciding at what price to sell, but in most cases the zone of discretion in pricing is quite narrow. The upper limit is determined by the prices offered by competitors for similar products. A firm which attempts to raise prices unduly will find its market position undermined by competition from existing products, by the development of substitute products, and by the entry of new firms.

The competitive nature of agriculture makes it difficult for farmers or even those marketing farm products to administer prices and especially to maintain them substantially above competitive equilibrium levels without government assistance.[4] If prices are to be raised, farmers and processors must accept some degree of control over supply (i.e., to limit sales or ration the right to produce). The only alternatives to limiting production are to develop secondary outlets for surplus commodities or to request the government to purchase whatever quantities cannot be sold at the higher price.

The objective of government-administered pricing in agriculture in some cases is simply to provide a floor under prices in years of large crops so as to limit price fluctuations, while in others it is to provide incentives to increase production, as during World War II, or to assure farmers of a "fair" or equitable price. The resource allocative function of prices is often sacrificed in order to achieve

[4] Food processors and food retailers, of course, administer prices in the sense that administrative decisions are involved in announcing or quoting prices. The amount of discretion these firms have in pricing is subject to some debate although the evidence indicates that such firms have relatively limited power to raise prices (National Commission on Food Marketing, 1966).

some welfare objective. There is no reason why society should not elect to do so, but if prices are to be used as an instrument to raise or maintain incomes, other methods must be employed to guide production or maintain consumption.

Conclusions

Pricing arrangements for agricultural commodities are extremely diverse. This diversity reflects differences in product characteristics, marketing channels, and contractual arrangements. The prices established as a result of individual negotiations and trading on organized markets are generally less stable, but they are more likely to approximate theoretical short-run equilibrium prices than those fixed as a result of administrative decisions made by government officials. The objective of some pricing mechanisms is simply to discover market-clearing prices, while for others it is to provide reasonable guides for future production or to raise farm incomes.

Underlying economic forces exert a powerful influence on prices regardless of the pricing mechanism employed. For this reason, changing the pricing mechanism—for example, from individual negotiation to collective bargaining—will not necessarily raise the average level of prices. In some cases, however, the substitution of one pricing method for another can help to reduce the frequency or amplitude of price changes and to reduce the time and cost involved in making pricing decisions.

Unfortunately, there is little empirical evidence on which to base firm conclusions about the relative performance of alternative price-discovery mechanisms. Furthermore, the available evidence is often inconclusive. In each case, one faces the perplexing problem of deciding what standards of performance should be applied, and if price behavior is judged to be "unsatisfactory" in some degree whether it is the fault of the pricing mechanism *per se* or merely reflects unfavorable supply and demand relationships.

References

Breimyer, Harold F. 1967. "Marketing Aspects of Farm Policy," *Agricultural Policy: A Review of Programs and Needs.* National Advisory Commission on Food and Fiber, Technical Papers, Vol. V (Aug.).

Caves, Richard. 1967. *American Industry: Structure, Conduct, Performance*. 2d ed. Englewood Cliffs, N.J.: Prentice-Hall.

Galbraith, J. K. 1952. *American Capitalism: The Concept of Countervailing Power*. Boston: Houghton Mifflin.

Kaplan, A. D. H., J. B. Dirlam, and R. F. Lanzillotti. 1958. *Pricing in Big Business*. Washington: The Brookings Institution.

Ladd, George W. 1964. *Agricultural Bargaining Power*. Ames, Iowa: Iowa State Univ. Press.

Manchester, Alden C. 1971. *Pricing Milk and Dairy Products: Principles, Practices and Problems*. Econ. Res. Ser., USDA, Ag. Econ. Report No. 207.

National Commission on Food Marketing. 1966. *Food from Farmer to Consumer*. Commission Report. Washington, D.C.: U.S. Govt. Printing Office.

Preston, Lee E. 1963. *Profits, Competition and Rules of Thumb in Retail Food Pricing*. Inst. Bus. and Econ. Res., Univ. of Calif., Berkeley.

Rhodes, V. James. 1971. "Pricing Systems—Old, New and Options for the Future," *Bargaining in Agriculture: Potentials and Pitfalls in Collective Action*. Ed. Harold F. Breimyer. North Central Regional Extension Publication 30, Univ. of Missouri. Pp. 8–13.

Rogers, George B. 1970. "Pricing Systems and Agricultural Marketing Research," *Ag. Econ. Res.*, 22:1–11.

Schultz, T. W. 1949. *Production and Welfare of Agriculture*. New York: Macmillan.

CHAPTER 12

Commodity Futures Markets: Their Mechanics and Price Relationships

This and the next chapter are devoted to a more detailed discussion of one pricing mechanism, namely, commodity futures markets. The discussion begins with a review of the mechanics of futures market operations but also provides additional depth with respect to the theory of price determination in such markets. Hopefully, these two chapters will enable the student to obtain greater insight into one method of price discovery and to understand more clearly why certain commodity prices behave as they do.

If equal weight is given to each of the large number of farm products produced in the world, then futures markets are important institutions only for a relatively small number of all such commodities. Further, in the United States, some commodities (in particular, the grains) for which futures markets exist are also influenced by government price-support programs. Nonetheless, the value of the volume of futures contracts traded in regulated U.S. markets was 114 billion dollars in the year ending June 30, 1971. Thus, the value of futures contracts traded is sometimes more than double the value of all farm-level cash sales in the United States.

A Description of Futures Trading [1]

Organized Market Places

A distinction must be made between cash sales and trading in futures contracts. Cash sales involve the actual delivery of the

[1] This section is intended as a review to facilitate subsequent discussion; for more detail see Gold, 1961.

commodity, and most cash sales are not made in central market places. Trading on futures markets involves buying and selling standardized *contracts* for the future delivery of the commodity. Trading in futures contracts takes place only on formally organized central market places. Typically, buyers and sellers do not intend to take or make delivery on the contract. Trading in futures contracts started in Chicago in the 1860's (for additional discussion of the historical evolution see Irwin, 1954).

An organized market provides a trading place, aids in disseminating market information, aids in trading mechanics, and helps regulate the business dealings of members—hence, helps settle disputes. In futures markets, trading must take place at a designated place and time by open outcry. The level of price and price changes are public knowledge. A market reporter continuously provides this information. A communications network swiftly distributes price information. The right to buy and sell in the specific market goes only to members of the exchange. (The Chicago Board of Trade is the largest futures market.) Nonmember traders place orders through a professional broker, who is a member, at established commission charges.

A futures contract is a legal contract, enforceable by the rules of the exchange on which it is traded, to deliver or accept delivery of a definite amount of a commodity during a specified month at a specified price. For example, on October 1, trader A buys 5,000 bushels of May wheat at $1.50 per bushel from trader B. A contract has been made in October for the delivery of wheat in May.

The contract calls for the delivery of a specific grade of the commodity at a specific location or locations. All contracts for a particular commodity on a given exchange are identical, but contract specifications may differ from market to market (e.g., wheat contracts at Chicago, Kansas City, and Minneapolis). In most cases, substitute grades may be delivered at discounts or premiums which are specified in the contract. Traders also understand that the definitions of a grade represent the minimal standards for the grade and that it is this minimal quality which usually is being priced.

Trading on futures markets is facilitated by the device of a clearing house whose purpose is to keep records and record each member's market position at the end of each day. The clearing house operation removes the individual responsibility of one member to another. In effect, the clearing house substitutes for the other party to the contract. Trader A, for example, may make both purchases and sales of contracts for the May delivery month for wheat during the course of the day. But trader A is responsible to the clearing house for his net position—not to separate individuals involved in the original trades. Trader A may sell contracts to B, who in turn subsequently sells to C, D, and E, but with the clearing house mechanism, trader A is not obligated to follow the movement of specific contracts which he has sold to other traders. The traders may make numerous transactions through time. As any particular delivery month approaches, however, the trader is responsible only for the net position with the clearing house. This responsibility is usually discharged by taking an offsetting position. A purchase "cancels" a previous sale.

The contracts are seller's option. The seller has the option of making delivery at any time during the delivery month. Notice of delivery must be given. "First notice day" usually is several days before the beginning of the delivery month. When traders who have net positions representing sales give notice of delivery, the clearing house in turn notifies a trader or traders with net positions representing purchases. In some cases, the notice goes to the trader with the oldest net purchases; in others, the notices are apportioned by the size of position. The trader receiving notice of delivery may be able to sell and pass on the notice, or he may choose to accept delivery. A very small percentage of the volume of transactions result in actual delivery. (Actual delivery is usually in terms of a warehouse receipt indicating that the commodity is at a designated location. The warehouse receipt is also the instrument of title transfer used in cash transactions. The person taking delivery can, of course, sell the commodity on the cash market.)

Types of Traders and Trading

Actual traders on the floor of the exchange include (1) floor traders buying and selling for their own account and (2) brokers trading for others. The floor traders and those placing orders through brokers are classified as "hedgers" and "speculators." However, an unambiguous definition of these terms is difficult because positions in a futures market often have elements of both speculation and hedging.

A perhaps oversimplified view of hedging is establishing a position in futures opposite from the one held in the spot (cash) market. A futures market transaction may be made as a hedge, however, even though the trader has no explicit position in a cash market. For example, a Maine potato grower may sell November futures contracts in the spring, while planting the crop. While no offsetting purchase of cash potatoes has been made, the sale of contracts is principally a hedge. The grower anticipates growing, and the subsequent sale, of potatoes. Holbrook Working (1953) defines a hedge as the use of a futures contract as a temporary substitute for a later transaction in the cash market. A selling hedge starts with the sale of futures contracts, and a buying hedge starts with the purchase of contracts.

In the "classical" example of a selling hedge, a grain warehouseman sells futures contracts as he buys grain for storage. Later, as the grain is sold out of storage, the warehouseman covers or offsets the original futures position by buying futures contracts. The main economic justification for futures markets rests with hedging. We elaborate on this topic subsequently.

Speculators take market positions with the expectation of making a profit. They do not take offsetting positions (explicitly or implicitly) in the cash market. For purposes of exposition, speculators may be divided into three groups. (1) "Scalpers" and "day traders" are professional speculators who trade frequently on small price changes. Their profits and losses are based on minute-to-minute and day-to-day transactions, rather than longer-time price trends. (2) "Position traders" take positions based on expectations about longer-term price movements. If the trader thinks a price is going to rise, he buys contracts hoping to sell at a higher price. Avocational speculators are typically position traders. There are also professional position traders. In practice, a continuum of speculators may exist based on the length of time positions are held, ranging from those offsetting positions every few seconds or minutes to those holding positions for weeks. (3) A "spreader" purchases one futures contract and at the same time sells another. This typically is done when the trader believes the difference in price between contracts will change.[2] For example, if a trader thinks the current price difference between the December and May contracts for corn is too large, then he would buy one and sell the other. *If the appraisal is correct and the spread subsequently narrows, then the speculator makes a profit by offsetting his initial transactions.*[3]

The spread between two delivery months for a given commodity is an interdelivery spread. Intermarket spreads involve contracts in different markets (e.g., Kansas City and Chicago wheat), and intercommodity spreads involve contracts for different commodities (e.g., oats and corn). Spreading tends to keep prices among contracts in "normal" (to be defined) alignment. Also, as we shall see, trading by speculators—especially the professional scalpers—provides market liquidity.

Market Positions and Volume of Trading

A trader may establish a market position by either buying or selling. It is *not* necessary to buy futures before selling. To be "short," a trader has sold contracts not covered by purchases. The seller simply has assumed a contractual obligation to deliver the specified commodity at a specified price and to receive the agreed-upon price. This is not unlike a tailor who agrees to make a suit of clothing for later delivery to a customer. A difference arises in that normally the seller of a futures contract offsets the short position by buying an equivalent amount of the same contract at a later date. This removes the obligation to make delivery. His net position with the clearing house is zero. To be "long," a trader has purchased contracts not covered by an equivalent amount of sales. He is obligated to accept delivery and pay for the contracted amount unless he subsequently offsets the long position with appropriate sales.

Assuming the trader does not make or take delivery, the cost of the futures trading includes commission charges to a broker and

[2] Other reasons exist for taking offsetting positions in different contracts; these are discussed in Chapter 13.

[3] Assuming the May contract price is above the December, the initial transactions are to buy December contracts and sell May. Subsequently, the trader makes the offsetting transactions; if the December price has risen relative to the May, the trader makes a profit.

the possible adverse price movement while holding the contract.[4] Because of the possibility of adverse price movements, traders are required to make a margin deposit. Margins vary from commodity to commodity and by type of trader (speculators pay higher margins). Margins are typically a small percentage (perhaps 5 to 15 per cent) of the total value of the contracts. This could amount to 10 cents per bushel ($500 for a 5,000 bushel contract) in absolute terms. The objective is to provide protection against default by the trader. Thus, a margin is not a down payment but is more like "earnest money." Margin calls occur with adverse price movements (e.g., a price decline for the purchaser).

The ideas associated with margins and margin calls are perhaps best clarified with an illustration. Suppose that the *initial margin* on a 5,000 bushel contract is 15 cents per bushel ($750) and that the *maintenance margin* is 10 cents per bushel. As prices fluctuate, the speculator's margin deposit fluctuates—the equity in the contract changes. If the trader holds a long position, a price increase is favorable and the margin is increased; a price decrease is unfavorable and the margin is decreased. Given an unfavorable price change, the trader is asked (margin call) to provide additional funds when the margin goes below the maintenance level. In our example (with the trader long), if price declines more than 5 cents per bushel, the trader is asked to deposit (within a certain time limit) sufficient funds to bring the margin back to the initial level of 15 cents per bushel. If the trader fails to meet the margin call, the broker will sell out the position.

"Open interest" is the number of contracts remaining to be settled for a particular contract. For example, if a trader with a net zero position buys a December contract from another trader with a net zero position, the open interest in this contract increases by one. If this trader subsequently sells a December contract, the open interest is reduced by one. The open interest is equal to the net number of long or short positions. The number of contracts long and short must be equal.

The "volume of trading" is the total number of transactions in a given time period, say a day. It may be quoted as number of

[4] A member of the exchange has purchased a "seat" on the exchange and pays a smaller fee; he trades for his own account.

contracts or physical volume in the contracts traded. A numerical example of volume of trading and open interest is given in Table 12-1.

Table 12-1. Illustration of open interest and volume of trading in a futures market for three "days"

Day	Transaction	Volume during day (number of	Open interest end of day contracts)
1	A sells 5 to B	5	5
2	C sells 10 to D		
	E sells 5 to F	15	20
3	F sells 5 to A	5	15

Establishing Price

A well-developed futures market comes close to exemplifying the economist's concept of a perfectly competitive market. There are many buyers and sellers dealing in a standardized commodity (the futures contract). Traders do not have perfect knowledge, but in principle, they have equal access to available information. For example, USDA crop-size estimates which may influence price are released at the end of the trading day. Traders have until the next day to "digest" this information. Prior to release, the USDA maintains strict secrecy so that traders have equal access to the available information. Exchanges facilitate the collection of information on factors influencing price.

The price at any point in time represents the *collective* judgments of buyers and sellers as indicated by their decisions to buy and sell. Potential buyers and sellers enter the market with numerous objectives (e.g., to speculate or to hedge various cash positions). However, the ultimate goal, one may assume, is to enhance profits. Traders, including hedgers, hope to make money on their transactions. Thus, potential traders know current prices, including the relationships among prices of different contracts, and they have some expectations, either implicit or explicit, about the future movements of prices. On the basis of this knowledge, purchases and sales are made, and price is the outcome.

Price Relationships: Seasonally Produced, Continuous Inventory Commodities

The relationships among the constellation of futures and cash prices for such commodities as wheat and corn are explored in this section. The relationships include the differences between prices at a point in time, and the movement of prices (and the differences) through time. The theory developed in this section is particularly relevant to those commodities produced once a year but stored and consumed throughout the year. Futures markets first developed for such commodities, and this type of market is more fully developed today than for other types of commodities. Price relationships for certain other commodities are considered in a subsequent section.

The Constellation of Monthly Prices

The annual (or seasonal) average cash price for a commodity is determined by the annual demand and supply conditions. A set of monthly prices is associated with the annual average. As explained in Chapter 9, the lowest price for seasonally produced crops occurs at harvest, and prices must rise through the year, on the average, by an amount to cover storage costs. Thus, a particular monthly price reflects (1) the average economic conditions for the crop year and (2) the specific conditions necessary for allocating inventories through time.

A hypothetical pattern of cash prices over a crop year is shown in upper Figure 12-1. If traders in futures contracts had perfect knowledge about forthcoming cash prices, then prices of the contracts would be stable reflections of the known future prices. Several such futures price patterns are also illustrated in Figure 12-1.

Prices of futures contracts for certain delivery months may be above the current cash price at a point in time. This is sometimes called the *premium* relationship (illustrated in lower Figure 12-1). A difference between a futures price and a cash price at a point in time is called a *basis*. A premium market has a positive basis. The basis narrows as the delivery month approaches. For a commodity with identical quality and location to that specified in the futures

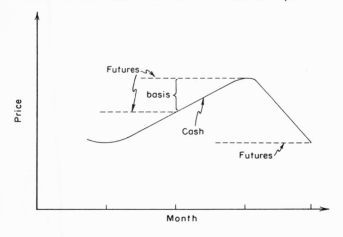

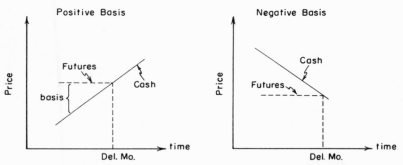

Figure 12-1. A seasonal pattern of cash prices with hypothetical futures prices superimposed

contract, the difference between the current cash price and the futures price is due to temporal differences. The narrowing basis is a reflection of the decreasing cost of storage as the delivery month approaches.

The current cash price also may be above the futures price; this is sometimes called a *discount* relationship (illustrated in lower Figure 12-1). This occurs when current inventories are small relative to expected supplies. For instance, at the end of the old crop year, the price of the futures representing the harvest month for the new crop may be below the current cash price.

In defining a basis, we will usually assume that the cash price is for the particular quality, location, and delivery conditions specified in the futures contract. Of course, the cash price for any particular lot of the commodity may vary from the futures price because of quality and location considerations. For instance, the farm price of wheat in a Kansas or Nebraska town differs from the Kansas City price by a transportation and handling differential.[5] Hence, to understand a particular empirical basis, the definition of the cash price used must be carefully compared with the price defined by the futures contract. These alternative definitions of the basis are of interest to the potential hedger for reasons which are explained in the next chapter.

The Supply of Storage

An economically rational merchant will hold inventories only if benefits are expected to equal or exceed the costs of storage between two points in time. The difference between the price for a future delivery month and the current cash price (or between the prices for two delivery months) defines the expected revenue from storage. This difference (the basis) may be defined as the price of storage.[6] It may be positive or negative.[7]

In its simplest form, the supply-of-storage concept states that the price of storage is mainly a function of the size of current inventories.[8]

$$P_f - P_c = f(I),$$

where $P_f =$ current price of a futures contract or, more generally, expected future price;

[5] On June 24, 1963, the closing cash price of number 2 winter wheat in Kansas City was $1.97½ per bushel. The price paid farmers at a local Nebraska elevator 150 miles distant was $1.77. The transfer cost between the two points was 19.3 cents, leaving a return of 1.2 cents to the elevator operation on that particular day.

[6] Holbrook Working wrote the fundamental paper on the supply of storage (1949). His empirical research used the difference between the prices of the last old crop and the first new crop futures as the price of storage. Brennan (1958), Cootner (1967), and Weymar (1966) have provided elaborations and extensions of the concept of the supply of storage.

[7] Other terminology includes "carrying charges" and "inverse carrying charges."

[8] The concept refers to the supply of the commodity as inventory, *not* to space available for storage.

P_c = current cash price;
I = current level of inventory.

The relation is analogous to the usual supply function; it may be viewed as derived from the marginal cost of storage. The form of the function (see Figure 12-2) is justified by a broad concept of costs. The direct costs of storage (e.g., the price of warehouse space) are thought to be constant over a fairly wide range of inventories, i.e., the added cost per bushel of additional inventory is approximately constant. However, in principle, inventories could approach the limit of available warehouse space, and at this point the marginal direct cost of storage would increase sharply. For instance, grain stored in inadequate facilities would deteriorate in quality. The supply-of-storage function becomes highly price inelastic as the limit of available space is approached.

Inventories have a convenience yield (Chapter 9), which is treated as a negative cost. The convenience yield is thought to be largest when inventories are smallest and to decline rapidly as inventories increase. At some point, merchants will carry added inventory only if the price of storage is expected to cover direct costs; the marginal convenience yield becomes zero. Thus, some in-

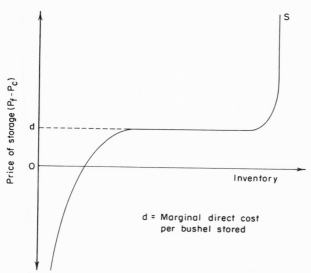

Figure 12-2.   Hypothetical supply-of-storage relationship

ventories are carried even with a negative price of storage, but the function rises rapidly as inventories increase (for additional elaboration see Cootner, 1967, pp. 68–73).[9]

Weymar (1966) hypothesizes that the price of storage is a function of the expected behavior of inventories over the time interval, say, from now to the delivery month. In other words, if expectations about the size and change in size of inventory over the time interval change, then the price of storage changes (pp. 1228f.).

$$P_f - P_c = f(I^*),$$

where $I^* =$ inventory level expected at a future time.

The level of current inventory is apparently a good proxy variable for expected inventory for seasonally produced commodities harvested over a short time period. Weymar argues that it is not such a good approximation for commodities where harvest is spread substantially through time; he uses the example of cocoa. By implication, the level of *current* inventories may not satisfactorily explain the price of storage of continuously produced commodities with inventories (e.g., pork bellies).

To this point, the concept of the supply of storage has been emphasized. Theoretically, the equilibrium level of the price of storage and the size of inventory at a point in time is jointly determined by the supply of and demand for storage. The demand for storage is related to consumption demand. Thus, the demand for

---

[9] The carrying of inventories also involves risks, and the marginal risk factor rises as *unhedged* inventories increase. Thus, the function may not be perfectly horizontal for moderate and large inventories; Brennan (1958, pp. 54–55) writes the net marginal cost (*m*) of storage as a function of three components, each a function of the size of inventory. Namely,

$$m = d + r - c,$$

where $d =$ marginal direct outlay (costs)
       $r =$ marginal risk aversion
       $c =$ marginal convenience yield.

However, the risk of adverse price movements does not increase on inventories hedged in futures contracts. This raises the question of whether speculators require a "risk premium" to take a position opposite the one held by hedgers. This is a question considered in the next chapter.

storage for a crop year is related to consumption demand for the
season and demand for inventory at the end of the season. With
the passage of time, the demand-for-storage function shifts. The
function shifts especially with changes in production in successive
years. Specifically, the demand for storage from period t to period
$t+1$ would increase with an increase in production in period t or
with a decrease in production in period $t+1$. A decrease in production in t or an increase in production in $t+1$ would reduce the demand for storage (Brennan, 1958, p. 52).

Empirical evidence suggests that the supply-of-storage function
is stable relative to the demand for storage. Shifts in demand are
largely the outcome of exogenous changes in production for the
seasonal crop. Thus, a scatter diagram of inventory level and price
differences gives an estimate of the supply function,[10] and it is appropriate, at least for a commodity like wheat, to view the price of
storage as a function of current inventory (see Brennan, 1958, pp.
63–67).

This theory, in effect, sets an upper limit to the positive price
of storage—namely, the positive marginal cost of storage. A basis
larger than the cost of storage would provide a large incentive to
store, and it is just this incentive and consequent competition to
acquire stocks which prevents the cash price from dropping below
the futures price by more than the cost of storage. (How a grain
merchant may use hedging to assure himself of the price difference
as a price of storage is illustrated in the next chapter.)

However, there is no theoretical limit to the size of the negative
price of storage. A current shortage of inventory may imply a very
high cash price relative to the price of a distant futures contract;
consequently, the price of storage will be a large (absolute value)
negative number. However, price-support programs with govern-
ment-owned stocks can place a practical limit on increases in cash
prices for some commodities. In the United States, the government
typically is able to sell out of its inventory when price rises to 115
per cent of the support level plus storage costs from harvest to the
current month. Hence, some grain markets have been character-

---

[10] For a fuller discussion of the interpretation of scatter diagrams involving
prices and quantities, the reader is referred to the section on "the identification problem" in Chapter 15.

ized by modest inverse carrying charges, reflecting current shortages of private stocks.

The theory outlined to this point implies a constellation of
prices, including the current cash price and the prices of progressively more distant futures. The *level* of the constellation of prices
may change with the passage of time, and the differences (prices of
storage) also may change. It is of interest to explore more fully the
nature of these changes.

Price Levels and Price Differences

Short-term changes. The constellation of prices at a point in time
represents the market's judgment of economic forces influencing
prices. With the passage of time, judgments change. New information on economic conditions becomes available, and the evaluation
of available information by market participants may change
(Working, 1958). Also, new information does not cause a single
once-and-for-all change in price level, but the effect is distributed
through time as a series of price adjustments. The forces influencing price are continually evaluated in a futures market. This does
not imply that past prices were "wrong." Market participants do
not have perfect knowledge; they do not have a diagram of appropriate supply and demand curves. Rather, they must make decisions in the light of information available at the time.

Thus, the prices of futures contracts are continually changing.
Since new information influencing price tends to occur randomly,
price changes appear to have elements of randomness. However,
since the influence on price is distributed through time, a price series typically has some correlation with itself through time; this is
called autocorrelation (Houthakker, 1961; Larson, 1960; Smidt,
1965; Working, 1967).[11]

The *level* of the constellation of prices is more variable through
time than the price *differences* (Working, 1942 and 1949). The
prices for various delivery months move up and down together
(e.g., in Figure 12-3). The concept of the supply of storage implies
that the price differences (the prices of storage) are approximately
fixed within a year by the size of available inventories. If, for ex-

[11] This simply means that prices in time t and $t+j$ are correlated, where
$j = 1, 2$, etc.

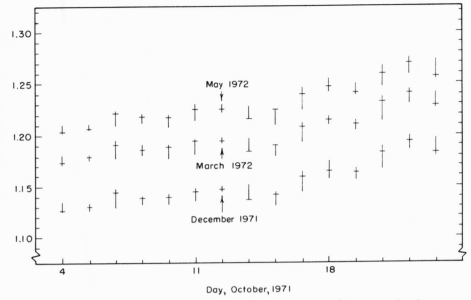

Figure 12-3. Prices of December, March, and May corn futures contracts, Chicago Board of Trade, October 4–22, 1971. Each vertical line shows a price range for a contract for a day and the horizontal "tic" mark gives the daily close.

ample, a dock strike is anticipated which will reduce export demand in a future month, this does not mean a decline only in price for the distant futures; rather, it implies, through the inventory linkage, a decline in the entire constellation of prices. In other words, changes in expectations change the current cash price and futures prices for the various delivery months by about the same amount; the differences among prices are a function of the size of current inventory. This view is in contrast to the opinion that current cash price and futures prices are not closely related because futures prices are determined strictly by expectations while cash prices are determined strictly by current conditions. This opinion is incorrect.

Of course, the prices of storage may change slightly through time. There is a close, but not a perfect, relationship among the constellation of prices. New information about the level of inventories, rates of use out of inventory, possible quality deterioration of inventory, and so forth, may influence the price of storage. Working (1942, p. 44) writes: "Variations from week to week in the relations between prices . . . appear mainly attributable to changes in the market estimate of the marginal cost of carrying." Further, as the price for the July future in the current year expires and the price for the next July future is established, the new price relationship may involve a substantial change in the price of storage (from one year to the next). This is a topic for the next subsection.

A dramatic change in information about a factor influencing price may cause a large change in the level of price, and this impact may be spread over several days. Most futures contracts have a limit on the size of price change which is permitted in one day. For example, trading in wheat is suspended if a price change reaches 10 cents per bushel in one day.

A common hypothesis is that futures prices tend to overreact to new information. For instance, "bullish" news is thought to cause price rises not warranted by the information; hence, prices subsequently decline to the "warranted" level. This type of behavior is sometimes called "price reaction." In general, the hypothesis implies a negative autocorrelation in a series of futures prices: price increases followed by decreases, and price decreases followed by increases. However, some evidence indicates that autocorrelations tend to be positive.[12] Prices appear to adjust gradually to new information and, on the average, do not represent overadjustments. This is not to deny that on occasion prices have overresponded to new information.

Large transactions also cause dips and bulges in prices on futures markets. For instance, a large selling hedge tends to depress price. The size of the price effect depends on the size of the transaction relative to the liquidity of the market, which illustrates the economic importance of speculation. A scalper makes his profit

[12] Autocorrelation coefficients involving lags greater than four days are consistently positive (Working, 1967, table 3). Another study (Brinegar, 1970) suggests that a slight reaction behavior (increases followed by decreases or the reverse) of futures prices exists over periods of one to two weeks but that, for longer periods, a clear tendency exists for gradual adjustments. Underreaction to new information with gradual price changes to the "correct" level, sometimes called price continuity, is also a form of imperfect price behavior. Labys and Granger (1970, chapter 3), in contrast, find that commodity price series obey a random walk or near random walk model (also, see footnote 14).

from the small price changes. For example, a scalper may take the opposite side of a large selling hedge for one-fourth cent less than the previous price. He hopes to resell the contracts gradually at the original or higher prices. The scalper, while making a profit on dips and bulges in price, is providing the service of temporally distributing the impact of a large transaction. It is this type of liquidity which minimizes the transactions cost (the price effect) of a large hedge (Gray, 1967; Working, 1967).

In sum, we started with a model of seasonal price variability and of "fixed" futures prices associated with perfect knowledge (Figure 12-1). However, knowledge is not perfect, and the level of this constellation of prices moves up and down through time with changing information.[13] Since changes in factors influencing price occur somewhat randomly through time, a time-series sequence of futures prices has the superficial appearance of a "random walk." [14] Nonetheless, such time-series data have systematic components. The differences between prices of successive delivery months (the prices of storage) are a function of the size of inventories. A price of storage tends to be stable relative to price level changes.

Year-to-year changes. The foregoing discussion emphasizes the character of *short-term* price behavior. One must be cautious in generalizing about year-to-year behavior, especially the price of storage.

As discussed in Chapter 5, the variability of the annual price of a seasonally produced crop depends (1) on the size of changes in supply and demand and (2) on the slopes of the functions. Thus, the season average price and the constellation of monthly prices about the average tend to move up and down from year to year, perhaps in some cobweb pattern. However, the size of inventories and hence the price of storage also may vary from year to year.

[13] Whether or not futures prices are unbiased estimates of cash prices in the subsequent delivery month is a controversial question and is considered in the next chapter. Loosely speaking, the question is whether or not the average of past futures prices for a contract equals the average cash price for that delivery month.

[14] If price changes are serially independent and have no trend, the price series form a random walk. Actual price series sometimes produce patterns that resemble a random walk, though chart traders believe that graphs have predictive significance. As suggested in footnote 12, some evidence of autocorrelation in price series does exist.

This implies that while the cash price varies annually in response
to changing general economic forces, the relationships among the
constellation of prices also may change.

In one year, a large inventory may be associated with a positive
price of storage; in another, a small inventory may be associated
with a negative price of storage. The contrast between a relatively
"fixed" price of storage within a year and the variable price of storage is illustrated in Figures 12-3 and 12-4. The movement of daily

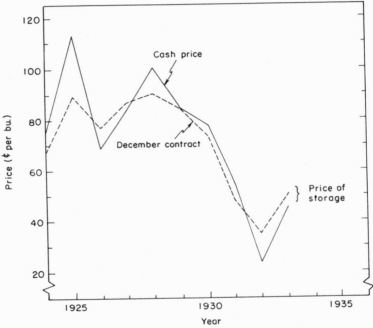

Figure 12-4. Closing prices of May and December corn futures, Chicago
Board of Trade, May 15, 1924–1933. Cash price is price of current May future on May 15; price of a contract near its expiration is essentially a cash
price. Data from Annual Reports of the Chicago Board of Trade.

prices for three futures contracts for corn is depicted in Figure 12-
3. Clearly, the prices are highly related, and price differences
among contracts are approximately constant.

The closing price on May 15 for the May and December contracts for corn over a period of years is graphed in Figure 12-4.[15]

[15] The years 1924–1933 are used to avoid the large influence of recent
price-support programs of the federal government on prices and inventories.

The price of the May contract on May 15 is essentially a cash price since the contract is being priced near its expiration. The difference between the December and May contract prices reflects the price of storage. These differences clearly change from year to year. As the price of one December contract expires, the price of the next December contract is being established, and this newly established price may imply a new price of storage. The new prices of storage reflect the changing inventory situation from the newly harvested crop.

An empirical consequence of the annually changing carrying charges is that futures prices apparently are somewhat less variable from year to year than cash prices. For instance, observations of the cash price on May 15 and the price of the December futures on May 15 over a period of years reveal that the cash price has a slightly larger variance (Tomek and Gray, 1970). Also, the price of the December future in May tends to be less variable than the cash price in December from year to year.

Futures prices are related to cash prices, but carrying charges are not constant from year to year. Further, a futures price is not going to be higher than a cash price at any point in time by more than the cost of storage, and in practice, the lowest cash price through time implies the lowest futures price. (The May price of a December future is not likely to be less than the lowest historical cash price observed in December.) On the other hand, a small inventory can mean a current cash price very much higher than a futures price in a particular year. In sum, a futures price can never be above a cash price by more than the cost of storage, but no such principle limits the cash price from being above a futures price. This contrast in annual variability is of interest in discussion of the stabilizing roles of futures markets (Tomek and Gray, 1970).

Price Relationships: Other Commodities

Since World War II, futures markets have developed for commodities which are not in the "traditional mold." These commodities don't fall into nice, clear-cut categories, but some classification is useful to illustrate that different models of price behavior are applicable. (1) Certain commodities for which futures are traded are seasonally produced but do not have continuous inventories (e.g., potatoes). (2) Another group of commodities are produced continuously, but have some seasonality of production and some stocks are carried (e.g., pork bellies). (3) Other commodities are continuously produced and no stocks, in the ordinary sense, are carried (e.g., fresh eggs). The remainder of this section is devoted to some general contrasts between these markets and the more traditional type. Many of the newer types of markets have not been fully developed for a sufficiently long period to permit careful empirical study.[16]

Intertemporal Price Relationships

Commodity markets differ in the degree to which they facilitate the carrying of inventories. The traditional grain markets might be called inventory-hedging markets. Inventories and inventory hedging play a lesser role in some of the newer markets. As the inventory-carrying role becomes less important, the close relation among the prices for various delivery months tends to decline.

A contrast between two markets is provided in the two parts of Figure 12-5. Daily closing prices for the May and November contracts of Maine potatoes are depicted in Figure 12-5 (bottom). Inventories are not carried from one crop year to the next for Maine potatoes, and the daily prices for the contracts for different crop years are not closely related. Daily closing prices for May and December contracts for Chicago corn are shown in Figure 12-5 (top). These prices are highly related even though two different crop years are represented by these prices.

The fact that current prices for different futures contracts are not closely related in some newer type markets does not imply that current prices of futures contracts are not related to particular current cash prices. For instance, the price of a six-month-distant beef cattle futures may be viewed as related to the current cash price of feeder cattle placements. Rather than a price of storage, the price difference defines a price of "feed-lot services," that is, gross returns to feeding cattle. The relationship is somewhat more complex in this example than for the supply of storage because feeder steers

[16] The volume of trading and the character of a market tends to develop over a period of years. Prior to full development, price behavior may be influenced by special circumstances of development.

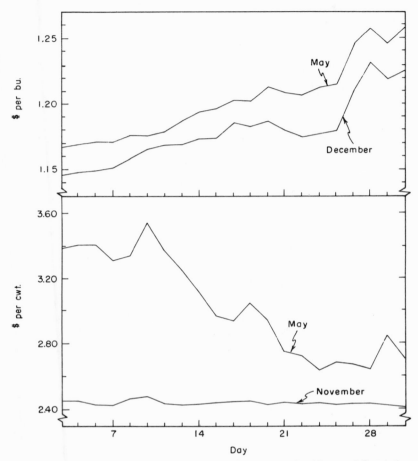

Figure 12-5. Top: Corn futures, daily closing prices for May and December contracts, April 1969. *Bottom:* Maine potato futures, daily closing prices for May and November contracts, April 1969

are being transformed into finished full-fed steers. The cost involved is that of feeding cattle instead of carrying inventory. Ehrich (1969) hypothesizes that the following relationship is appropriate:

$$P_f - P_d = (P_f - C) \, (1 - \frac{W_f}{W_d}),$$

where P_f = price of fed cattle futures, dollars per 100 pounds;
$\quad\quad$ P_d = current price of feeder cattle placements, dollars per
$\quad\quad\quad\quad$ 100 pounds;
$\quad\quad$ C = total cost per 100 pounds of gain;
$\quad\quad$ W_f = weight of finished fed cattle;
$\quad\quad$ W_d = weight of cattle placed on feed (e.g., 500 pounds).

This price difference defines a return to feeding cattle. For given costs of production and a given price of feeder cattle, the producer can approximately fix the returns to cattle feeding through hedging. However, the reader should note that the price difference in this case is based on a change in the *form* of the commodity priced. In the supply-of-storage concept, the same form is being priced; the price difference reflects a *time* difference. This has implications for the relationships among various prices through time.

Short-Term Price Changes

Price changes may still be viewed as responding to changing information and re-evaluation of available information. Since changes in factors influencing price occur sporadically through time, a time series of daily prices of futures contracts will still look somewhat like a series of random numbers. However, as implied above, the relationship between the prices for various delivery months may be less closely related than for a seasonally produced, continuous inventory commodity.

For example, the current cash price of beef is a function mainly of current supply and demand. The price of a six-month-distant beef cattle futures is related to expected supplies and demands. Expected supplies are related to current placements of feeder cattle. Thus, a more direct relationship between the distant future price would be with the current price of feeder cattle and a less close relation with the current price of finished fed cattle.

For potatoes, the prices of current crop year futures depend on current supply and demand. The prices of futures for the next crop year depend on expectations about that year. A change in expected demand in the new crop year, for instance, will have little influence on current price because current inventories cannot be carried over to the new crop year. Prices in adjacent crop years might be somewhat related through the cobweb phenomenon. However, empirical analysis suggests that potato prices for the forthcoming crop year futures are principally an "average" of past prices (Tomek and Gray, 1970).

One should not infer from this, however, that the prices of adjacent delivery months are completely independent. They have, after all, some common influences, especially where inventories are carried; a change in a factor which influences price in May is also likely to have some impact on price in July.

Year-to-Year Price Variability

Cash prices vary from year to year with changes in factors influencing price. As discussed above, futures prices for the seasonal, continuous inventory commodity are tied to cash prices through the supply-of-storage concept. Thus, while futures prices are likely to be somewhat less variable from year to year than cash prices, they are still highly variable for the seasonal, continuous inventory product.

In contrast, futures prices in the newer-type markets are less closely tied to current cash prices for the same form of the commodity. Although they depend on how expectations are formed, futures prices may be substantially less variable from year to year than cash prices (Tomek and Gray, 1970). For example, if price for a distant futures contract (e.g., a contract for the subsequent crop year) is simply an "average" of past prices, then the price of the contract for the distant delivery month may be very stable from year to year even though cash prices are highly variable. Specifically, the price of November potatoes on April 30 may be highly stable from year to year even though the cash price on March 15 (or on November 15) is highly variable from year to year.

On the other hand, the expectations about the price of a six-month-distant live beef cattle futures may be formed on the basis of current prices of placement feeder cattle and various inputs which would supply the finished product six months later. Thus, the price of a distant live cattle contract could be as variable from year to year as the prices of the major inputs.

References

Brennan, Michael J. 1958. "The Supply of Storage," *Am. Econ. Rev.*, 48:50–72.

Brinegar, Claude S. 1970. "A Statistical Analysis of Speculative Price Behavior," *Food Res. Inst. Studies*, 9:1–58 (Supplement).

Cootner, Paul H. 1967. "Speculation and Hedging," *Food Res. Inst. Studies*, 7:65–105 (Supplement).

Ehrich, R. L. 1969. "Cash-Futures Price Relationships for Live Beef Cattle," *Am. J. Ag. Econ.*, 51:26–40.

Gold, Gerald. 1961. *Modern Commodity Futures Trading*. 2d rev. ed. New York: Commodity Research Bureau.

Gray, Roger W. 1967. "Price Effects of a Lack of Speculation," *Food Res. Inst. Studies*, 7:177–194 (Supplement).

Houthakker, H. S. 1961. "Systematic and Random Elements in Short-Term Price Movements," *Am. Econ. Rev.*, 51:164–172.

Irwin, Harold S. 1954. *Evolution of Futures Trading*. Madison, Wis.: Mimir Publishers.

Labys, Walter C., and C. W. J. Granger. 1970. *Speculation, Hedging and Commodity Price Forecasts*. Lexington, Mass.: D. C. Heath and Co.

Larson, Arnold B. 1960. "Measurement of a Random Process in Futures Prices," *Food Res. Inst. Studies*, 1:313–324.

Smidt, Seymour. 1965. "A Test of the Serial Independence of Price Changes in Soybean Futures," *Food Res. Inst. Studies*, 5:117–136.

Tomek, William G., and Roger W. Gray. 1970. "Temporal Relationships among Prices on Commodity Futures Markets: Their Allocative and Stabilizing Roles," *Am. J. Ag. Econ.*, 52:372–380.

Weymar, F. Helmut. 1966. "The Supply of Storage Revisited," *Am. Econ. Rev.*, 56:1226–1234.

Working, Holbrook. 1942. "Quotations on Commodity Futures as Price Forecasts," *Econometrica*, 10:39–52.

——. 1949. "The Theory of the Price of Storage," *Am. Econ. Rev.*, 39:1254–1262.

——. 1953. "Hedging Reconsidered," *J. Farm Econ.*, 35:544–561.

——. 1958. "A Theory of Anticipatory Prices," *Am. Econ. Rev.*, 48:188–199.

——. 1967. "Tests of a Theory Concerning Floor Trading on Commodity Exchanges," *Food Res. Inst. Studies*, 7:5–48 (Supplement).

CHAPTER 13

Commodity Futures Markets: Their Functions and Controversies

With the background of Chapter 12, we may turn to a discussion of the functions of a futures market. The general function is to facilitate various types of resource allocation through hedging and through the provision of forward prices. Within this context, speculators play a role in facilitating hedging.

Trading in futures contracts has resulted in controversies about, among other things, the influence of futures markets on cash prices received by producers and paid by consumers. We review some of these controversies and such evidence as is available in answering these questions. The chapter closes with brief discussions of price manipulation, regulation, and biases which make some markets unsuccessful.

Functions of Futures Markets

Temporal Allocation of Seasonally Produced Commodities

The carrying of inventories of seasonally produced commodities is facilitated by the existence of a futures market and is perhaps the role most emphasized by economists. The accumulation and decumulation of inventories is often accompanied by hedging. In addition, forward cash sales made without inventories on hand are frequently offset by buying hedges (as are forward requirements of processors).

Decisions by grain merchants with respect to inventory carrying and hedging are related to the constellation of prices observed by them. The price of storage is a minimum return which is essen-

257

tially assured through hedging; it is an incentive or disincentive to store. To illustrate, using a hypothetical example, the merchant might observe on September 1 the following price relationship:

Cash wheat at $1.90 per bushel and

May wheat futures at $2.00 per bushel.

The positive price of storage is 10 cents per bushel, and the merchant may view this price as sufficient for profitable storage. If so, he buys wheat and sells an equivalent quantity of May futures contracts.

The initial positive price of storage and the narrowing of the basis through time can provide a 10-cent-per-bushel return for storage. The merchant is, in a sense, "guaranteed" a minimum return of 10 cents per bushel. If, for instance, price is $2.00 per bushel in May (the cash and futures price are identical in the delivery month for identical quality, location, and delivery conditions), then the merchant is able to sell the wheat at a 10-cent increase in the cash price and is able to buy back the futures contracts at no gain or loss. However, this return is not contingent on cash prices rising to $2.00. For example, if price declined to $1.88 in May, then the hedger still gains at least 10 cents per bushel. The final set of transactions is

a cash sale of wheat at $1.88 and

purchase of futures contracts at $1.88.

The 2-cent loss on the cash transaction is offset by a 12-cent gain on the futures market transaction. The direct costs of storage, of course, are constant whether prices move up or down.

In addition, the merchant hopes to sell and, in fact, typically does sell the inventory through private transactions to buyers at cash prices which reflect gains beyond those guaranteed by the hedging transaction. The typical merchant has no intention of holding his entire inventory, say, through to May to sell on the central market or to make delivery on the futures contracts at the then prevailing price. (However, it is the *potential* to deliver on the contracts which results in the observed price relationships.) Rather, the trader will be alert to various merchandising opportunities to sell wheat at a gain above that implied by the initial basis. This possibility exists because the merchant often has grain of a quality or in a location of special advantage to a particular buyer and the seller.

If the grain merchant is faced with inverse carrying charges, then the incentive is not to store (although, as previously noted, there may be a convenience yield in carrying some inventories). However, the merchant may have an opportunity to make a contract for delivering grain in some future month without having grain in inventory. This forward cash sale can be covered by the purchase of futures contracts—a buying hedge.

For example, a merchant might contract in March to deliver corn in November at $1.35 per bushel, and at the same time offset this forward contract by the purchase of December corn futures at $1.24. If on October 10 the merchant buys corn at $1.25 (to deliver on the forward contract) and sells December futures at $1.20 (to cover the hedge), he has gained 10 cents in the cash transaction and lost 4 cents on the futures market transaction for a gain of 6 cents on the net transaction. These particular figures are hypothetical, but they illustrate the principle that an inverse carrying charge combined with a narrowing basis is an incentive for this type of merchandising transaction (i.e., a buying hedge covering a forward cash sale).

In sum, both positive and negative carrying charges provide incentives for particular types of transactions by grain merchants. The positive carrying charge reflects ample current inventories and an incentive to carry stocks. Negative carrying charges reflect current shortages of stocks relative to forthcoming supplies and a disincentive to carrying stocks, and in addition, there is an incentive for merchants to make forward contracts covered by a buying hedge. Since the trader can take advantage of these price relations through hedging, a futures market is an institutional mechanism which facilitates temporal allocations of seasonally produced commodities.

Risk Aversion

Holbrook Working (1953) has emphasized that most hedging does *not* have the objective of pure risk aversion or pure price insurance. Rather, hedging is a tool which the user hopes to employ in making a profit. The intelligent hedger knows that the basis tends to narrow as the delivery month approaches. This changing basis, which may be positive or negative, may work in favor of or

against various hedges. The hedger is unlikely to employ a hedge
which has the potential of being unprofitable.

To illustrate, the oversimplified textbook example of pure risk
aversion (perhaps more accurately risk shifting) frequently assumes
a constant basis. Thus a selling hedge is placed as follows:

Buy cash wheat at $1.90 per bushel and

sell futures contracts at $2.00 per bushel.

Later, the hedge is lifted.

Sell wheat at $1.85 (loss of 5 cents) and

buy futures at $1.95 (gain of 5 cents).

With the constant basis, the loss in the cash market is just offset by
the gain in the futures market.

Given the same initial transaction with a positive carrying
charge of 10 cents, however, the hedger is protected against a price
decline, and a narrowing basis works in favor of the inventory
holder. The selling hedge also would assure a gain if prices had increased and the basis had narrowed. For instance, the final offsetting transactions might have been

sell cash wheat at $2.05 (gain of 15 over 1.90) and

buy futures at $2.12 (loss of 12 from 2.00).

Notice that, if the hedge had not been placed, the gain in the cash
transaction would have been 15 cents per bushel. Thus, while a
selling hedge assures a minimum return from holding inventories
with a positive basis, it also precludes larger returns when prices
rise. The potential hedger has an incentive to make a judgment
about the direction of price changes. The case of rising prices with
a selling hedge is an illustration of a "speculative element" of
hedging.

The selling hedge, as implied by previous discussion, is less
effective with inverse carrying charges. In contrast, the buying
hedge works best with inverse carrying charges and provides protection against price increases. A buying hedge precludes potential
profits if price declines, and it is not an effective hedge with positive carrying charges. The student should develop examples of
these various alternatives to more fully understand the applicabil-
ity of the buying hedge under alternate situations.

The basis often remains fairly constant over short time periods,
and a hedge can be placed purely as insurance against an adverse

price movement over a short time span, even if the basis is adverse. Working's argument is that the *typical* motive for hedging is not pure price insurance. The placement of a hedge depends on (1) the purpose of the hedge in relation to (2) the size of the basis and (3), to some extent, the expected movement of the constellation of all prices. An inverse carrying charge implies that the cash price will eventually decline relative to the distant future and a positive basis implies the opposite.

The ability of a hedge to achieve its purpose depends, in part, on the degree of association between the cash and futures prices involved in the transactions. Assuming the same quality, location, and delivery conditions for the cash commodity as specified in the futures contract, the two price series move up and down together in a closely related fashion with the basis narrowing as the delivery month approaches. However, the hedger may have grain of a different quality or in a different location such that the cash and future prices are less closely related. This implies a less perfect hedge, which may work in favor of or against the hedger. He may, as previously implied, be able to take advantage of the imperfections by completing the hedge on more favorable terms than suggested by the initial basis.

A hedge may be less than perfect also because futures contracts specify the delivery of fixed quantities (say, 5,000 bushels per contract) which may differ somewhat from the quantities involved in the cash transactions. In addition, the typical hedging example assumes that the hedge can be placed and lifted at two points in time. In practice, the purchase of grain and the sale of futures contracts and the subsequent offsetting transactions may not precisely coincide. Thus, the usual textbook examples tend to oversimplify the real situation.

Operational and Margin Hedging

Processors and other purchasers of farm commodities may use futures markets as a part of their business operations. For example, a flour miller may buy wheat without having offsetting forward flour sales. Thus, he may temporarily sell wheat futures contracts; eventually, the miller hopes to cover the wheat inventory with forward flour sales, and he can then lift the hedge on the wheat inventory.

Or, the miller may make a forward flour sale without having a wheat inventory. This forward sale can be covered by the purchase of wheat contracts. Covering forward flour sales with purchases of wheat contracts assumes flour and wheat prices are closely related, which they are.

Soybean processors can, in principle, hedge their processing margins directly because futures contracts exist for whole soybeans, soybean oil, and soybean meal. A 60-pound bushel of beans is processed into about 48 pounds of meal, about 11 pounds of oil, and approximately one pound of waste (these numbers are rounded to simplify computations). If the processor bought beans at $2.05 per bushel and if he sold meal at $50 per ton (2.5 cents per pound) and oil at 10 cents per pound, then the gross margin would be 25 cents per bushel.[1] Clearly, the possibility exists for a soybean processor to hedge stocks of beans in bean contracts or by the sale of oil and meal contracts, to buy bean contracts and sell oil and meal contracts in anticipation of subsequent purchase and processing of beans, and so forth. In other words, the processor has a chance, through hedging, to "fix" the gross processing margin.[2]

These potential uses of the futures market further illustrate Working's definition of a hedge in futures as a temporary substitute for a later transaction in the cash market.

Price Discovery and Forward Pricing

A principal justification for futures trading for the seasonally produced, continuously held commodity has been, and is, the hedging of stock carrying and processing activities. Price discovery can be viewed as essentially a by-product of the main function of

---

[1]
48 lb. × 2.5 cents	= $1.20 for meal
11 lb. × 10.0	= 1.10 for oil
total value	= 2.30 per bushel
cost of beans	= 2.05 per bushel
gross margin	= 0.25

[2] In practice, meal and oil prices often have not been high enough relative to bean prices to cover processing costs. Apparently, losses in processing have been more than covered by gains from holding stocks of beans—the inventory has been an asset which has typically increased in value (for more detail see Paul, 1966). Henry Arthur (1971) provides further discussion of business uses of futures.

inventory-hedging markets. The views of many buyers and sellers are focused on a single market. They have diverse objectives in terms of hedging and speculation, but the process leads to a continual appraisal of price-making forces. This might be viewed as a complementary function of inventory-hedging markets.

New futures markets are developing which appear to have as a main objective price discovery and the establishment of forward prices. The carrying of inventories may be of little or no importance. Such markets might be termed forward-pricing markets. Examples include futures markets for fresh eggs, live cattle, and iced broilers. Futures markets, one may hypothesize, are an economical method of establishing a forward price even when hedging of inventories is not of primary importance.

Whether futures markets are primarily inventory-hedging, primarily forward-pricing, or have dual but equal roles,[3] the forward-pricing functions can be useful to producers and buyers. A producer might use futures prices as a guide to production decisions; he may sell futures contracts at the beginning of the production process to cover the production decision. This is analogous to margin hedging.

A processor may selectively hedge ingredient requirements. In particular, if he believes prices are likely to rise in the future, the processor can buy futures and then sell them as he actually acquires the commodity. This is sometimes called anticipatory hedging. Where appropriate, viable markets exist, a food chain might hedge anticipated product requirements. Of course, if prices decline rather than rise, then the transactions in futures would result in a loss to the anticipatory hedger. Another example is the meat packer who makes forward (cash) contracts with livestock growers at fixed prices and who protects this agreement through a sale of appropriate cattle or hog futures contracts. Likewise, a producer of livestock and livestock products could anticipate feed needs

[3] The reader should recall that we argued in the previous chapter that the "type" of market does influence the behavior of prices, where the type of market is related to commodity characteristics. These differences in price behavior can influence the usefulness of the markets for particular purposes. For instance, futures prices in inventory-hedging markets vary almost as much from year to year as cash prices, and hence routine hedging in such markets by producers is less likely to reduce the variability of their annual revenue.

through the purchase of appropriate futures contracts. Thus, futures markets have the potential to facilitate many types of decisions other than those involving inventories.

Seasonal Patterns in Hedging Positions

If the main justification for futures trading rests with hedging use (i.e., if futures trading is not a "game" in which traders engage at random), then hedging open interests for seasonal crops should have seasonal patterns, and indeed they do. Wheat illustrates the "classical" inventory-hedging market. With seasonally large inventories immediately following harvest, short hedging is large, and as inventories decline seasonally, short hedging positions also decline (Table 13-1).

Table 13-1. Aggregate open short hedging positions on 15th of month for Chicago wheat and Maine potatoes, 1967–1968

Month	Short hedging positions	
	Wheat (mil. bu.)	Potatoes (1,000 carlots)
July	87.8	2.7
August	117.4	3.1
September	106.8	3.7
October	94.7	4.6
November	76.8	4.5
December	77.1	5.0
January	70.4	5.2
February	64.3	5.2
March	45.8	4.5
April	41.2	4.1
May	22.0	1.7
June	33.4	1.7

Source: Commodity Exchange Authority, *Commodity Futures Statistics, July 1967–June 1968*, USDA Stat. Bul. No. 432 (Washington, D.C., 1968), table 20.

Maine potatoes represent a more complex situation. With discontinuous inventories, this market plays only a forward-pricing role from late spring to the next harvest. The seasonal build-up of short hedging positions during this period represents forward-price hedging by growers. At harvest, the potato market also starts to play an inventory-hedging role. Hence, the short hedging position typically continues to increase seasonally until February and then declines rapidly to the end of the storage period in late May. The pattern for one year is given in Table 13-1.

The Role of Speculators—Some Further Comments

Speculators, in a sense, provide two types of liquidity. As we have just observed, particular types of hedging tend to be seasonal, and hence it is unrealistic to expect short hedging to be completely offset by long hedging. When short hedging is seasonally large, this must necessarily be offset in large part by long speculation. Further, it is unrealistic to expect a potential long hedger to enter the market at precisely the same moment as a potential short hedger, nor are their hedges likely to be of the same size. Hence, traders who take the opposite side of such hedges are needed. In a well developed market, these traders are primarily professional speculators.

The objective of the speculator is, of course, to make a profit. The decision to buy or to sell is based on expectations about the forthcoming movements of price—in a rather general sense, a forecast. However, some evidence suggests that a significant proportion of speculation is not based on formal forecasts of longer-term price level changes (Olson, 1970, p. 17; Working, 1967). Rather, speculation tends to respond directly to the (small) price changes implied by the placement of hedges. The position taken by scalpers is essentially that the current market-determined price is correct, that a large transaction (usually a hedge) can cause a deviation from this price, but that price will return to its previous level. Thus, for example, a scalper may buy on a ¼-cent price decline, hoping to resell the contracts, perhaps a few at a time, at higher prices over the next few minutes. This speculator is providing liquidity and is temporally spreading the effects of a large transaction.

Clearly, the market price can show "trends" of a few minutes, days, or weeks. A speculator trading on a minute-to-minute basis must be proficient in recognizing the longer trends to cut losses quickly when necessary. Hopefully, gains and losses from longer trends will balance for the scalper. In a well-developed market, professional speculators specialize their activities. Working (1967, pp. 17f.) classifies scalpers as (1) those who devote attention primarily to the smallest dips and bulges, (2) day traders who give most of their attention to dips and bulges of more than unit size, yet occurring fairly often within a day, and (3) day-to-day scalpers who give attention to price changes of such size and duration that positions are carried through several days. Working concludes, "it must be largely, if not almost wholly, scalping that contributes to the fluidity of the market"(p. 19).

Some speculators, of course, are trading on expectations of price changes over a longer time period. These traders contribute less to market liquidity, but they help in the continual appraisal of factors influencing price. These traders take positions based on new information or the re-evaluation of old information.

Some people seem to believe that speculators are free to drive prices up (to the detriment of consumers) or to drive prices down (to the detriment of farmers), getting rich in the process. A large speculator may on occasion attempt to "corner the market" (see subsequent section) and influence price; this is illegal and a relatively infrequent occurrence. Futures prices are typically the outcome of numerous transactions by many buyers and sellers and hence represent a collective evaluation of market forces. Since futures markets have zero sum returns (gains equal losses), not all traders are getting rich on futures markets. The evidence (Hieronymus, n.d.; Stewart, 1949; Wise, 1962) suggests that small, nonprofessional speculators are, on balance, losers. A study of 462 speculator customers of a large commission firm for one year found that 164 made profits totaling $462,123, while 298 lost a total of $1,127,-355. However, regular traders, as defined in the study, did better than the occasional traders (Hieronymus, pp. 7–8). It seems likely that professional speculators and perhaps hedgers are gainers. This is their vocation. They are likely to be better informed and can place more "timely" trades than the nonprofessional.[4]

One other class of speculator deserves comment, namely, the "spreader." These are professional speculators who place offsetting

[4] If the small speculator faces a high probability of loss, why does such speculation continue? This question is considered in a subsequent section of this chapter.

transactions in different futures contracts. These positions are based on the supposition that the price difference between the two contracts will change. These differences, as previously discussed, tend to be more stable, at least in inventory-hedging markets, than price level changes. The interdelivery spread (the price of storage) is related to the size of inventories. The intermarket spread, say, between wheat contracts in Minneapolis and in Chicago is related to space (transfer costs) and quality differences. The intergrain spread, say, between oats and corn contracts is a function of the substitutability between the two grains. If the price spreads are viewed as functions of certain economic variables, then the spreader by trying to recognize potential profit opportunities from changes in price differences plays the role of keeping the price differences consistent with prevailing economic conditions—that is, in "normal" alignment.

In addition, spread positions are held by scalpers in the course of their trading, and a position trader may spread to another contract to "hold" a profit. For instance, if a trader is long March contracts and if he has a profit from a price rise but does not wish to take it by selling, perhaps because of tax considerations, then he may sell May futures. The prices of March and May futures, of course, tend to move together; hence, with a spread position, the gains in one contract tend to be offset by losses in the other. It is in this sense that a spread may hold a profit.

In sum, speculators enter a futures market to make a profit, although many do not. One consequence is an increase in market liquidity, which assists hedgers. In addition, speculators contribute to the process of price discovery.

Some Theoretical and Empirical Issues

To this point, we have presented a majority viewpoint, among professional economists, of the "facts" of futures trading; we now turn to a few of the controversies.

Risk Premiums and the Supply of Speculative Services

Until the 1950's, economists tended to view hedgers as purchasers of price insurance from speculators (in contrast to the emphasis in this book). Grain merchants were thought to hedge inventories solely as protection against price declines. Speculators were presumably induced into taking long positions (against the short hedges) by some clear indication of a positive return. If hedgers are typically short and speculators are typically long, then positive returns to speculators must come from an increase in price through time to the maturity date of the contract. In other words, hedgers "pay" speculators to absorb a price risk (on the average), and it is this risk premium that attracts a supply of speculative services to the market. If this view is correct, then futures prices are *not* unbiased estimates of forthcoming cash prices but are biased downward to induce speculators to take long positions (as shown in Figure 13-1).

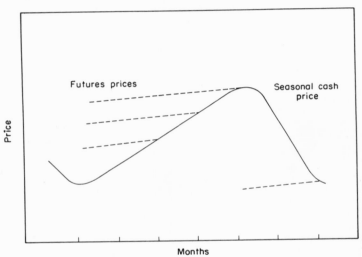

Figure 13-1. Hypothetical biased relationship of futures prices to cash prices under the assumption of a risk premium

Keynes (1923) and Hardy (1923) apparently were the first to discuss the issue. Keynes believed that speculators received positive returns; Hardy (p. 225) states, "it [that hedgers pay speculators] does not seem probable." Considerable empirical research has been devoted to the question of the existence of a risk premium. The majority view is that a risk premium is nonexistent (Gray, 1961; Rockwell, 1967; Telser, 1967), but several researchers (Cootner,

1967; Houthakker, 1957) believe that a small positive risk premium does exist.

If a risk premium is not transferred, if the majority of speculators are losers, and if hedgers are not hedging purely against price declines, then what induces speculation? Successful speculators are, by definition, persons who make a profit on speculation. However, they are a minority of the total number of speculators, and their profits do not necessarily come from a risk premium. As previously discussed, profits are a return for providing liquidity (Working, 1967). But some professional speculators presumably are successful in forecasting price level or price difference changes, and this implies that some professional speculators have developed special skills in making certain types of forecasts.[5]

While the avocational amateur speculator typically is a loser, there is a possibility of making a large gain, and the amateur speculator may gain pleasure from the process of speculation. "To these amateurs speculation represents a 'good' for which they are willing to pay and not a 'bad' for which they must be paid to undertake. The losses of speculation, if any, are made up by other sources of income. Amateurs who cannot sustain the losses and who leave the market are replaced by others; a rapid turnover of amateurs is compatible with the maintenance of a large stock of them. Thus to the amateurs speculation in commodities is comparable to the purchase of a lottery ticket which has a small probability of a large gain" (Telser, 1967, p. 132).

Influence of Futures Trading on Cash Prices

The public, as represented by the Congress of the United States, seem to believe that trading futures contracts "adversely" influences cash prices.[6] This belief has taken many forms. Futures trad-

---

[5] The issue under discussion has in fact been stated in terms of a forecasting problem (see Houthakker, 1957; Rockwell, 1967). In reviewing the literature, the reader should be reminded that Keynes' term "normal backwardation" is analogous to the concept of an inverse carrying charge; however, he viewed this carrying charge as including a risk premium.

[6] For example, trading in onion futures was declared illegal by an act of the Congress in 1958. Of course, such laws tend to reflect the views of certain special-interest groups (e.g., onion growers) rather than those of the general public. The public image of futures markets is in contrast to the views of most

ing is thought to influence the *level* of cash prices. Thus, high wheat prices in 1947 were blamed on futures trading (Wise, 1962), but, on the other hand, relatively low potato prices in Maine also were thought to be due to futures trading (Bagnell, 1963). Further, futures trading, some argue, increases the *frequency* and *magnitude* of the variation of cash prices.

Before discussing specific allegations, it is useful to try to put them in a general perspective. First, cash and futures prices in inventory-hedging markets are highly correlated. Also, cash prices and futures prices for nearby delivery months in forward-pricing markets are related. However, current cash prices and prices for distant futures in forward-pricing markets are not closely related. We have discussed theoretical reasons for these various levels of correlation. In other words, logical reasons exist for the correlations in futures and cash prices in some markets, and this does not somehow imply that these prices are inconsistent with existing economic conditions.

Second, where high correlations exist, the allegations imply that cash prices would behave differently without the institution of a futures market and that this behavior would in some sense be "better" without futures trading. The source of adverse price behavior is alleged to be excess speculation in futures. Clearly there are difficult problems involved in judging performance. What is "adverse" price behavior? If it can be identified, is its source in the futures market? If so, would the different behavior be "better" or "worse" than the alternative behavior? What is "excess speculation"? And so on. We now turn to some specific questions.

Does trading in futures contracts influence the level of annual average prices? In other words, would these commodity prices be significantly higher (or lower) without futures trading? Logically, the answer is no. A futures market is a price-discovery mechanism interpreting economic forces; it is these forces which determine the level of price. But like any other pricing mechanism, a futures market's "unbiasedness" depends on a lack of market imperfections. High-quality information about price-making forces should minimize bias. Empirical evidence also suggests that the answer to the above question is no (Emerson and Tomek, 1969). Occasionally, an

---

professional economists, who typically argue that such markets serve useful purposes.

illegal manipulation may influence price over relatively short time periods. Futures markets have shown substantial ability to compensate for such "artificial" price movements. It is also true that a few futures markets have had persistent price biases (see below).

Does trading in futures contracts increase the magnitude of the variance of annual cash prices? The variability of prices from year to year, as we have seen, depends on the magnitude of shifts in supply and demand and on the slopes of these functions. Thus, for instance, the large variability of onion prices (for which no futures trading now exists) is mainly a function of a highly price inelastic demand and variable supplies. Futures markets may, in some instances, be stabilizing influences by providing relatively stable forward prices. Stable forward prices may help stabilize acres planted and hence reduce annual price variability (Gray, 1964). In addition, available evidence (see previous chapter) suggests futures prices tend to have smaller annual variances than cash prices. The influence of futures markets on annual variability of cash prices, if any, would seem to be in the direction of reducing them.

Does trading in futures contracts influence the variance of seasonal price patterns? There is some logic and evidence which implies that futures trading reduces the variability of seasonal price fluctuations. Futures trading, through its inventory-hedging function, should contribute to an "optimal" distribution of a seasonally produced commodity through the marketing year. Hedging by reducing the price risk of carrying inventories in a sense reduces the costs of storage. One may hypothesize that without futures trading "too little" of the commodity would be stored with consequent lower prices at harvest and higher prices at the end of the storage period. Active trading in onion futures followed by the (legally required) abandonment of this market provided a test of the hypothesis, and the evidence supports it (Gray, 1963).

Does futures trading influence the day-to-day variability of cash prices? The answer apparently is both yes and no, depending on the particular market. Futures markets with liquidity and a good balance between the demand for short and for long positions have relatively stable daily prices. "Adequate demand by speculators for futures contracts often contributed to short-run price stability" (Nathan Associates, 1967, p. 3). Day-to-day price changes were considerably smaller when the percentage of total volume attributable to scalpers was relatively high (p. 88). On the other hand, a lack of market balance and of the liquidity provided by scalpers helps explain day-to-day price changes (for more detail see pp. 84–89).[7] Thus, if cash prices received by farmers are tied closely to futures prices and if the futures market has substantial daily variability, then the futures market has the potential to increase daily price variability.

Clearly, a sufficient volume of speculation must exist in a market to provide liquidity. Whether or not there are too many speculators, leading to unnecessary price instability, or too few speculators to insure liquidity, which also may lead to instability, is extremely difficult to determine. Speculators are more likely to be active in markets in which price changes are occurring than in stable markets. Thus, a positive association between the volume of trading and the magnitude of price changes within each day, such as found by Olson (1970), would be expected. But, the effect of increased trading activity may be to damp down price fluctuations rather than to accentuate them. Working's theory of floor trading (1967) implies that hedging demand typically attracts whatever volume of speculative trading is required to provide liquidity.[8]

Regulation and Price Manipulation

The Commodity Exchange Authority (CEA) of the USDA is the regulatory agency for most futures markets. Actually, their authority is limited to markets in which U.S. (domestic) agricultural commodities are traded, and it even excludes a few of them; it does not

---

[7] The study cited defines day-to-day price change as the difference between the closing and opening prices. The empirical analysis is for the prices of the May 1961 soybean contract in Chicago in February and March 1961. This was a period in which the Commodity Exchange Authority collected daily reports on the classification of reporting traders and other daily data. The concept of "market balance" can be approached in several ways. One is the approximate equality of the ratios long hedging/short hedging and short speculation/long speculation. These ratios typically are below one because short hedging and long speculation tend to dominate futures markets. Values between zero and 2.5 have been observed. The concept of a "thin market" may be defined by the ratio volume traded/open interest. The market is thin when the ratio is small.

[8] However, we subsequently point out that some futures markets are characterized by bias, which precludes a balanced volume of trading.

cover trading in commodities originating in other countries (e.g., sugar, cocoa, and coffee). The CEA collects statistics, conducts studies, and promulgates regulations with respect to futures markets. The regulations cover such things as licensing exchanges, client-broker relationships, and price manipulation. In addition, each exchange has a set of by-laws or regulations which cover the operations of members of the exchange.

While there is relatively little fraud, it may be of interest to briefly describe certain illegal activities. A trader may attempt to "corner" the market (1) by taking a large long position in futures and (2) by gaining control of the physical supplies which could be delivered on these contracts. Thus, this trader is in a position to prevent those short futures to cover their position by buying futures or to obtain supplies to deliver on the contracts *at existing prices.* In other words, he is in a position to force up prices of the contracts he owns. Traders with an open interest of over 200,000 bushels must report their position to the CEA.

A "bear raid" involves manipulative selling to force down price. This would be attempted when the manipulator indentifies a situation in which his selling can precipitate a price decline. For instance, those long futures may have stop-loss orders under their contracts so that a price decline sets off a wave of sales. If the sale by the manipulator sets off more sales and the price declines, then he is able to cover his sales with purchases at lower prices.

A viable futures market with a large volume of trading has substantial built-in resistance to price manipulation. It takes large financial resources to move price, and unless a special situation like a "corner" exists, price will return to its original position as quickly as it moved away when the manipulator tries to take his profit. A few wealthy, but uninformed, traders have run up prices by huge purchases, but prices go right back down because the offsetting volume of sales to take "profits" lowers price. Price has been temporarily manipulated but not necessarily to the benefit of the manipulator.

What Makes a Successful Futures Market?

The factors which result in a successful futures market are not absolutely clear. Economists have argued that the commodity involved should be seasonally produced and reasonably storable. This assumed that the major use of futures markets was inventory hedging. However, successful futures markets have developed for other types of commodities, and there are seasonally produced commodities without futures.

A successful market does have many buyers and sellers—hence, liquidity and balance. A single trader does not have a large impact on price. The commodity also must be "suitably" described in the contract. This does not mean that the commodity is perfectly homogeneous. Rather, it is a question of describing deliverable grades in the contract. The *contracts* are homogeneous.

Biases may exist which result in little or no use of a futures market, although in principle—if one were unaware of the bias—such use might seem desirable. (1) The terms of the contract may result in market imbalance. For instance, the delivery terms may favor the buyer or the seller. Consequently, only buyers or only sellers attempt to use the market, leading to lack of balance and price bias. (2) Buyers and sellers may not use a market simply from lack of experience or historical precedent. Farmers have typically not used the forward-pricing feature of futures markets. The "bran and shorts" (wheat milling by-products) market apparently died because feed manufacturers were less disposed to use the market than flour millers. (3) Programs external to futures markets may reduce use. A price-support program reduces the need for inventory hedging. Extreme inflation or government attempts to control price are examples of other external factors. Such factors apparently explain the persistent bias in the coffee market (for full detail see Gray, 1960).[9]

Markets have declined in use as their main economic justification has declined. The storage egg contract is an example. The seasonality of egg production has been reduced. Hence, the need

---

[9] The existence of a continual bias through time in price leads one to ask why it continues to exist. For instance, coffee prices were biased downward consistently. This implies that a trader should make a large profit by consistently buying the contract, holding it, and then selling as the delivery month approaches. Of course, if enough traders did this, the bias would be eliminated—hence, the question, why has the bias persisted? Apparently, the uncertainty from inflation and potential devaluation, which would lower futures prices, prevented buyers from entering the market.

to store eggs and to hedge these inventories has decreased. Price-support programs, likewise, have reduced the hedging needs for commodities when prices are near the support level, and hence the volume of trading has declined when this situation has prevailed.

In contrast, a futures market can grow as potential hedgers identify the economic usefulness of the market. Trading in soybean and Maine potato futures, including hedging use, increased greatly in the 1950's. For a futures market to be successful, it apparently should fulfill an economic (hedging) need. Concurrently, it must attract sufficient speculators for liquidity. However, potential hedgers may not use the market for various reasons. Such vague considerations as personal attitudes of potential hedgers, tradition, timing of the start of the market, location of the market, and so on seem to influence the success of a market. For example, experience by potential hedgers in making forward contracts in a cash market seems like a useful prerequisite. Some important research remains to be done before we can clearly identify the factors influencing the success of new futures markets.

References

Arthur, Henry B. 1971. *Commodity Futures as a Business Management Tool*. Boston: Harvard Univ. Graduate School of Business Administration.

Bagnell, Douglas B. 1963. "Irish Potato Futures Trading," *Hearing before a Subcommittee of the Committee on Agriculture and Forestry, United States Senate*, 88th Congress, 1st Session on S. 332, Sept. 30, 1963, pp. 43–54.

Cootner, Paul H. 1967. "Speculation and Hedging," *Food Res. Inst. Studies*, 7:65–105 (Supplement).

Emerson, Peter M., and William G. Tomek. 1969. "Did Futures Trading Influence Potato Prices?" *Am. J. Ag. Econ.*, 51:666–672.

Gray, Roger W. 1960. "The Characteristic Bias on Some Thin Futures Markets," *Food Res. Inst. Studies*, 1:296–312.

——. 1961. "The Search for a Risk Premium," *J. Pol. Econ.*, 69:250–260.

——. 1963. "Onions Revisited," *J. Farm Econ.*, 45:273–276.

——. 1964. "The Attack upon Potato Futures Trading in the United States," *Food Res. Inst. Studies*, 4:97–122.

Hardy, C. O. 1923. *Risk and Risk-Bearing*. Chicago: Univ. of Chicago Press.

Hieronymus, Thomas A. N.d. *Commodity Speculation as an Investment Medium*. New York Coffee and Sugar Exchange, Inc., pamphlet.

Houthakker, H. S. 1957. "Can Speculators Forecast Prices?" *Rev. of Econ. and Stat.*, 39:143–151.

Keynes, J. M. 1923. "Some Aspects of Commodity Markets," *Manchester Guardian Commercial*, section 13, March 29.

Nathan Associates. 1967. *Margins, Speculation and Prices in Grains Futures Markets*, Econ. Res. Ser., USDA.

Olson, Wayne L. 1970. *The Extent and Price Effects of Floor Trading on the New York Mercantile Exchange Potato Futures Market*. Commodity Exchange Authority, USDA.

Paul, Allen B. 1966. "Pricing below Cost in the Soybean Processing Industry," *J. Farm Econ.*, 48 (Part II):2–22 (Aug).

Rockwell, Charles S. 1967. "Normal Backwardation, Forecasting, and the Returns to Commodity Futures Traders," *Food Res. Inst. Studies*, 7:107–130 (Supplement).

Stewart, Blair. 1949. *An Analysis of Speculative Trading in Grain Futures*, Econ. Res. Ser., USDA Tech. Bul. 1001.

Telser, Lester G. 1967. "The Supply of Speculative Services in Wheat, Corn, and Soybeans," *Food Res. Inst. Studies*, 7:131–175 (Supplement).

Wise, T. A. 1962. "Do You Have a Future in Commodity Futures?" *Fortune*, April, pp. 120–121, 200–206.

Working, Holbrook. 1953. "Hedging Reconsidered," *J. Farm Econ.*, 35:544–561.

———. 1967. "Tests of a Theory Concerning Floor Trading on Commodity Exchanges," *Food Res. Inst. Studies*, 7:5–48 (Supplement).

CHAPTER 14

Government Intervention
in Pricing Farm Products

Governments now attempt to influence the prices of at least some farm products in nearly every country of the world. Political considerations obviously play a dominant role in the decision to support or not to support the price of a particular commodity. Although government price-support programs remain controversial in the United States, a majority of those in Congress have voted in favor of continuing such programs over the past forty years. Support programs in some form have been maintained since the 1930's for most grains, cotton, tobacco, oilseed crops, wool, sugar, and milk. These commodities account for about half the cash receipts of farmers in the United States. Prices of commodities which account for the remaining half of gross farm receipts, including poultry and eggs, beef, pork, fruits, and vegetables, have not been supported directly, although the prices of these commodities have been influenced by support programs on grains, and to a modest degree by government purchase programs and marketing orders for a few commodities.

The objective of this chapter is to provide a framework that will enable the student to appraise the economic consequences of alternative forms or degrees of government intervention in pricing. While policy decisions are inevitably influenced by political pressures and social considerations, economists can play a useful role by pointing out which groups are likely to gain or lose if a particular policy is adopted. In this chapter, we illustrate how economic principles and a knowledge of demand and supply relationships (or elasticities) can be used to predict the consequences of alternative policies on such variables as the level and stability of farm

prices and incomes, consumer prices, the magnitude of surpluses or
deficits, the volume of imports, and government costs.

Objectives of Government Intervention

Governments generally intervene in pricing farm products to
achieve one or a combination of the following objectives:
(1) to reduce price and income instability,
(2) to improve the allocation of resources,
(3) to increase self-sufficiency in food and fiber,
(4) to raise the average level of prices and incomes.
As we have observed, farm prices tend to fluctuate more than
the prices of many nonfarm goods and services. This can lead to
cycles in production with excess resources being devoted to certain
commodities during some periods and can lead to underutilization
of processing and marketing facilities during others. Consumers
gain relatively little from price instability, especially if it leads to
fluctuating supplies. Under reasonable assumptions regarding the
nature of utility functions, it can be demonstrated that consumers
generally are better off with relatively stable rather than fluctuating supplies of farm products (Johnson, 1947, pp. 151–153). Waugh
(1944), on the other hand, argues that consumers are made worse
off if the price of a commodity is stabilized at the arithmetic mean
of the fluctuating prices. This argument is based on the concept of
consumer surplus (approximately equal to the area under the demand curve). With a downward-sloping demand curve, gains in
consumer surplus at a price below the mean will exceed the loss in
consumer surplus from an equal price change above the mean
level.
Unstable prices also may have an adverse effect on the demand
for agricultural raw materials. For example, in periods of high
prices for fibers, textile manufacturers are likely to switch to synthetic materials. Once processors and consumers have become ac-
customed to the substitute materials, it may be difficult to regain
markets even when prices subsequently fall. A compelling case can
be made for collective action on the part of producers or for the introduction of public policies designed to reduce price fluctuations

under such circumstances. Alternative methods of stabilizing supplies are discussed in a subsequent section.

Government intervention in pricing also has been advocated by some economists to provide producers with better guides for planning. Current or past prices, as pointed out in Chapter 11, do not always provide reliable guides for the future. Such prices may be depressed or abnormally high as a result of temporary shifts in demand or supply. This may lead producers to make what turn out to be unwise production decisions. Where local market prices are depressed, perhaps as a result of an overvalued exchange rate or export taxes, Krishna (1967) sees a need for what he refers to as a "positive price policy" to provide the incentives for farmers to increase output. Gunnar Myrdal (1968) likewise believes that government intervention may be needed in some less developed countries to maintain appropriate prices for planning purposes. He views price policy as an instrument of planning which will help to bring about a more rational allocation of resources.

Efficiency in the use of capital also may be enhanced through government intervention in pricing. Unstable or unpredictable prices can inhibit investment. Uncertainty produces what Johnson (1947) calls "capital rationing." This means that creditors refuse to lend as much money as farmers could profitably invest or, alternatively, that farmers borrow smaller amounts than they might productively use because of discounting for uncertainty, partly associated with unstable prices. Johnson argues that resource allocation can be improved by announcing "forward prices" based on long-run equilibrium prices prior to the time production decisions need to be made. If actual market prices fall below these guaranteed prices, he would then have the government make up the difference through the use of deficiency payments. There is considerable evidence to indicate that price guarantees do encourage farmers to make additional investments. Insofar as such investments increase output and efficiency, consumers ultimately gain.

A major purpose of introducing support programs in some countries is to increase self-sufficiency in food and fiber production, to reduce dependence on imports, and perhaps to improve the balance of payments. This has been one of the compelling arguments for maintaining guaranteed prices to producers of farm products in the United Kingdom above potential import prices (McCrone, 1962, pp. 14–20, and Hallett, 1968, pp. 206–208). Widespread support for expanding home agriculture developed as a result of the experience with shortages and food rationing during two world wars. A number of economists in England also argued in the 1950's that agricultural price policies could make a contribution to reducing their persistent balance-of-payments deficit. By offering incentives to expand home agriculture, they pointed out that England would need to spend less of their limited foreign exchange on food imports, and this, in turn, might enable her to buy any required imports at somewhat more favorable prices. Postwar policy decisions in the United Kingdom were based in part on the assumption that food supplies available for export would be limited by rising population and income in the traditional exporting countries, a forecast that turned out to be inaccurate. Food supplies became more abundant in the 1960's and prices fell below the levels prevailing in the late 1940's and early 1950's.

In most industrial countries, including the United States, the major purpose of government intervention in pricing farm products has been to improve the welfare of farmers. The argument most frequently advanced to justify support programs in the United States is that farm incomes would be too low in the absence of such programs. Proponents of support programs call attention to the fact that even with a substantial degree of government intervention, farm incomes in the United States have averaged well below those of employed nonfarm workers over most of the past thirty-five years.[1] Similar arguments are heard in the European Economic Community where, despite even higher support prices than in the United States, farm incomes still lag well behind those of the nonfarm population. The social consequences of abandoning supports also are of concern. Some believe that, in the absence of government intervention, farm prices would fall to a point where

[1] Although *average* farm incomes are relatively low in the United States, the top third of U.S. farmers, who account for over 85 per cent of the value of all farm products sold, earned incomes in the late 1960's which were approximately equal to those obtained by comparable nonfarm groups.

more people would be forced off the land, migration to urban areas would increase, and rural towns would become derelict.[2]

Methods of Reducing Price Instability

Fluctuations in prices received by producers can be reduced through the use of buffer stocks (i.e., by storing a portion of the crop in years of large production and low prices and then releasing stocks in years of high prices) or by creating a stabilization fund. Under the latter scheme, funds are accumulated by paying producers less than current market prices in favorable years. This money is then used to make supplementary payments to producers in low-priced years. In theory, either type of stabilization program could be operated by a producer organization created without the assistance of the government, although, in practice, such schemes are usually initiated and carried out by some agency of the government or a monopoly marketing organization such as a marketing board.

A buffer program that succeeds in reducing the amplitude of price fluctuations (without government subsidies) does not necessarily reduce instability in producer revenue. Under some circumstances, a storage program may even increase instability in annual returns. When prices are free to fluctuate in response to changing supplies, high prices are normally associated with small crops and vice versa. If the price elasticity of demand is equal to -1.0, price changes are just sufficient to compensate for quantity changes, and hence total revenue is constant regardless of the level of production. The inverse relationship which normally prevails between price and quantity tends to stabilize revenue. In contrast,

[2] Studies were made in the 1960's of the possible effects of eliminating all price and income support programs in the United States, and they indicated that average farm prices would fall substantially in the short run, perhaps by as much as 10 or 20 per cent. One of the consequences would be to encourage the consolidation of farms; land values also could be expected to decline but there probably would not be a mass exodus from agriculture. Migration from farms has been shown to be influenced much more by the age of farmers and the availability of nonfarm job opportunities than by the level of farm product prices (Robinson, 1970; Tweeten, 1969).

a buffer-stock program which stabilizes prices (but not farm sales) will increase income instability over a wide range of elasticities. Gross receipts will be more unstable with freely fluctuating prices than with stable prices only if the elasticity of demand is less than -0.5 (in absolute value). Under such circumstances, small crops bring considerably higher revenue than large crops. With stable prices, the reverse is true, but the fluctuations are smaller in the case of a severely inelastic demand with a stabilization program than without one.

The effect of a buffer-stock scheme on total revenue to producers over a period of years depends on possible shifts in the demand curve between the time of acquisition and the time of sale of stocks, on storage costs over the intervening period, and on the price elasticity of demand when stocks are withheld relative to the elasticity when they are released. In general, farmers gain from a storage program only if demand shifts by enough to cover storage costs or if the price elasticity of demand at the time of sale of stocks is greater than at the time of acquisition (Thomsen and Foote, 1952, pp. 212–215; Gislason, 1959, pp. 594–597). With a linear demand function, it pays producers to accumulate stocks in years of low prices and sell them in years of high prices.

The effects of withholding stocks in years of high production and selling them in years of short crops when the demand function is linear are illustrated in Figure 14-1. Assume that a monopoly selling organization knows the shape of the demand curve and that high-production years are normally followed by low-production years so that it is possible to acquire stocks in the first period for sale in the second. If production in t_1 (represented by Q_3 in Figure 14-1) were sold in that year, price would be equal to P_1 and total revenue as shown in the right-hand diagram would be R_1. But by withholding $Q_3 - Q_2$ of the product in t_1, price would be raised to P_2 and total returns to R_2. In the following period, with production equal to Q_1, the accumulated stocks could be sold. This would drive down the price from P_3 to P_2, but total revenue would rise to R_2 (since demand over this range is price elastic, total revenue rises with an increase in sales). At the price P_2 and volume Q_2, total revenue is maximized. Thus, producers would benefit by acquiring stocks any time the price fell below P_2 and releasing them

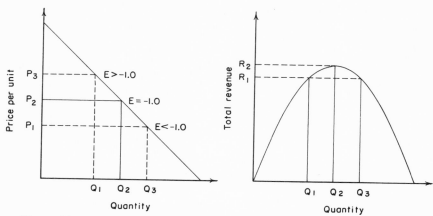

Figure 14-1. Effect of a buffer-stock scheme on average prices and total revenue with a linear demand function

whenever the price exceeded P_2. In this case, they benefit from both the acquisition and the release of stocks, a special situation which is attributable to the fact that demand is inelastic over the low range and elastic over the upper range of prices.

Producer returns are reduced by a storage program designed to equalize supplies when demand is inelastic at high prices and elastic at low prices; producer returns are increased by a stabilization program when the opposite elasticity conditions prevail. Whether or not it pays producers to stabilize supplies and prices, once the demand curve is known, can be determined simply and directly by noting the shape of the total revenue function (price multiplied by quantity) (Eckstein and Syrquin, 1971). If the total revenue function is curved downward so that it falls below a line joining the two points on the revenue function which show the total returns obtainable with fluctuating supplies and prices, producers are worse off (receive a lower average revenue over a period of years) with a stabilization program.[3] This situation is illustrated in Figure 14-2. The average revenue over a two-year period with production

[3] The total revenue function has this general shape when the price elasticity of demand is constant and less than unity in absolute value. Eckstein and Syrquin (1971, p. 332) point out that with constant elasticity functions (admittedly a special case), "farmers' revenue will rise as a result of supply fluctuations when price elasticity is *smaller* than unity and fall when it is greater."

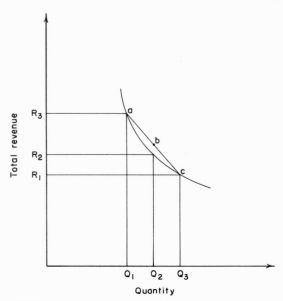

Figure 14-2. Difference in average revenue between two periods with fluctuating and stable supplies and prices

at Q_1 and Q_3 is represented by point b, the midpoint of the line ac joining R_1 and R_3. If sufficient supplies were withheld in the high-production year and sold in the low-production year so as to maintain supplies at Q_2, the average revenue in the two years would be R_2. This clearly falls below point b. The opposite would be true if the total revenue function is curved upward, as shown in the right-hand side of Figure 14-1.

Past experience with stabilization schemes has been mixed. Consumers in the United States as well as some in other countries benefited in the 1940's when the government-financed Commodity Credit Corporation sold excess stocks of grains and cotton which had been acquired in the 1930's. In this case, producers also gained since the government absorbed storage costs and any losses on the commodities held off the market. If excess stocks must be held for long periods before being sold, the cost of storage may more than offset any gains realized from shifts in demand. Gislason (1959) concluded that Canadian wheat producers did not gain from storage operations of the Wheat Board in the 1930's and 1940's despite the fact that the average price of wheat when sold was considerably greater than when it was acquired. Storage costs (which were not subsidized by the government) exceeded the gains from higher prices.

Buffer-stock schemes cannot be operated successfully unless commodities are storable and production is sufficient to acquire stocks before prices rise. International buffer-stock schemes have been proposed from time to time for agricultural commodities, but the tin agreement is the only international agreement negotiated thus far that makes use of buffer stocks. The experience with this agreement indicates the importance of having adequate funds to acquire whatever quantities are needed to stabilize prices. In 1958, the administrators of the tin agreement were unable to keep prices from falling below the range specified in the agreement because they had exhausted the funds available. Later, when demand conditions improved, they were unable to prevent prices from rising above the upper limit because the stocks they had previously acquired were inadequate (Hallett, 1968, p. 197).

Without accurate forecasts, it is difficult to decide when to acquire stocks, how much to store, and when to liquidate. If the general trend of prices is downward, a storage scheme may prove to be extremely expensive. A commodity stabilization program is more likely to be successful if prices fluctuate around a stable or reasonably predictable trend.

Price stabilization funds have been used in Australia and New Zealand in an attempt to reduce fluctuations in returns from selling on export markets where prices are often unstable. Such schemes also may turn out to be devices to support rather than stabilize prices if the funds accumulated in high-priced years are exhausted and returns to producers remain low. In the case of the wheat stabilization scheme in Australia, the government stepped in to underwrite losses in the late 1950's and early 1960's when export prices fell and remained below the guaranteed price (Campbell, 1964). Furthermore, serious equity problems may arise when a long lag exists between the time funds are accumulated and the time they are dispersed. If farms change hands, those who were taxed initially lose at the expense of those who acquired farms at a later date and became eligible for payments from the fund. The major advantage of a stabilization fund over a buffer-stock scheme is that the former is less expensive to operate since funds are not tied up in commodities; however, it offers no advantages to buyers since supplies are not stabilized.

Price-Support Programs in the United States

An extremely complicated array of support programs has evolved in the United States over the past forty years as a result of periodic revisions of the Agricultural Adjustment Acts that were adopted in the 1930's. Intervention in pricing has been selective. Support levels also have varied widely over time and among commodities. Support prices for wheat and cotton, for example, were maintained well above the prices that would have prevailed in the absence of government intervention during the 1950's and 1960's, while support levels for other commodities such as soybeans were held close to or below long-run equilibrium prices. Congress has been unwilling to extend supports to perishable commodities for a number of reasons, including the unwillingness of producers to accept controls on production or sales, especially for livestock products, and the potential high cost to the government of extending support to these commodities. Part of the reluctance to extend supports to perishable farm products is traceable to the unfortunate experience with the attempt to maintain the prices of eggs and potatoes above equilibrium levels during and immediately after World War II. Costs proved to be so high that support programs for these commodities were abandoned in the late 1940's.

During the 1940's and 1950's, support prices for most commodities were closely linked to parity prices. Parity prices, as defined in legislation adopted in the 1930's, are those prices which give farm products the same purchasing power with respect to articles farmers buy as they had in 1910–1914 (USDA, 1970, p. 22). The major mover in the parity formula is the Index of Prices Paid by Farmers. When this index goes up, all parity prices rise. This means that support prices, insofar as they are tied to parity prices, are adjusted up or down on the basis of an index which includes the prices of items used in farm homes as well as machinery, fertilizer, feed, interest, taxes, farm wage rates, and other items used in production. The current parity price for any commodity is obtained by multiplying the base price (originally but no longer the average price received by farmers in the period 1910–1914) by the most recent index of prices paid by farmers (also on a 1910–1914 base) divided by 100. Thus, if the base-period price of a commodity such as wheat is 70 cents per bushel and the current index of prices paid is 350, the parity price is $2.45 per bushel ($70¢ \times \frac{350}{100}$).

A number of attempts have been made to improve the parity formula since it became obvious in the 1940's that the original formula led to overpricing some commodities, in relation both to costs of production and to the prices of other commodities. A new or modernized parity formula was adopted in 1948. Current parity prices are calculated using adjusted base prices rather than actual market prices prevailing in the period just preceding World War I. Adjusted base prices reflect price relationships prevailing among commodities in the most recent ten-year period.[4] But even the modernized version has shortcomings as a basis for establishing support prices. It fails to take account of changes in efficiency or costs of production that have occurred over the past half century. Moreover, changes in relative demand and efficiency among commodities are reflected in parity prices only insofar as the ten-year moving averages of actual market prices reflect these changes. The formula does not provide an equitable method of establishing prices for different commodities. If all farm products were to be supported at a fixed percentage of modernized parity prices, returns to producers would be much higher for some products than for others.

Both Congress and successive Secretaries of Agriculture have recognized the limitations of the parity formula. As a result, there has been a move away from tying support prices to parity prices in recent years. During World War II and for a considerable period

---

[4] Adjusted base prices are calculated by computing an average of actual market prices for the most recent ten-year period, and then adjusting these back to the 1910–1914 base by dividing each ten-year average price by the Index of Prices Received by Farmers for the same ten-year period (USDA, 1970, pp. 26–28). The effect of this is to raise the base price of any commodity that goes up faster than the average of all farm products and to lower the base price of commodities that go up more slowly.

immediately following the war, the Secretary of Agriculture was compelled by law to maintain supports on most commodities at not less than 90 per cent of parity (Robinson, 1970). Subsequently, a flexible or sliding scale was adopted which permitted the Secretary to adjust individual commodity support prices downward to as low as 75 per cent of parity, depending on the relationship between total supplies, including carryover stocks, and estimated demand for each commodity. In the 1960's, the Secretary was given even more discretionary authority in establishing price-support loan rates for grains and cotton in order to avoid the need for export subsidies and to encourage consumption. Farmers who agree to participate in supply-adjustment programs have been compensated in part for reductions in price-support loan rates by payments made from the treasury.

Alternative Methods of Supporting Prices

The economic effects of programs designed to support farm prices depend on the level of support in relation to equilibrium prices and the method used to make supports effective. If a country produces less of any commodity than it consumes, internal prices can be maintained above import prices simply by imposing tariffs or by restricting imports. This is the method of support most commonly used in food-deficit nations. In countries where actual or potential production at the support or guaranteed price exceeds consumption, the government has the choice of purchasing the excess production (presumably for disposal abroad or in some market that does not compete with normal commercial sales), subsidizing consumption so as to shift the demand curve to the right, restricting production to what can be sold at the support price, or making deficiency payments to producers. The costs to the government of maintaining a given level of support will differ depending on the support method used and the elasticities of demand and supply. In practice, of course, governments frequently use a combination of devices to maintain or raise prices.

Tariffs, Variable Levies, and Import Restrictions

The United States makes use of tariffs on such commodities as meat and wool to maintain domestic prices above import prices. In addition, quotas are employed to restrict imports of frozen beef, dairy products, sugar, and a number of other supported commodities. Most European countries make use of similar devices, along with variable levies, minimum import prices, and compulsory mixing requirements, to maintain internal farm prices well above those of the major exporting countries, including the United States. For most temperate-zone products there is no longer a single world market but rather a series of national markets with widely varying levels of protection.[5] In the mid-1960's, for example, the price for wheat ranged from less than $1.50 per bushel in some countries to more than $4.00 in others.

The effect of most protectionist policies is to raise internal prices, thereby encouraging domestic production and reducing the market for potential exporting nations. The degree to which internal production and consumption are affected by the imposition of a tariff depends on the slopes or elasticities of the demand and supply curves in the importing nation: the more elastic these relationships are, the greater will be the impact on residual exporters for a given tariff or import duty. This assumes that import supply is perfectly elastic at the import price. If it is not, the imposition of a tariff will affect the import price as well as the internal market price.

The potential effect of an import duty on domestic production, consumption, and imports is illustrated in Figure 14-3. The supply of an imported commodity such as feed grains is assumed to be perfectly elastic at the price P_1. In the absence of any tariff or other protectionist measures, domestic production will be equal to Q_1 and consumption will be equal to Q_4, with imports making up the difference between total consumption and domestic production $(Q_4 - Q_1)$. If a tariff is imposed on imports such that the domestic price rises to P_2, producers will eventually increase output to Q_2

[5] Johnson (1964, pp. 922–923) has estimated the average degree of protection afforded agricultural producers in a number of countries in the early 1960's using a method devised by McCrone (1962, pp. 50–57). The level of protection is computed by valuing output at national or internal prices and then dividing this total by the same output valued at import prices. According to Johnson's estimates, the degree of protection (i.e., the percentage that the internal value of agricultural production exceeded the import value) ranged from over 50 per cent in Norway and Sweden to between 10 and 20 per cent in Belgium, Netherlands, France, and the United States.

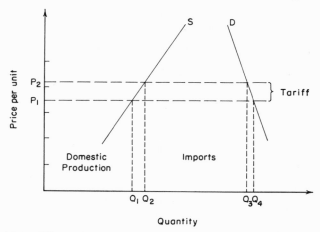

Figure 14-3. Effect of a tariff on domestic production, consumption, and imports

and consumers will reduce purchases to Q_3. These changes are usually referred to as the production and consumption effects of a tariff policy. If the import price remains the same, costs to consumers will rise by the full amount of the tariff and imports will decline from $Q_4 - Q_1$ to $Q_3 - Q_2$. Obviously, the flatter the slopes of the supply and demand curves, the more production and consumption are affected, and the greater is the reduction in imports. If only a small proportion of the total requirements are imported, even modest changes in the degree of protection can have a large impact on residual exporters.[6]

As long as some quantity is imported, tariffs have the additional advantage of creating a source of government revenue. Consumers

[6] The elasticity of demand for imports is often used to indicate the percentage effect on the quantity imported of a one per cent change in the import price (or the equivalent percentage effect on the internal price of a change in the tariff or an import quota). The elasticity of import demand can be high even though the price elasticities of demand and supply within the importing country are quite low. This is attributable to the fact that the elasticity of import demand is a multiple of the combined elasticities of domestic demand and supply in the importing country. The weights or multiples used to derive the import elasticity of demand are equal to the ratio of total consumption to imports for the domestic demand elasticity and the ratio of domestic production to imports for the internal supply elasticity. Assume imports make up one-fifth of the total supply and domestic production four-fifths and that the elasticity of domestic demand(E_d) is equal to -0.2 and domestic supply (E_s)

clearly pay the full cost of supporting agriculture if this is done through the use of tariffs or import restrictions. The same effect on prices as shown in Figure 14-3 could be obtained simply by restricting imports by means of a quota to the amount $Q_3 - Q_2$. In this case, however, the government would obtain no revenue. The benefits of higher prices would accrue to the exporting country granted the privilege of selling in this particular market. During the 1960's, only certain countries were permitted to ship butter to the United Kingdom, and the amount they could sell was restricted. This enabled selected dairy surplus–producing countries —notably Denmark, Ireland, New Zealand, and Australia—to obtain higher returns but restricted the volume they were permitted to sell. The United States has used a similar procedure to limit sugar imports. Selected countries have been granted quotas to export sugar to the United States where it is sold at prices higher than those normally prevailing in the residual or free market. During the 1960's, the countries who had been granted quotas obtained several hundred million dollars more for their sugar than they would have received if they had sold it elsewhere (Horton, 1970).

With a fixed or *ad valorem* tariff rate on imports of agricultural commodities, exporting countries can maintain the existing volume of sales simply by reducing their own export prices. If this occurs, the internal price may not increase or will rise less than the amount of the tariff. But if the importing country makes use of variable levies which are adjusted up or down to compensate for any change in import prices, there is no way (short of negotiating for a guaranteed share of the market) that exporters can increase sales. This type of protection was adopted by the original members of the European Common Market so as to assure their own farmers a

---

is equal to 0.15. The elasticity of import demand (E_i) is then equal to -1.6. Specifically,

$$E_i = \frac{consumption}{imports}\,(E_d) - \frac{production}{imports}\,(E_s) = \frac{5}{1}\,(-0.2) - \frac{4}{1}\,(0.15) = -1.6.$$

If only one-tenth of the total supply had been imported with the same internal elasticities, the import elasticity of demand would be still higher (-3.35).

guaranteed minimum price for grains and most livestock products. The variable levy system has been widely criticized by exporting nations, including the United States.

Government Purchases

Protectionist policies are not sufficient to maintain producer prices above equilibrium if potential supply exceeds demand at the support or guaranteed price. A country which produces surpluses above domestic needs, such as the United States, must then rely on some other method to maintain prices above equilibrium. Support prices have been made effective in the United States by offering farmers price-support loans or the opportunity to sell surplus commodities to the government (acting through the Commodity Credit Corporation). The price-support loan rate is, in effect, a buying price if the market price falls to the loan level. Farmers who comply with acreage restrictions or other supply-control measures are eligible to obtain price-support loans on storable commodities such as grains and cotton. Such loans need not be repaid. If a farmer does not repay his loan, the government simply takes title to the commodities pledged as security for the loan. Thus, commodities that cannot be sold at or above the loan rate eventually become the property of the government. The government also may acquire surplus commodities by direct purchases, as with dairy products. Any surplus stocks which the government acquires can be resold if the price rises at least 15 per cent above the loan rate. In addition, the government makes available surplus commodities to welfare recipients or public institutions in the United States and, under some circumstances, may donate them for relief overseas or sell them outside the normal channels of trade. Commodities which cannot be disposed of in this way are retained in storage.

The economic effects of a government purchase or acquisition program are illustrated in Figure 14-4. Assume the support price is maintained at P_2, which is above the equilibrium price P_1. In the absence of effective supply controls, an amount Q_2 will be produced in response to the favorable support price. In order to maintain the price at P_2, the government will have to acquire an amount represented by the shaded area, which is the difference between Q_2 and Q_1. Total consumer expenditures are represented by the unshaded rectangle ($P_2 \times Q_1$). Producers will receive the sum of what consumers spend plus the value of government purchases.

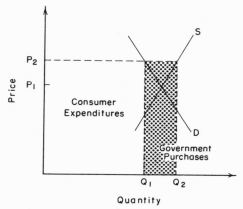

Figure 14-4. Consumer expenditures and government costs of supporting prices above equilibrium through a government purchase program

Initial government costs will depend on the price elasticity of demand, the level of support in relation to the equilibrium price, and the price elasticity of supply if production is uncontrolled or the effectiveness of control measures when an attempt is made to hold down production. The more elastic the demand and supply curves are, the higher the cost to the government of maintaining a given level of support. Ultimate losses incurred by the government depend on how long the commodities are held before being resold (or given away) and the recovery value of commodities which are sold. The government may even gain if demand shifts by more than enough to cover storage costs or a series of unfavorable crop years reduces production.[7] Storage and associated handling costs are relatively high, however, especially for semiperishable commodities like dairy products. They are lower for grains, but annual

[7] This occurred in the mid-1930's in the United States, for example, when two years of severe drought made it possible for the government to unload accumulated stocks. Surpluses acquired in the late 1930's were used to meet emergency needs during and immediately after World War II. Proponents of such programs argue that in an uncertain world in which drought or insect and disease damage may cut production or food aid demands may suddenly increase, it is desirable for the government to maintain emergency reserves.

costs may still amount to as much as 10 per cent of the initial value of commodities acquired. For this reason, the government is likely to incur losses on stored commodities if they must be held for several years before they can be sold.

Subsidized Consumption

Surpluses of farm products can be avoided, even if prices are maintained above free-market levels, provided the government is willing to subsidize domestic consumption or exports. This is equivalent to shifting the demand curve to the right. Producers generally prefer programs that make use of farm products rather than those that compel them to limit output. The welfare of certain nonfarm groups also may be enhanced by programs designed to increase consumption, such as the school lunch program and the food stamp plan.

The economic effects on producers of a domestic food-subsidy program depend on the amount of the subsidy and how it is spent, that is, whether it is used to buy additional food or more services. If the subsidy simply enables consumers to substitute public for private expenditures on food, their welfare is increased, but farmers do not gain. At least a part of the additional purchasing power made available under a domestic food-subsidy program is normally used to pay for packaging and marketing services rather than for more farm products. Any benefits accruing to agriculture also are likely to be distributed very unevenly among producers of different commodities. Only those producing commodities with relatively high income elasticities of demand such as meat, cheese, snack foods, and certain fruits and vegetables can expect to gain. Such programs offer little to those producing wheat, rice, dry beans, or cotton. Domestic food-subsidy programs can be used to improve nutrition and the welfare of certain consumer groups, but the benefits to agriculture are likely to be modest in relation to the total amount of public funds allocated to such programs.

Export subsidies have been more widely used than domestic food-subsidy programs in an effort to minimize or eliminate surpluses of farm products. The European Common Market countries have sought to dispose of surpluses of wheat and dairy products in this way, while the United States has, on a number of occasions, subsidized exports of grains and cotton or has offered these and other commodities under very favorable terms to food-deficit countries. Substantial quantities of U.S. surpluses of farm products have been disposed of since 1954 under the provisions of Public Law 480, sometimes known as the Food for Peace Act. This act authorizes the United States to sell surplus commodities under long-term credit arrangements or to donate commodities for relief in emergency situations. Competing exporting nations have raised objections to this program. To the degree that it has displaced normal commercial imports, competing exporting nations unquestionably have been disadvantaged; however, many of the countries benefiting from P.L. 480 shipments would not have been able to pay for commercial imports because of foreign exchange limitations. The use of export subsidies is quite rightly regarded as a form of unfair competition by low-cost countries who can compete on the basis of price but who cannot afford to subsidize their own exports.

Limiting Production or Sales

The government can hold prices above equilibrium levels in the short run simply by accumulating surpluses in storage, but unless additional outlets can be found, this becomes very expensive. In the long run, it is cheaper for the government to limit production, or even to pay farmers not to produce, rather than to purchase commodities and then attempt to dispose of them.

Supply-adjustment programs have been a major feature of agricultural support programs in the United States since the 1930's. In theory, the supply of any agricultural commodity can be limited simply by assigning each producer a sales or marketing quota with sufficiently high penalties to discourage anyone from exceeding the quota, but in practice, it has proven difficult to gain political support for sales quotas except for tobacco. Instead, the government has relied mainly on acreage-control or land-retirement programs in an attempt to curb production. It is much easier to administer an acreage-allotment or land-retirement program than to enforce sales quotas or to check on the use of other inputs. Land restrictions are relatively easy to police using maps and aerial photographs. But it is generally conceded that limiting the area of land that can be planted to certain crops is a relatively inefficient method of attempting to restrict production. Large areas of land must be held out of production to compensate for the fact that farmers will remove the poorest land first and use additional fertilizer plus other inputs to increase yields on the remaining acreage. An acreage-allotment or land-retirement program can effectively reduce production, but only if the acreage planted is cut back substantially.

Farmers benefit from reducing the output of a commodity only if the demand for that product is price inelastic. In the short run, the demand for most of the major crops produced in the United States is sufficiently inelastic so that returns can be increased by cutting back on production, or at least preventing production from rising as fast as it otherwise might. But, over a period of years, the demand for a controlled commodity may become more elastic as alternative sources of supply or substitute products are developed. Thus, an effective supply-control program ultimately may lead to a serious loss of markets, especially for commodities which are exported. Cotton is a good example of a commodity that has been adversely affected by the loss of markets, owing to persistent overpricing made possible by an effective supply control program. Other commodities such as wheat, tobacco, rice, and peanuts have been much less seriously affected than cotton.

Any additional revenue obtained by farmers under a supply-control program comes directly from consumers. Such programs, if effective, provide a relatively low-cost (from the standpoint of the government) means of raising farm prices and incomes, unless, of course, farmers are compensated for keeping land idle. If production or marketing limitations are sufficiently comprehensive and enforced, the government need not purchase any commodities. All that is required is that either total output or the amount sold be limited to whatever consumers will purchase at the support price (Q_1 in Figure 14-4). Producers obtain less total revenue under a sales-quota program than with a government-purchase or subsidized-consumption program, but the loss in revenue presumably would be offset in part by lower production costs since total output would be smaller. Farmers could be expected to purchase less fertilizer, gas, insecticides, and other inputs; marketing firms and handlers, likewise, would process, store, and transport a smaller volume. Thus, agribusiness firms supplying services to farmers would be adversely affected. This is the reason such firms usually are opposed to the adoption of effective supply-management programs.

Supply-control programs, if applied to only one or a few crops, can have undesirable consequences from the standpoint of producers of noncontrolled crops. Resources withheld from the production of wheat or corn, for example, may be used to produce other commodities. This is precisely what happened when acreage-allotment programs were reintroduced in the United States in the mid-1950's. Land formerly used to produce crops such as wheat and cotton was diverted to the production of grain sorghum, barley, and soybeans. Thus, a selective acreage-control program can lead to surpluses or depressed prices for other crops. A selective sales-quota program could have similar consequences. For example, if the amount of milk that could be sold were restricted, dairy farmers might use their excess forage supplies and grain to produce beef.

The secondary effects on other producers of selective acreage-control programs can be minimized by imposing comprehensive restrictions on all commodities or by adopting a general land-retirement program. Successive administrations have opted for the latter approach in the United States since the late 1950's. Opposition to limiting production has been minimized by making participation in supply-management programs voluntary and by paying farmers to keep part of their cropland idle. This gives farmers who want to plant additional land the option to do so, although they forego substantial cash benefits if they do not sign up to participate in the various programs that are offered. It has proven relatively expensive to attract sufficient participation to have any significant effect on total production; however, the programs adopted made it possible for the government to reduce excess stocks of wheat, feed grains, and cotton during the decade of the 1960's.

The benefits accruing to producers under a successful supply-control program tend to be capitalized into the value of the rights to produce or to sell the controlled commodity. Where acreage allotments or the right to receive payments go with the farm, the original owners of land with such rights reap most of the gains. The market price of the factor of production which is restricted rises because producers are willing to bid for the privilege of obtaining the right to higher returns. This applies equally well to allotments, bases, or marketing quotas. The capitalization problem, of course, is a feature of all programs in which the rights to obtain higher returns are restricted and negotiable. By restricting land rather than labor, supply-control programs in the United States have contributed more to raising land values over the past three decades than they have to raising labor incomes.

Deficiency Payments

By making use of compensatory or deficiency payments, it is possible to maintain above-equilibrium prices to producers while permitting market prices to fall to whatever level is necessary to equate production and consumption. The government is responsible for making up the difference between market-clearing prices and those guaranteed to farmers. Storage, handling, and disposal problems are eliminated. Consumers benefit from increased supplies of commodities and lower market prices, but some families will pay more in taxes. In contrast to supply-control programs, deficiency payments make the cost of supporting agriculture a visible item in the government's budget. If the money to finance deficiency payments is raised through a progressive income tax, low-income groups benefit at the expense of upper-income families.

One of the obvious advantages of shifting away from support methods which keep market prices high to a method involving deficiency payments is avoiding the loss of markets. This is particularly important for those products faced with close substitutes as well as those which must compete with imports or exports from other suppliers.

The economic effects of an unlimited deficiency-payment program (i.e., one with no restrictions imposed either on production or on the total amount of money that can be paid to an individual producer) are illustrated in Figure 14-5. Assume the price guaranteed to producers (P_3) is above the equilibrium price (P_2). Total supply is determined by the point at which the guaranteed price intersects the supply schedule. The total amount produced (Q_2) is then placed on the market and will be consumed at a price P_1.

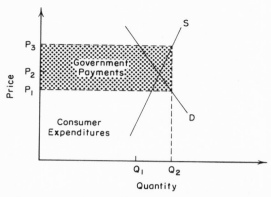

Figure 14-5. Consumer prices and expenditures and government costs of supporting farm prices above equilibrium by making deficiency payments

Under these circumstances, the government will be obligated to make payments equal to the difference between P_3 and P_1 on each unit sold. Total government costs are represented by the shaded area in Figure 14-5. Consumers pay below-equilibrium prices while producers receive above-equilibrium returns. Thus, in a sense, both producers and consumers are subsidized out of general tax revenue. Consumers obtain more for less money than they would spend for food if producer prices were supported by government purchases or a supply-control program.

A deficiency-payment program is likely to cost the government more than any of the alternative methods of supporting prices that have been discussed, although this will not always be true. For a given level of support, the cost of a deficiency-payment program depends on the elasticities of demand and supply. If the supply curve is elastic so that producers respond to the guaranteed price by adding substantially to total output, and if the demand is price inelastic, much lower prices are required to induce consumers to purchase the added output. On the other hand, if the supply function is relatively price inelastic and the demand function elastic, it is less expensive for the government to place the added volume on the market and make deficiency payments than to hold up market prices by purchasing whatever quantities could not be sold at the guaranteed price (Schickele, 1954, pp. 217–221, and Shepherd, 1952, pp. 216–227). The cost of a purchase program, as previously discussed, is equal to $Q_2 - Q_1$ multiplied by the support or guaranteed price. With the slopes of the demand and supply schedules shown in Figure 14-5, it would be cheaper to purchase the required volume of commodities than to make deficiency payments, but with a steeper supply curve and a flatter demand curve, the relative costs would be reversed. In general, for a given level of support, the more elastic the demand schedule, the lower is the cost of a deficiency-payment scheme relative to a purchase program.

The government's liability under a deficiency-payment program can be limited in a number of ways. For example, payments can be restricted to something less than 100 per cent of the total output of each farm or to an individually assigned farm base or quota. If payments are limited in this way, the marginal price (which in turn affects the willingness of producers to increase supply) becomes the actual market price, not the guaranteed price. Thus, a payment program limited to a fixed base is likely to lead to a smaller increase in output than is an unrestricted payment program.

Few governments have been willing to offer unlimited deficiency payments to producers. In the United States, payments made under programs adopted in the 1960's have been tied to supply-control measures, except for those made under the wool support program. Only those farmers who plant within their allotments or agree to keep a certain proportion of their cropland idle have been eligible to receive payments. The purpose of these payments has been twofold: first, to compensate farmers for lower loan rates; and second, to induce farmers to participate in voluntary supply-management programs. Thus, they have not been "pure" deficiency-payment programs but rather a means of buying adjustments in production.

For food-deficit countries that want to protect home agriculture or increase their degree of self-sufficiency, a deficiency-payment scheme has a number of advantages over tariffs or import quotas. Domestic production can be encouraged by making payments to producers above the prices of imported goods, but consumers continue to benefit from the relatively low market prices at which commodities can be imported. Exporters are less adversely affected by a deficiency-payment scheme than by tariffs or import quotas, since consumption is not reduced; they will, however, lose markets insofar as domestic production expands in response to the guaranteed prices. This method of supporting domestic agriculture was used in the United Kingdom prior to its entry into the Common Market.

Conclusions

Government intervention in agriculture now takes many forms. In most instances, governments have attempted to maintain prices above equilibrium levels, either to encourage production or to improve the incomes of farmers. In the United States, support programs have been used successfully to transfer income from the nonfarm sector of the economy to agriculture. Such programs also have contributed to the growth of output, and, by providing farmers with additional income, have enabled them to make productive investments leading to increases in efficiency. This has provided some long-run benefits to consumers, although such programs clearly have held prices above where they otherwise might have been in the short run.

While income unquestionably can be transferred to agriculture by supporting prices, most economists would argue that this is not the most efficient or socially desirable means of improving the welfare of the farm population. The benefits of support programs usually are distributed among farmers roughly in proportion to sales, which means that a high proportion of the gains go to the larger farms. Few low-income farmers are likely to be liberated from poverty by programs which result in raising the average level of farm prices. Furthermore, the benefits of farm programs tend to be capitalized into the value of farms. Thus, subsequent landowners may be no better off with higher product prices than they would be with lower prices.

The effects on welfare and government costs of maintaining farm prices above equilibrium depend on: (1) the level of support; (2) the mechanism used to make supports effective; (3) the price elasticity of supply, unless production is controlled; and (4) the price elasticity of demand. The social costs of overpricing farm products are likely to be less serious if the supply and demand curves are relatively inelastic than if they are elastic. The allocation of resources is not seriously distorted and welfare losses to society are modest if neither consumption nor production is materially altered by raising prices.[8] Under such conditions, prices can be maintained above equilibrium by either a supply-control program or a government purchase and diversion program at a cost to the treasury which is low in relation to the amount of money transferred to agriculture.

Countries that are residual suppliers of farm products on world markets are among those who have been most seriously affected by the widespread adoption of national support policies. Partly in response to these policies, a number of countries have made efforts to raise the prices of commodities they export, including coffee, sugar, and wheat, by entering into international commodity agreements. Thus, even export prices of many farm products are now influenced by government intervention.

References

Campbell, Keith O. 1964. "National Commodity Stabilization Schemes: Some Reflections Based on Australian Experience," *International Explorations of Agricultural Economics.* Ed. Roger N. Dixey. Ames, Iowa: Iowa State Univ. Press. Pp. 55–63.

Cochrane, Willard W. 1965. *The City Man's Guide to the Farm Problem.* Minneapolis: Univ. of Minnesota Press.

Eckstein, S., and M. Syrquin. 1971. "A Note on Fluctuations in Supply and Farmers' Income," *Am. J. Ag. Econ.,* 53:331–334.

Gislason, Conrad. 1959. "How Much Has the Canadian Wheat Board Cost the Canadian Farmers?" *J. Farm Econ.,* 41:584–599.

Hallett, Graham. 1968. *The Economics of Agricultural Policy.* Oxford: Basil Blackwell.

Horton, Donald C. 1970. "Policy Directions for the United States Sugar Program," *Am. J. Ag. Econ.,* 52:185–196.

Johnson, D. Gale. 1947. *Forward Prices for Agriculture.* Chicago: Univ. of Chicago Press.

———. 1964. "Agriculture and Foreign Economic Policy," *J. Farm Econ.,*

[8] At least some of the welfare costs of overpricing farm products can be neutralized or offset by using nonprice allocative mechanisms to limit supply and by subsidizing consumption. For an excellent discussion of the concept of welfare costs applied to agricultural support programs and the relative social costs of alternative support methods, see Wallace, 1962.

46:915–929. Reprinted in *Agricultural Policy in an Affluent Society*. Ed. Vernon W. Ruttan *et al.* New York: W. W. Norton and Co., 1969. Pp. 264–281.

Krishna, Raj. 1967. "Agricultural Price Policy and Economic Development," *Agricultural Development and Economic Growth*. Ed. H. M. Southworth and B. F. Johnston. Ithaca, N.Y.: Cornell Univ. Press. Pp. 497–540.

McCrone, Gavin. 1962. *The Economics of Subsidising Agriculture*. London: George Allen and Unwin Ltd.

Myrdal, Gunnar. 1968. *Asian Drama*, Vol. III. New York: Pantheon. Appendix 5, pp. 2031–2039.

Robinson, K. L. 1970. "Commodity Policies and Programs," *Contours of Change*. 1970 Yearbook of Agriculture, USDA. Pp. 117–123.

Schickele, Rainer. 1954. *Agricultural Policy: Farm Programs and National Welfare*, New York: McGraw-Hill.

Shepherd, Geoffrey S. 1952. *Agricultural Price and Income Policy*. Ames, Iowa: Iowa State College Press.

Thomsen, Frederick L., and Richard J. Foote. 1952. *Agricultural Prices*. 2d ed. New York: McGraw-Hill.

Tweeten, Luther G. 1969. "Commodity Programs for Agriculture," Technical Paper prepared for the National Advisory Commission on Food and Fiber, Reprinted in *Agricultural Policy in An Affluent Society*. Ed. Vernon W. Ruttan, *et al.* New York: W. W. Norton and Co. Pp. 99–115.

USDA. 1970. *Major Statistical Series of the U.S. Department of Agriculture*, Vol. 1: *Agricultural Prices and Parity*. Ag. Hb. 365.

Wallace, T. D. 1962. "Measures of Social Costs of Agricultural Programs," *J. Farm Econ.*, 44:580–594.

Waugh, Frederick V. 1944. "Does the Consumer Benefit from Price Instability?" *Quart. J. Econ.*, 48:602–614.

IV

INTRODUCTION TO
EMPIRICAL PRICE ANALYSIS

Two subjects are stressed in this section: (1) the formulation of models to explain the behavior of agricultural product prices or related variables and (2) the use and appraisal of the results of quantitative price analyses. Our intent is to provide sufficient discussion of model building to show how the economic principles presented in the earlier part of the book can be combined with statistical methods to produce useful empirical results. In addition, an objective is to enable the student to understand and interpret empirical studies. We do not present a formal discussion of statistical inference, although some prior background in statistics, particularly in regression analysis, would be helpful. Excellent references in econometrics are available.

CHAPTER 15

Background for
Price Analysis

The term "price analysis" usually refers to the quantitative study of demand-supply-price relationships. Much of price analysis is simply applied econometrics.[1] However, quantitative analyses may range from the construction of tables and graphs to the use of a variety of rather advanced mathematical tools. No attempt is made here to survey all available quantitative methods.

Two reasons for engaging in price analysis are (1) to estimate specific economic coefficients (parameters) such as price and income elasticities of demand and (2) to provide forecasts of prices or the variables affecting prices. As mentioned in previous chapters, estimates of elasticities are necessary to determine the effects of alternative policies such as a supply-control program. Forecasting is the objective of an important part of the price analysis work done by the U.S. Department of Agriculture, by extension economists in land-grant universities, and by economic research departments in private industry. In addition, price analysis is sometimes used simply to describe the behavior of prices and related variables. For example, one may want to determine whether or not

[1] Econometric techniques found rather early and wide use in agricultural economics, particularly in the estimation of demand and price relationships. Henry L. Moore (1914; 1917) is considered to be the founder of statistical estimation of economic relationships. Over the past 50 years, a large literature has developed with much of today's research firmly based on the pioneering research of the 1920's and 1930's (e.g., Schultz, 1938; Warren and Pearson, 1928; H. Working, 1922). A paper by Haavelmo (1943) produced a major change in econometrics in the 1940's. Both techniques and empirical results are discussed in Foote, 1958; Fox, 1953; Johnston, 1972; Stone, 1954; and Wonnacott and Wonnacott, 1970.

there are persistent trends, cycles, or other regularities in the price series.

This chapter is devoted to a discussion of alternative techniques of analysis, procedures in formulating models, sources of data, and the identification problem. More detail concerning the interpretation and use of results will be presented in the next chapter. This should enable the student to see the relationship between certain economic principles outlined earlier and empirical work. We hope that this will also help the student to gain an appreciation of the complexities of price analysis as well as some of the uses and limitations of statistical studies based on time-series data.

Alternate Techniques

Some individuals appear to have the ability to judge events qualitatively without the aid of formal methods of analysis, but it usually helps to have at hand the results of quantitative studies. Quantitative approaches to price analysis are emphasized in this book, but of course judgment is important in all types of analysis. Among other advantages, quantitative studies serve the purpose of making relationships among variables explicit.

A common type of quantitative analysis is based on persistent patterns of behavior in time-series data. Thus, price forecasts might be based on observed trends, seasonals, or cycles. One of the simplest approaches in forecasting is to assume that the recent past trend will continue in the immediate future. Other models could be based on the assumption of a changing rate of change, such as a diminishing rate of increase in production. Graphic methods provide a simple means of identifying trends or other persistent patterns of behavior. The most common procedure is to graph the variable of interest (such as price) on the vertical axis with time on the horizontal axis. In this way, the behavior of the variable through time can be observed (Figure 15-1). Of course, linear trend lines, harmonic functions, and so forth may be fitted or moving averages computed. These relatively simple procedures often yield surprisingly accurate forecasts for the short run. But, forecasts based on trends miss all of the turning points (changes of direction) for the variable. Such changes can be extremely impor-

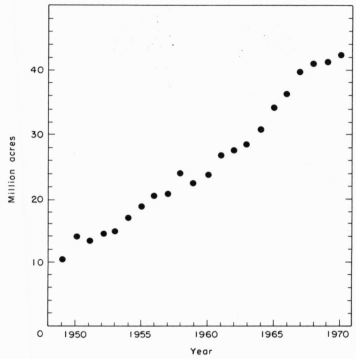

Figure 15-1. Acreage harvested, soybeans, United States, 1949–1970. Data from U.S. Dept. of Agriculture, *Agricultural Statistics 1971*, p. 132.

tant in economics. The simpler techniques of analyzing patterns of behavior in time-series observations (trends, seasonal indexes, and moving averages) are developed in numerous introductory text-books in statistics.

The "balance-sheet approach" is sometimes used by private business firms to summarize information which will help to indicate whether surpluses or deficits in supplies are likely to exist in the forthcoming year if current prices prevailed (see Ashby, 1964). Thus, an informed judgment can be made about whether or not prices in the future are going to rise or fall from current levels. The technique is essentially a method of organizing large quantities of data, especially for important farm commodities in international trade. The accuracy of the method depends mainly on the judgment and experience of the user.

A third quantitative approach to price analysis is to consider the relationships among variables.[2] Demand and supply functions are examples of particular economic relationships. Relationships among variables might be examined graphically, or they may be explicitly estimated by statistical methods. Scatter diagrams, which show relationships visually, are often a useful preliminary step in the analysis.

Regression analysis provides a method of estimating relationships among variables. A multiple linear regression equation considers the net relationship between each explanatory variable (X) and a dependent variable (Y). Specifically,

$$Y_t = \beta_0 + \beta_1 X_{t1} + \beta_2 X_{t2} + \ldots + \beta_K X_{tK} + e_t,$$

where Y_t = observable dependent variable,
X_{tk} = observable independent variables, K in number,
e_t = unobservable error or disturbance term,
β_k = unknown population parameters to be estimated,
and $t = 1, 2, \ldots, T$ observations on the variables.

The equation states that Y_t depends linearly on the observed X_{tk} and on the unobserved disturbances e_t. One statistical problem is to estimate the parameters $(\beta\text{'s})$ given the observations on the variables in the equations. Naturally, an estimation technique which provides "good" estimates is desired, and ordinary least squares is a commonly used method. The appropriate technique, however, depends on how the observations on Y_t and X_{tk} are generated (see Johnston, 1972, chapters 3 and 5; Wonnacott and Wonnacott, 1970, chapter 3).

The analyst must specify the variables in the equation and the logical relationship among the variables, obtain the observations on the variables, estimate the coefficients $(\beta\text{'s})$, and appraise and use the results. It may, of course, require more than one equation to describe and analyze a particular problem.

[2] Other quantitative techniques available to economists include operations research methods like linear programming. We concentrate on the formulation and use of simple econometric models, but this does not imply that other approaches are poorer methods of analysis. Each has its place, depending on the problem to be analyzed.

Getting Started

Some General Comments

The first step in model specification is problem definition. For example, the growers of a particular commodity may want to know whether or not a supply-control program might raise their income. Hence, the analyst would need to test the hypothesis that the demand for the commodity is price inelastic in the relevant range of prices—one of the requirements for the proposed program to raise total revenue.

The second step in the analysis is to formulate a model that is oriented toward solving the stated problem. The model should be consistent with the logic and theory underlying the commodity sector being analyzed. The term "model" implies some abstraction from the real world. A model of a particular economic sector may be thought of as one or more equations that describe the important relationships among the variables.

Model building may be viewed as having two parts. One involves the specification of the economic model, that is, the general economic relationships. Economic theory can be thought of in terms of functions and certain variables within these functions. The second part of model building involves the explicit definition of equations which are to be estimated. For example, what variables appear in a particular equation, and how are these variables explicitly defined? Is the relationship linear or nonlinear? Out of the answers to these and other similar questions, explicit equations are defined.

Given the equations to be estimated, the next step is to obtain observations on the variables and to estimate the coefficients which relate the variables. In practice, the specification of the equations to be estimated is likely to be influenced by the data available. The final step in analysis is to evaluate and use the results. The evaluation includes appropriate statistical and logical "tests." The use of results may include computation of elasticities, preparation of forecasts, and so forth.

There are perhaps three requirements for doing a good job of price analysis. First, a good knowledge of economic theory aids the researcher in model formulation. Second, the analyst needs to have a thorough knowledge of the economic sector being analyzed. This helps to provide specific details for the model, prevent errors, and correctly interpret the results. A third requirement is a good knowledge of statistical principles and methods, which is essential for correct estimation and hypothesis testing.

Economic Models—Some Elementary Examples

Economic theory suggests the general types of functions that may be appropriate for a particular research problem and also the economic variables that should appear in each equation. For example, in a demand relation, quantity is assumed to be a function of the commodity's own price, the prices of substitutes, income, and perhaps other variables. Theory also often suggests how these variables are related. The commodity's quantity and price are expected to be inversely related (negative sign); income and quantity would be positively related for most products. Theory typically does not tell us the precise functional relationship among variables, nor does it specify the magnitude of the coefficients which relate one variable to another. Thus, while price and quantity demanded are inversely related, we do not know whether a straight line or a curvilinear relationship is most appropriate.

To illustrate the use of models, we begin with a simple model of competitive price determination using linear demand and supply functions. The static equilibrium situation, which simultaneously determines price and quantity, can be defined by two equations with the third equation specifying that quantity demanded must equal quantity supplied in equilibrium.

$$Q_t^d = \alpha - \beta\, P_t \text{ (demand equation)}.$$
$$Q_t^s = \delta + \gamma\, P_t \text{ (supply equation)}.$$
$$Q_t^d = Q_t^s.$$

The subscript t indicates that P and Q are observed within some specific time period.

The first modification to make the model more realistic would be to permit changes in supply and demand, that is, shifts in these functions. For instance, assume R is a variable, say rainfall, which influences the level of supply but which is not in turn influenced by supply. Given these assumptions, the supply equation can be re-written as

$$Q_t^s = \delta + \gamma \, P_t + \pi \, R_t.$$

As R increases the level of Q increases and vice versa (Figure 15-2). Other supply shifters may include variables like factor prices and technology.

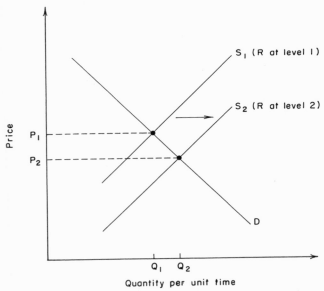

Figure 15-2. Changes in price and quantity as the result of changes in the variable R

Other elements of realism may come from the analyst's personal knowledge. Theory does not exhaust the factors that explain the level of supply in a particular time period, but hopefully theory does include the important, systematic variables influencing sup-ply. There also may be "random" or "special" factors (e.g., a dis-ease affecting yields) which have an impact on supply. If e_t is set equal to these disturbances or equation errors, then the supply equation can be rewritten as

(1) $Q_t^s = \delta + \gamma P_t + \pi R_t + e_t.$

In addition, total supply may equal production in the current period, stocks carried over from the previous period, and net imports. That is,

(2) $S_t = Q_t^s + C_t + I_t,$

where   S = total supply
         Q = current production
         C = carryover stocks
         I = imports.

It may be appropriate to have separate equations to explain Q, C, and I, rather than one equation to explain S. Again, this comes from the analyst's special knowledge of the economic sector rather than from economic theory.

In the terminology of econometrics, equation (1) is an example of a behavioral equation. Demand, consumption, and investment functions are other examples of behavioral equations. They contain parameters to be estimated, and since they are not exact functions, a disturbance term (designated e_t) is added. Equation (2) is a definitional equation. It is an exact relationship. Just as one plus one equals two, we are saying in equation (2) that by definition total supply equals the sum of current production, carryover stocks, and net imports.

Returning to the model depicted in Figure 15-2, the equations are (ignoring the disturbances for the moment):

(3) $Q_t^d = \alpha - \beta P_t$
(4) $Q_t^s = \delta + \gamma P_t + \pi R_t$
(5) $Q_t^d = Q_t^s.$

If the model is a correct approximation of the real world, then price does not determine quantity nor does quantity determine price; rather the two are simultaneously determined within time period t. When R changes, both P and Q change, and over a discrete time interval, P and Q interact to determine the new equilibrium. Price influences quantity and quantity is influencing price.

If this takes place within time t, then P and Q are, in effect, simultaneously or jointly determined. In this oversimplified model, the different levels of P and Q are generated by the shifts in supply resulting from changes in R. The variable R is assumed to be determined by outside conditions. If R is rainfall, then its level is determined by hydrological factors and certainly not by P and Q.

Equations (3), (4), and (5) form a simple simultaneous equations model. The variables that are simultaneously determined are called jointly determined or endogenous variables. Their values are determined simultaneously within the sector being studied. Variables that influence the endogenous variables but whose own level is determined by factors entirely outside the economic sector under consideration are called exogenous variables. In our illustration, R is exogenous, and P and Q are endogenous.

The cobweb model exemplifies a recursive system of equations such as those presented in the appendix to Chapter 9. In a recursive system, the endogenous variables are determined sequentially as a chain through time rather than simultaneously. In the cobweb model, quantity supplied in t is hypothesized to be a function of lagged price (not current price). The level of price in the previous period is determined by events at that time; it is a lagged endogenous variable. Exogenous and lagged endogenous variables are grouped under the general heading of predetermined variables.

The parameters of equations in a recursive system often can be appropriately estimated by a simpler method than the analogous parameters in a simultaneous model. Fortunately, a recursive model is appropriate for numerous agricultural commodities. A supply equation which is part of a recursive system, for example, can be treated as a single equation without specifying the other equations in the model.[3] Thus, in general, when an equation can be considered part of a recursive system, some useful simplifications in specification and estimation are often possible.

[3] The analyst must decide whether or not single equation procedures are appropriate for his particular problem. If price and quantity are simultaneously determined within the time period covered by each observation, then the demand equation cannot be ignored, though the main interest is in the supply equation. The simultaneity in the determination of price and quantity should be taken into account in estimating the supply relation. A discussion of methods for estimating equations which are part of a simultaneous system are discussed in standard econometrics textbooks (e.g., Johnston, 1972, chapter 12).

Diagrams

The economic structure of agricultural commodities is more complex than the elementary models discussed so far. But the important economic relationships can be clarified through the use of a diagram. Rectangles represent variables; sometimes circles are used to represent price. Arrows show the direction of influence among variables (one-way or two-way), with heavy lines indicating the major paths of influence and dashed lines indicating the negligible or occasional paths.

A diagram for a simple recursive model is illustrated in Figure 15-3. In this illustration, production is determined by lagged endog-

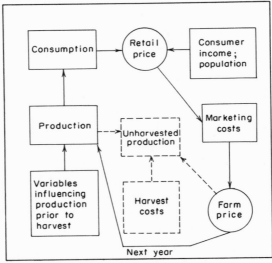

Figure 15-3.   Simplified demand-supply structure for perishable commodity

enous and exogenous variables (the one-way arrows). The commodity is perishable; no stocks exist; consumption depends solely on the level of production. Usually, the quantity produced is consumed, but occasionally prices may be so low relative to harvesting costs that a part of the crop is abandoned (the dashed lines). Retail price is depicted as a function of the quantity available for consumption and certain demand variables. The one-way arrow from income to price is technically not correct. The level of national income depends on prices and quantities of sales. Assuming that the product in question is a small proportion of the national economy, income is often treated as a predetermined variable.[4]

A diagram such as Figure 15-3 summarizes the analyst's knowledge, and of course the diagram is no better than the information going into it. The model would be more complicated if the product could be used in alternative ways. Producers may have a choice in selling their crop for fresh use or for processing. Under these circumstances, quantities sold for different uses and the corresponding prices would be simultaneously determined although total output would still be predetermined by past events.

The scatter diagram (Figure 15-4) is a particularly useful tool in price analysis. It is relatively easy to construct and read, and it can help answer questions such as the following: Are changes in prices associated mainly with one variable such as changes in volume? Does the relationship appear to be linear or curvilinear? Is there evidence of systematic shifts in demand? When time-series data are used, it is useful to label each dot so as to see any systematic changes associated with the passage of time.

In Figure 15-4, we have added linear regression lines for three subperiods to highlight the shifts in the price-quantity relationship for pork. The backward shift from 1955–1959 to 1960–1965 is perhaps partly the result of increased availability of substitutes, such as beef and broilers, at lower prices.

The scatter diagram depicts the simple relationship between two variables, but as we shall see, the "net" relationship between two variables, after taking account of the influence of other variables, differs from the simple two-variable relationship. Thus, while the two-dimensional diagram is a very useful tool, it is also subject to misuse.

Data Sources

In economics, the observations on variables typically are *not* generated by a formal experiment.[5] Rather, economic behavior is re-

[4] Klein (1962, p. 69) points out that the absolute size of the error made by using this assumption may be small but that the relative bias can be large.

[5] In an experiment, if $Y = f(X)$, then the experimenter can control X and observe the outcome Y. Occasionally, an economist can rely on an experiment to generate data for a specific problem.

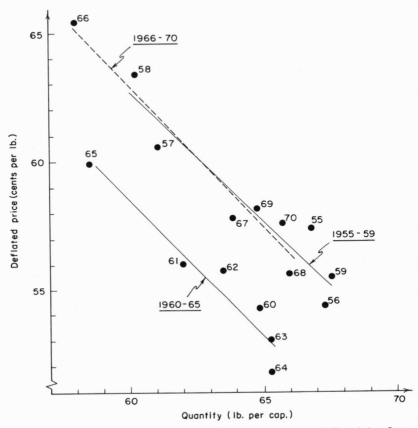

Figure 15-4. Relationship between retail price of pork deflated by Consumer Price Index and consumption of pork, United States, 1955–1970.
Computed from data in *Livestock and Meat Statistics,* USDA Stat. Bul. No.
333 (1963), tables 201 and 212, and subsequent annual supplements.

flected in various nonexperimental data sources. Such data are the
outcome of the many complex interactions of the real world.

Two major types of data are used in economic analyses: time
series and cross section. Time-series data are sums or averages collected with the passage of time, e.g., monthly or annual average
prices. The use of time-series data is emphasized here because such
data are the cheapest and most readily available observations for
most economic analyses. Cross-section observations are obtained
from some population at a point in time. For instance, a sample of

households in New York State might be interviewed over a short period of time with the objective of obtaining observations on household income, other household characteristics, and expenditures on various items.

Regardless of the source, the analyst should become thoroughly acquainted with the data, including the sources and methods used to constuct the series. For example, how is beef "consumption" computed?[6] It is also important to make sure that the series being used accurately reflects the desired concept. If the objective is to develop a price-forecasting equation for apples used in processing, one should not use the average prices based on combined fresh and processing sales.

Agencies compiling data sometimes change the definition of a variable or the method of obtaining and computing it. For instance, the states included in a particular region might be changed, and consequently the production reported for a commodity in this region would change. Obviously, the reason for the change in production is a change in definition of the region and has nothing to do with the economics of supply. Therefore, an analysis of production in this region could be very misleading unless the analyst were familiar with the change in definition.

In another example, the "marketings" of cattle and calves in the United States have exceeded "production" by about 10 billion pounds in recent years (Statistical Reporting Service, 1971, p. 30, table 40). The casual user who did not examine the definitions of these variables might assume that production (by his intuitive usage of the term) exceeds marketings. The careful user would study the definitions of both variables to determine the one appropriate for the analysis.

If more than two sources exist for the observations on a particular variable, then the most recent source should be used. It presumably contains any recent revisions. Thus, in obtaining data, the analyst should start with the most recent source and work back as necessary, checking, where possible, for consistency in the different

[6] The USDA does not conduct a survey to measure consumption directly. Rather, data on beginning inventories, domestic production, exports and imports, and ending inventories are used to compute "domestic disappearance" during a given time period. This quantity is assumed to be "consumed."

sources. Observations issued by a particular agency, say the Bureau of the Census, may be reprinted in a variety of other sources. It is usually a good policy to go to the original source to obtain the observations.

The Identification Problem

Assume the problem is to estimate a market demand function based on annual observations. The data are nonexperimental time-series observations. Thus, price is an annual average and quantity is an annual total for each year. The price may be viewed as an average equilibrium price and quantity as the equilibrium quantity exchanged. In this example, the identification problem is whether or not a demand equation can be estimated from the observed prices and quantities. It is possible to compute coefficients that relate price and quantity, but the question is whether the coefficients obtained really are estimates of the true demand coefficients. This is not an easy question to answer. The discussion which follows assumes that a competitive market structure is appropriate.

If the economy were perfectly static, then the observed outcome would be a single price and quantity—the point of equilibrium. In this case, it would be impossible to estimate either a demand or a supply function since an infinite number of curves could be constructed to go through the equilibrium point.

With the passage of time, supply and demand functions are expected to change (shift), and these changes may help identify one or the other or both of the relations. However, this is not guaranteed because these average equilibrium points may form a "shotgun pattern" (Figure 15-5), and without specific information on how the pattern was generated, neither relationship can be inferred from the data. In other words, the scatter of observations may have been the result of many combinations of changes in demand and supply. These changes "do not carry any labels accommodating to analysts which explain whether they were due to demand forces or supply forces" (Breimyer, 1961, p. 56). This means that additional information must be obtained (or assumed) about how the observations were generated.

If the demand curve shifted through time and the supply curve

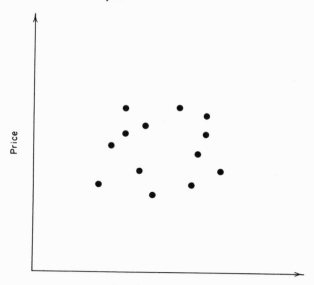

Figure 15-5.   Scatter diagram with no identifiable relationship

remained stable, then the observations trace out a supply curve (Figure 15-6). If the supply curve shifts (either for systematic or random reasons) and the demand curve remains stable, then the observations would trace out a demand curve (similar to Figure 15-2). The additional information necessary to achieve identification in these cases is the knowledge that one function is stable while the other is changing (E. Working, 1927).

However, even if the observations form a definite pattern on a scatter diagram, it is still possible that neither function can be identified. This occurs if the shifts in the functions are highly or perfectly correlated, as they might be if both were shifting to the right through time with changes in population and technology. In Figure 15-7, the shifts in the functions are negatively correlated; the observations form a negative slope; but the function connecting the dots clearly is not a demand function.

Thus, (1) if the demand function is relatively stable and the supply function shifts and (2) if the shifts in the two functions are not highly correlated, then the demand function is identified. An anal-

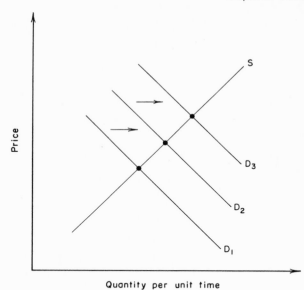

Figure 15-6. A supply relation identified

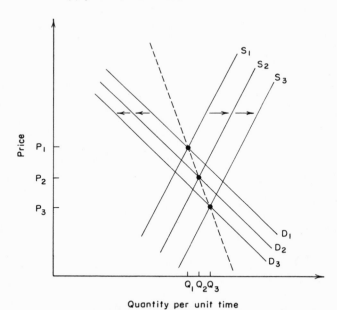

Figure 15-7. Correlated changes in supply and demand and neither a supply nor a demand curve identified

ogous argument can be made for the identifiability of the supply equation.

The preceding discussion is based on the simplest possible simultaneous equations model. With more complex models, the question of whether or not the equations in the model are identified is handled in an explicit mathematical fashion (see Johnston, 1972, chapter 12; Wonnacott and Wonnacott, 1970, chapter 8).[7]

The identification problem is a general one in the estimation of economic relationships, but it is in simultaneous-equations models that the identification problem is explicitly considered. The question of identification also arises for equations in a recursive system. Fortunately, equations in a "true" recursive system are identifiable, and the question of identification typically is not explicitly considered (however, see Klein, 1962, pp. 75–81). Thus, assuming current supply is solely dependent on lagged price and other predetermined variables, estimates of the coefficients relating these variables (using an appropriate technique) are estimates of the true supply coefficients. This means that as long as the equations considered subsequently can be viewed as part of a recursive system, they are identified.

Equations in a Recursive System

The price structure for some agricultural commodities is best represented by a recursive model. As previously discussed, current production is a function of lagged prices as well as exogenous factors, and this quantity, once produced, is a principal factor determining current price. Annually produced crops often fall within this framework. Fox's research (1953) suggests that the supply of certain types of livestock also is largely predetermined for any given year. For example, on January 1, the number of pigs in various age categories is known and fixed. The size of the coming

[7] Identification is achieved through knowledge about the explicit predetermined variables which are "shifters" in the various functions. We argued that identification might be achieved if one function changed relative to the other and if these changes were uncorrelated. This is typically achieved when the functions have different predetermined variables. For instance, in Figure 15-2, R is assumed to be a systematic predetermined variable in the supply equation, and these shifts in supply trace out a demand function.

spring pig crop also can be estimated and essentially is fixed by the number of sows already bred. Thus, the quantity of hogs marketed in one year is largely predetermined by the events of the previous year.

Recursive models, if applicable to a problem, are appealing. The parameters of the model are identifiable, and generally the relatively simple method of least squares can be used to estimate the parameters. Thus, we turn to some details of specifying equations. Numerous decisions must be made by the analyst in building a model. We can only convey information about the types of decisions to be made, but no precise guides exist to determine "the" appropriate model. Model building is partly an art which must be refined by experience, and the correctness of a particular model depends on the objectives of the analysis.

Market-Supply Equations

The complex, chainlike process of production in agriculture permits substantial latitude in building supply equations. Careful definition of terms is essential. Total supply in a specific time period may depend not only on current production but also on carryover stocks and imports and exports. The analyst may wish to develop separate equations to explain storage stocks and net imports. In this section, we concentrate on equations relating to current production.

Production in a given time period equals yield per unit multiplied by the number of units. Units may be acres or animal numbers. For instance, total milk production equals the number of producing cows multiplied by average pounds of milk per cow. Thus, while the analyst may consider making total production dependent in one equation, it may be more appropriate to consider yields and units separately in two or more equations. Using total production as the dependent variable is simpler since only one equation is involved, but some detail is lost in the process. There are often several measures of production, including total production, harvested production, and sales to particular markets (e.g., for fresh or for processing uses). Total production presumably is not related to current price because of the lag in the production process. However, current price may influence quantities harvested or allocated to various uses.

The producer usually has more control over units (say, acres) than over yields. Thus, acres planted (sows farrowing, etc.) is often used as the dependent variable in analyzing producers' supply response to various factors. Yields, on the other hand, may be largely influenced by factors which the producer cannot control (moisture, temperatures, pests). Some factors, like level of fertility, can be controlled, but yield equations typically are difficult to specify, and they frequently exhibit strong underlying trends.

We especially consider, then, equations which explain units like acres or cow numbers. The general nature of the independent variables is suggested, in part, by theory. The product's price, the prices of other products competing for the same production resources, and input prices are logical explanatory variables, but with the substantial lag between the decision to produce and the actual realization of production, a problem exists in specifically defining the price variables to which producers respond. One hypothesis is that production responds to expected prices and costs and that expectations are based on current or recent experience. Thus, assuming the dependent variable is acres planted in the current time period, then the independent variables for prices and costs typically are those for the previous year. Other hypotheses about the appropriate definition of variables, of course, are possible. Prices lagged two or more periods also might be considered; other alternatives include some weighted average of past prices or perhaps prices of contracts for future delivery of the product.

Two considerations in specifying the time lag between prices and quantity are the units of time (month, year, etc.) in which the variables are observed and the actual biological lag in the production process. There are clearly differences in the speed of response possible in egg production on the one hand and milk on the other. Producers in both cases can control the rate of culling from existing herds or flocks rather quickly, but new additions to producing units can be made much faster for chickens than for cows.

Equation specification must emphasize the major factors thought to influence supply. It is not possible to include an exhaustive set of variables. For instance, the price of a single major input or an index of input prices is commonly used to represent costs. The price of corn in a pork supply equation represents the major input in pork production. Similarly, prices of one or two major substitutes (on the production side) might be included, e.g., the price of corn in a soybean supply equation.

Supply schedules for many agricultural commodities have shifted because of technological change. In fact, changes in technology often seem to be the dominant factor in explaining supply changes, but unfortunately there is no direct measure of "changes in technology." We must resort to the rather unsatisfactory device of a proxy variable. The most common proxy is a trend variable, e.g., the numbers 1, 2, . . . , T. This specification assumes a smooth change in technology of equal amounts each time period. Sometimes general measures of changes in productivity are used, such as an index of changes in productivity (changes in output per unit of input).

Current production is usually highly correlated with production in the previous time period. We noted in Chapter 4 that the production of various farm commodities in particular regions is influenced by physical and climatic considerations. For example, many acres devoted to wheat simply have no viable alternatives over a wide range of prices. Further, large changes in production tend to be restricted by factors like resource fixity, managerial ability of farmers, and habitual production patterns. As a result of such considerations, some researchers have specified the dependent variable lagged one time period as an independent variable (if Q_t is dependent, then Q_{t-1} is independent).[8] This simply says that current production is influenced by the level of production in the previous period, and current production may be viewed as changing from the previous level in response to various price and cost factors. Unfortunately, the lagged dependent variable often tends to be highly correlated with the influence of technology and other trending ex-

[8] The inclusion of the lagged dependent variable as an independent variable may also be justified by means of distributed lag concepts which are beyond the scope of this book. The distributed lag view implies that if Q_{t-1} is an appropriate variable, then expected price (to which producers respond) is a geometric average of all past prices (Nerlove, 1956).

planatory factors; in such cases the lagged variable simply becomes a proxy for trend. Therefore, another approach to supply analysis is to use first differences of variables (i.e., changes from the preceding period) or to use deviations from trend rather than the actual observations.

When specifying yield or total production equations, independent variables may include noneconomic factors influencing the dependent variable. Such factors might include rainfall at critical growth periods, soil moisture reserves, or a weather index. An illustration of a supply relation is given in Chapter 16.

Market Demand and Price Equations

If prices and quantities are indeed determined recursively, then price is the logical dependent variable in the demand equation while the quantity of the commodity as well as the quantities of the major substitutes are specified as the independent variables. However, the quantity variables for some agricultural commodities are not predetermined. Production of an annual crop is predetermined, but the quantity harvested may be influenced by price. Imports and exports also may be influenced by current prices. Furthermore, a commodity like broilers has a sufficiently short production period so that supply and price may be jointly determined within a twelve-month period. Nonetheless, the quantity available for domestic consumption of a number of agricultural products appears to be largely predetermined for periods of twelve months or less. The analyst, of course, must make the ultimate decision as to whether or not the quantity variable is predetermined for the commodity he is considering.[9]

Income is thought to be one of the important demand "shifters," and is often included as an independent variable. Again, the regression model assumes that income influences the dependent variable but not vice versa. This is technically not correct because the level of income in an economy is influenced by the quantities and prices of all (final) goods and services which are sold. Hence, in-

[9] Waugh (1964), a greatly respected price analyst, takes the position that the objective of most studies should be forecasting, and hence that the variable to be forecast naturally determines the variable to be treated as dependent.

come is jointly determined with prices and quantities. However, any one commodity typically is a very small part of the economy, i.e., makes a small contribution to income. For example, a change in the marketings and price of beef changes the level of national income, but the change is small relative to the total. Therefore, income is typically treated as if it were a predetermined variable in demand equations for agricultural commodities.[10]

The most commonly used measure of income is consumer-disposable income—income after taxes. The consumer can presumably use this income among many alternatives. However, most consumers have fixed commitments like utility bills and rents to pay. Therefore, some economists have suggested that a measure of discretionary income—that part of income over which the consumer has discretion—is most appropriate in demand analysis. Other variables like tastes and preferences can change systematically with the passage of time. It is sometimes difficult to separate statistically the effects of the upward trend in income and other systematic changes on demand. If income alone is treated as the major demand shifter, then the influence of income on demand may be understated or overstated depending on the correlation of income with the other variables which are omitted. If other variables that change systematically are included, they are often so highly correlated with income that it is impossible to estimate accurately the separate effects of each variable. This is the problem of multicollinearity (high intercorrelation) among the independent variables of regression analysis.

Changes in population have a direct influence on market demand relations. The population variable is commonly taken into account by putting the quantity and income variables on a per capita basis (dividing total quantity and income by population). Sometimes a question of the relevant population arises. Typically, this is the population of the entire country, but for a commodity like beer the relevant population might include those 18 years and older. Changes in the distribution of the population by age, occupation, or region may have an impact on demand. For example, the

---

[10] In some economies, national income can depend largely on one commodity so that this would be an incorrect assumption. (Also, see comment and citation in footnote 4, this chapter.)

relatively large number of young people in the United States in the 1960's is thought to have helped maintain the demand for fluid milk. Hence, a variable measuring the proportion of people in a particular age category might be considered.

Substitutes and complements probably have important impacts on demand, but these effects are often difficult to measure. There are two reasons for this. The first is that individual substitutes or complements may have only a small influence on demand, and the second is that the variables measuring the influence of substitutes are often highly correlated. The common practice is to include one or two variables representing major substitutes. If price is the dependent variable, then a quantity variable for the substitute is usually used. The assumption is that this variable is predetermined. For example, the price of pork could be made a function of the quantity of beef. Sometimes an aggregate measure of substitutes is used. This might be the sum of several variables. For example, substitutes in a pork demand equation might be measured by the aggregate consumption of all other meats. Index numbers of prices or quantities of substitute commodities are occasionally constructed. This approach attempts to take account of a number of substitutes in one variable, but it does not permit the measurement of the separate influences of individual commodities.

In a price equation for an individual state, the analyst must not forget that the most important substitute for the product grown in the state is the same product grown in other states. The farm price of apples in New York State depends on New York production and production in other states. Similarly, the most important substitute for a particular grade of a commodity is other grades of the same commodity.

Changes in tastes and preferences may influence demand, and such changes are perhaps the most difficult to handle in statistical demand analyses. There is no direct measure of tastes. Hence, the researcher must either assume that there was no change in tastes and preferences during the period analyzed or use a proxy variable. The most common proxy variable is simply a linear trend. This approach assumes that tastes have changed in a continuous and regular fashion over the period analyzed. An analyst may believe in some cases that the change in tastes is associated with such factors as urbanization or shifts to more sedentary work. This suggests the possibility of using a proxy variable like the percentage of the labor force in blue-collar jobs.

Depending on the objective of the study and on the commodity sector being studied, other variables might be considered. If the equation is a derived demand (say, farm-level) equation, then it is appropriate to consider the effects of a change in the marketing margin. Or, the analyst may wish to consider the influence of advertising by using a measure of the amount of money spent advertising a particular commodity or the space devoted to advertising.

With the passage of time, the average level of all prices tends to change (see Chapter 10). For example, the price level as measured by an index might rise 20 per cent in 10 years. If during the same period the price of the commodity being analyzed rose 5 per cent, then it declined *relative* to the movement of all prices. If at the same time consumer (money) incomes rose 30 per cent, then clearly real incomes also rose but not by as much as money incomes. Thus, in demand analysis one can argue that the important variables are measures of changes in relative prices and real incomes. With this in mind, a common practice is to deflate (divide) the observed price and income series by a general price index. For example, in a retail-level demand equation for broilers, the price and income variables could be divided by the Consumer Price Index.

$$X_{i1} = \frac{P_{i1}}{I_i},$$

where P_{i1} = observed price of broilers (say per year);

I_i = Consumer Price Index for each year;

X_{i1} = deflated price;

i = years over which observations are obtained.

The deflating procedure raises two basic, but interrelated, questions: What is the appropriate deflator? Assuming the appropriate deflator is used, what is the model implied by deflating? The objective of deflating a price or income series is to purge that series of the effects of changes in the general price level without introducing distortions in the relationship which is to be estimated. The selection of an appropriate deflator obviously is critical. If a series is deflated by an inappropriate index, then it will be difficult or impossible to measure the true relationship, say, between per capita consumption and prices in constant dollars. The use of a volatile price index to deflate a relatively stable price series, for instance, may purge more than general price level effects from the individual price series.

The macro (general price level) and micro components of an individual price series, however, are not easy to separate. The general price level component of various individual price series presumably differs from series to series. Thus, it is an oversimplification to assume that a single price index is the appropriate deflator for all price series. Nonetheless, a common practice is to use the Consumer Price Index as the deflator, particularly when deflating retail-level prices. The Consumer Price Index also may be the appropriate deflator for farm-level demand functions provided that the equation also contains a measure of the marketing margin (Foote, 1958, p. 28). In general, however, the appropriateness of a particular deflator depends on the problem under analysis.

If the index used in the deflation procedure contains the price series being deflated, then the coefficients relating the deflated variable to other variables are likely to be biased. The amount of bias depends on the relative weight which the price series being deflated has in the index. If it is a large component of the index (e.g., the price of beef in an index of meat prices), then the bias is large. A regression equation with price as a function of quantity illustrates the point. A small quantity produced implies a high product price and this also means a larger price index. The larger index, however, means that the ratio P/I is too small. In other words, since the index changes because of the change in this particular commodity's price, deflating by that index tends to "cancel" the influence of the price change. Consequently, the regression coefficient relating quantity to deflated price is biased.

The assumption underlying deflation is that the appropriate demand function is defined by the relationship of relative prices and real income to quantity. For instance, if the price index and the individual prices doubled (relative prices remain constant), then the demand for the product is assumed to be unchanged, and indeed deflated prices have not changed. Relative prices and real incomes are specified to be the correct variables. If, however, changes in the general price level have an "illusion effect" on the demand for the product being analyzed, then deflating does not provide the correct model. An example of an "illusion effect" is a change in demand for a product induced by a change in the general price level even though real prices have not changed.

In addition, deflating price may be inconvenient and unnecessary when the objective of the analysis is to forecast price. Usually, the analyst wants to forecast the nominal (actual) price, not a deflated price. The simplest procedure in such cases is to make the undeflated price the dependent variable in the forecasting equation.

An alternative to deflating is to include the price index as a separate independent variable. However, since price indexes often have strong trends, they are often highly intercorrelated with other explanatory variables. Such intercorrelation, as discussed in the next chapter, can create problems in estimating the equation.

Some of the foregoing comments can be illustrated by the following price-dependent demand equation for pork. Mnemonic notation, rather than conventional Y's and X's, is used.

$$\left(\frac{P}{I}\right)_t = \beta_0 + \beta_1 \left(\frac{Q}{L}\right)_t + \beta_2 \left(\frac{Q_b}{L}\right)_t + \beta_3 \left(\frac{Y}{LI}\right)_t + e_t,$$

where $P =$ retail price of pork, cents per pound,
         $Q =$ consumption of pork, pounds,
         $Q_b =$ consumption of beef, pounds,
         $Y =$ disposable personal income, dollars,
         $I =$ Consumer Price Index,
         $L =$ July 1 U.S. population,
         $t = 1, 2, \ldots, T$ observations,
         $e =$ unobserved disturbance or error term.

This specification states that the deflated price of pork is a linear function of the per capita quantity of pork, the per capita quantity of beef, real per capita disposable income, and a disturbance term.

The simple scatter diagram for deflated price and per capita quantity of pork on an annual basis is given in Figure 15-4.

The equation represents one possible specification. Numerous other alternatives are available. The analyst, for instance, might wish to consider other substitutes, such as broilers, or to consider alternate functional forms.

Assuming the specification is correct, the analyst obtains the necessary data (observations on the variables) and estimates the values of the unknown β's. If the explanatory variables are predetermined, then the most commonly used estimation method is ordinary least squares (for a discussion of the method see Johnston, 1972, Chapters 2 and 3).

Time-Series Data

We have previously noted that the selection of variables, how accurately the series are measured, and whether or not they are deflated and by what index, has a bearing on the results. Among the additional decisions that have to be made in using time-series observations are the following:

(1) What specific years should be covered (included) by the analysis? Dropping some years and adding others may alter the results.

(2) Should one make use of annual, quarterly, monthly, weekly, or daily observations?

Two conflicting factors enter into the decision as to what historical time period to use. One consideration is the number of observations. Other things being equal, we prefer a long time series simply to increase the number of degrees of freedom—that is, we prefer a large number of observations relative to the number of variables in the equation. A second factor, however, is the desire to have the analysis cover a relatively homogeneous time period, which would yield results relevant to the immediate future. This usually implies a recent, relatively short, series. It is desirable to have, say, at least ten observations. "Abnormal" years, including war years or periods with special government programs, may sometimes be excluded. If this is done, it should be based on logic prior to the analysis and should not involve dropping observations simply to improve the fit.

A second question is the choice of time unit for analysis. The researcher may have access to daily, monthly, or quarterly, as well as annual, observations. Which should be used? The objectives of the study usually dictate the choice. Obviously, annual observations would not be appropriate if the objective is to estimate seasonal demand relations. Observations for short time units do require more complex models; seasonal and other short-time variations must be explained. Conversely, annual observations which are essentially averages of short-time variations may make it possible to use somewhat simpler models.

Most price-analysis studies are based on annual observations. This is a natural period for summarizing data, and hence annual data are readily available. If the objective is to make specific short-term forecasts, then it is essential to have monthly or quarterly data. Recent studies have included more complex models using shorter units of time. Of course, such data increase the number of observations (as compared with annual observations).

A third problem with time-series data is that of consistency. There are calendar, crop, and fiscal years. The researcher, if he is not careful, may inappropriately obtain quantity observations on a crop-year basis and prices on a calendar-year basis. Also, the data should be obtained at the same market level: farm, wholesale, or retail. And, as previously mentioned, the researcher should be sure that the definition or method of construction of the variable has not changed over the time period being considered.

Alternative Algebraic Forms of Equations

The researcher also must decide which specific functional form is appropriate for the equation being estimated. If possible, the decision should be made on the basis of logic prior to the analysis. For example, consumption functions for individual foods are thought to have a curvilinear relationship because as incomes rise it seems logical that the incremental growth in food purchases becomes smaller. Thus, consumption might be made a function of the logarithm of income. However, theory often does not dictate the specific functional form which is most appropriate, and a purely empirical approach must be used. This might involve inspecting scatter diagrams or comparing alternate estimates derived from equations based on different functional forms.

The most common specification is to assume the relationship is linear. This assumption is represented by the following equation:

$$Y_t = \beta_0 + \beta_1 X_{t1} + \beta_2 X_{t2} + \ldots + \beta_K X_{tK} + e_t.$$

The net relation between each independent variable and the dependent variable is specified to be a straight line. The net slope is a constant, β_k. However, this specification implies a changing percentage relationship between Y_t and X_{tk} and hence changing elasticity.

The linear specification has the virtue of simplicity. The relationships may indeed be straight lines, and over modest ranges of the data a straight line may be a reasonable approximation, even if the "larger" relation is curvilinear.

The most common method of allowing for curved relationships is by transforming variables to logarithms. In arithmetic values, the equation for the observed variables in such cases is as follows:

$$Y_t = \beta_0 X_{t1}{}^{\beta_1} X_{t2}{}^{\beta_2} \ldots X_{tK}{}^{\beta_K} e_t.$$

The transformed relation, used for estimation, is

$$\log Y_t = \log \beta_0 + \beta_1 \log X_{t1} + \ldots + \beta_K \log X_{tK} + \log e_t.$$

The regression coefficients are based on the logarithms of the variables. This functional form assumes a constant percentage relation between Y_t and each X_{tk}. The slope at any point on the curve for a simple two variable relationship can be computed as follows:

$$\frac{dY}{dX} = \beta \frac{Y}{X}.$$

There are many other alternative specifications, but they are less commonly used. Johnston (1972, chapter 3) describes some of these alternate functional forms.

Perhaps the most important point to recognize is that the selection of a particular functional form automatically places some type of restriction on the nature of the slope and elasticity coefficients. The log-log transformation, for instance, permits the slope to change over the range of the variables, but the function is such that the percentage relationship (elasticity) between variables remains constant. As long as the analyst is cognizant of the limitations of any given function, then no problem need arise.

A Final Comment

A major problem in building econometric models is that many alternative specifications are more or less consistent with the theory undergirding the model. Either a linear or a curvilinear relationship may be appropriate for a demand equation. More than one measure of the income variable exists; income may or may not be deflated; and so on almost *ad infinitum*. Thus, in selecting a model, the analyst is faced with numerous choices, and sometimes no clear guides exist for making choices.

The problem of choice is compounded by the "requirements" of statistical inference that the model be specified, the sample data collected, the estimates made, and the hypotheses tested. It is (from the viewpoint of statistical inference) inappropriate to experiment with alternate models, using one set of data, until good results are obtained. Clearly, if a sufficiently large number of alternate specifications are tried, then some specification is likely to be found that gives "good" (but perhaps spurious) results.

Since specification of the best model prior to estimation is nearly impossible for many problems in economics, some experimentation is generally necessary. The judgment of the analyst is critical in model selection, although different models sometimes give similar results. The problem of choice is further considered in the next chapter.

References

Ashby, Andrew. 1964. "Forecasting Commodity Prices by the Balance Sheet Approach," *J. Farm Econ.*, 46:633–643.

Breimyer, Harold F. 1961. *Demand and Prices for Meat—Factors Influencing Their Historical Development.* Econ. Res. Ser., USDA Tech. Bul. 1253.

Foote, Richard J. 1958. *Analytical Tools for Studying Demand and Price Structures.* Econ. Res. Ser., USDA Ag. Hb. 146.

Fox, Karl A. 1953. *The Analysis of Demand for Farm Products.* Econ. Res. Ser., USDA Tech. Bul. 1081.

Haavelmo, T. 1943. "The Statistical Implications of a System of Simultaneous Equations," *Econometrica,* 11:1–12.

Johnston, J. 1972. *Econometric Methods.* 2d ed. New York: McGraw-Hill.

Klein, Lawrence R. 1962. *An Introduction to Econometrics.* Englewood Cliffs, N.J.: Prentice-Hall.

Moore, Henry L. 1914. *Economic Cycles: Their Laws and Causes.* New York: Macmillan.

——. 1917. *Forecasting the Yield and Price of Cotton.* New York: Macmillan.

Nerlove, Marc. 1956. "Estimates of the Elasticities of Supply of Selected Agricultural Commodities," *J. Farm Econ.,* 38:496–509.

Schultz, Henry. 1938. *The Theory and Measurement of Demand.* Chicago: Univ. of Chicago Press.

Statistical Reporting Service. 1971. *Livestock and Meat Statistics.* Econ. Res. Ser., USDA, Supplement for 1970 to Statistical Bul. 333.

Stone, Richard. 1954. *The Measurement of Consumers' Expenditure and Behaviour in the United Kingdom.* Cambridge: Cambridge Univ. Press.

Warren, G. F., and F. A. Pearson. 1928. *Interrelationships of Supply and Price.* Cornell Univ. Ag. Exp. Sta. Bul. 466.

Waugh, Frederick V. 1964. *Demand and Price Analysis: Some Examples from Agriculture.* Econ. Res. Ser., USDA Tech. Bul. 1316.

Wonnacott, Ronald J., and Thomas H. Wonnacott. 1970. *Econometrics.* New York: John Wiley and Sons.

Working, Elmer. 1927. "What Do Statistical 'Demand Curves' Show?" *Quart. Jour. Econ.,* 41:212–235.

Working, Holbrook. 1922. *Factors Determining the Price of Potatoes in St. Paul and Minneapolis.* Univ. Minn. Ag. Exp. Sta. Bul. 10.

CHAPTER 16

Using Results
of Price Analysis

This chapter provides a basis for interpreting and using the results of price analysis based on regression techniques. An ultimate appraisal of results depends in part on the basic objective of the analysis and how well the analysis fulfills the objective. This chapter must of necessity be more general, but it does suggest tools for using and appraising specific studies. The first section discusses selected regression statistics, and a second section considers methods of appraising results.[1] The computation of elasticity coefficients is briefly considered. The final section is devoted to topics related to forecasting from regression equations.

Interpreting Estimated Parameters

Net Regression Coefficients

Using the notation of the previous chapter, the unknown relationship among variables is represented by the following equation:

$$Y_t = \beta_0 + \beta_1 X_{t1} + \beta_2 X_{t2} + \ldots + \beta_K X_{tK} + e_t.$$

The equation estimated by least squares may be written

$$Y_t = b_0 + b_1 X_{t1} + \ldots + b_K X_{tK} + u_t.$$

Also, $\quad \hat{Y}_t = b_0 + b_1 X_{t1} + \ldots + b_K X_{tK},$

---

[1] The intent, as in the previous chapter, is not to give a rigorous statistical treatment, but to provide an intuitive review and some insights into uses and appraisal of quantitative economic analyses.

where the computed residuals, which are estimates of the disturbances, are

$$u_t = Y_t - \hat{Y}_t.$$

The $b_1, \ldots, b_K$ are estimates of the net relationship between the respective X_{tk} and Y_t. Each is an estimate of the change in the dependent variable in response to a one-unit change in the particular X_{tk}, the other independent variables held constant. This interpretation holds regardless of how Y_t and X_{tk} are measured. However, the magnitudes of the estimated coefficients do vary with the units (e.g., pounds or tons) used to measure the variables. For this reason, the absolute magnitudes of the estimate coefficients are not measures of the "importance" of the independent variables.[2]

Interpretation is easier if the variables are in comparable units, e.g., quantities in bushels and prices in dollars per bushel. However, variables should be of roughly similar orders of magnitude to help insure computational accuracy. Adjusting variables by powers of 10 only influences the placement of the decimal in the coefficient (Friedman and Foote, 1957, p. 6).

Multiple regression equations are quite flexible in incorporating different functional forms, but this can lead to incorrect interpretations. For the quadratic form, the independent variable and the square of the independent variable both appear as regressors. The effect of a change in this variable must be evaluated by using the coefficients of both regressors (X_t and X_t^2). Another specification sometimes uses the level of a variable and its change from last period (e.g., the current level of income and the change in income are separate regressors).

$$Y_t = b_0 + b_1 X_t + b_2 (X_t - X_{t-1}) + \ldots$$

In this case, the net effect of X_t must be computed from $b_1 X_t + b_2 X_t = (b_1 + b_2) X_t$, that is, $b_1 + b_2$.

[2] Three measures of the relative importance of independent variables in the regression are the level of significance of the coefficients of the variables (to be discussed), partial r^2 coefficients, and beta coefficients (Ezekiel and Fox, 1959, pp. 192f. and 196).

The estimate of the intercept coefficient b_0 places the level of the equation. Technically, it estimates the level of the dependent variable when all of the independent variables are zero. Often the intercept has little meaning because the range of observations of the X_{tk} usually does not extend back to zero. Hence, it is not reasonable to assume a linear relation between Y_t and X_{tk} from zero to the beginning of the observations on the variables. For example, annual per capita beef consumption has ranged upward from 80 pounds in recent years. A linear relationship perhaps exists between the price of beef and the per capita consumption of beef in the range from 70 to 120 pounds. However, it is unrealistic to project a linear relation to zero pounds per capita. Hence, an intercept coefficient in a price-quantity equation for beef has little meaning except to place the level of the equation.

In the first difference transformation, all of the variables are expressed as the change from the previous period ($\Delta Y = Y_t - Y_{t-1}$). The net slope coefficients have the same interpretation as in an untransformed equation, but the intercept coefficient has a different interpretation. It is an estimate of the trend per unit of time, if any, in the dependent variable. Assuming first differences of the original observations, a negative intercept (b_0) says that the (period-to-period) change in Y_t is the estimated negative coefficient net of the influence of the independent variables.

The following supply equation for onions in the United States (Suits and Koizumi, 1956) illustrates the use of first differences. In this case, differences in the logarithms of the variables are used.

$$\Delta \log Q_t = .0123 + .324 \, (\Delta \log P_{t-1}) - .512 \, (\Delta \log C_{t-1}),$$

where Q_t = quantity onions available for harvest, 50 lb. sacks,

         P_{t-1} = farm price onions, previous year,

         C_{t-1} = prices paid (cost) index, previous year, and hence
$\Delta \log Q_t = \log Q_t - \log Q_{t-1}$, etc.

A one-unit change in the log of price (in the previous year) changes current quantity by 0.3 log unit in the same direction. The logarithmic changes can be interpreted as percentages. Hence, a one per cent change in price is estimated to change quantity supplied 0.3 of one per cent. This is the price elasticity of supply for onions. The cost variable receives an analogous interpretation, except that an inverse relation exists between costs and supply.

The intercept coefficient states that log Q changes .0123 unit each year even if price and cost changes are zero. There is a positive trend in logarithmic terms and hence a constant percentage increase each year. The annual rate of increase can be estimated as follows:

$$\text{antilog} (\log b_0) = b_0, \text{ or in the example}$$
$$\text{antilog} .0123 = 1.029.$$

Let r be the estimate of percentage trend, and then

$$r = b_0 - 1, \text{ or}$$
$$r = 1.029 - 1 = .029.$$

Onion production is estimated to be increasing 2.9 per cent per year during the period of analysis, net of changes in prices and costs.

Standard Errors

Courses in introductory statistics emphasize the concept of the variance and standard deviation of a single variable. These statistics are based on the variability of the individual observations about their mean. For the variance, the individual deviations from the mean are computed, squared, summed, and divided by "degrees of freedom."

The variance of regression is simply an extension of the single variable concept. The variance of regression measures the variability of the observed Y_t about the computed regression "line" (the $\hat{Y}_t$). For T observations and $K+1$ parameters, the regression equation has $T-K-1$ degrees of freedom. Thus, the variance of regression is

$$s_u^2 = \frac{\sum\limits_{t=1}^{T} u_t^2}{T-K-1} = \frac{\Sigma (Y_t - \hat{Y}_t)^2}{T-K-1}.$$

s_u^2 is an estimate of the assumed constant variance of the disturbances (see Wonnacott and Wonnacott, 1970, for assumptions
underlying this computation).

The standard error of estimate is the square root of the variance
of regression. This provides a measure of variability in the same
units of measure as the dependent variable. Naturally, the analyst
would like to have a relatively small standard error of estimate.[3]
This is consistent with a high degree of "explanation" of the dependent variable by the independent variables. However, it is possible
for a particular economic sector to have large random variations
which are not susceptible to systematic explanation.

The standard errors of the regression coefficients (s_b) also may
be interpreted by analogy with the standard deviation of a variable. Each b is an estimate of an unknown β. The conceptual possibility of repeated samples means that many possible estimates of β
exist, and these alternate estimates are likely to be distributed about
the true value. In practice, one sample is available, but nonetheless the standard error of the distribution of each b_k can be
estimated. This arises from the assumptions that the variance of regression is a constant and that the disturbances are normally distributed about the regression line. Intuitively, we recognize that
this sets "limits" on the probable values of the b_k. It is important to
note that the estimates of the variances and standard errors of the
coefficients (as well as the associated statistical tests) are based on
the underlying assumptions of the statistical model. If the assumptions are not met, then the estimated standard errors and the associated statistical tests may not be appropriate.

The analyst would like to have a small standard error of each regression coefficient relative to the size of the respective coefficients.
Loosely speaking, this means that the analyst can have considerable confidence that the true, but unknown, parameter is within a
relatively small range of the estimate. The importance of small
standard errors relative to the regression coefficients is also emphasized in a following section on statistical tests.

---

[3] The standard error of estimate is not the appropriate statistic for computing a confidence interval of the forecast of Y_t. This is discussed in a subsequent section.

Coefficients of Determination

The coefficient of multiple determination, R^2, is a measure of the degree of linear association between the dependent variable and the collective independent variables. A measure of the total variation in Y_t is the variance of Y_t. This variance can be partitioned into that associated with the variability in the X_{tk} and the residual variance, s_u^2. Thus,

$$R^2 = \frac{\text{variability in } Y \text{ associated with } X\text{'s}}{\text{total variance of } Y}$$

or

$$R^2 = 1 - \frac{\text{"unexplained" variability in } Y}{\text{total variance of } Y}.$$

R^2 is a ratio with a range from zero to one. For example, if $R^2 = 0.75$, then 75 per cent of the variability in Y_t is estimated as being associated with the variability of the X_{tk}.

Adding independent variables tends to increase R^2 at least slightly even if there is no "true" relationship between the added independent variable and the dependent variable. Also, as the number of independent variables increases, the degrees of freedom of the equation decrease. Thus, for instance, two observations exactly determine the regression line for a simple two-variable equation; there are no degrees of freedom, and $r^2 = 1$. In general, $R^2 = 1$ in a multiple regression when degrees of freedom is zero. Intuitively, a R^2 near one with very few degrees of freedom suggests a misleading overestimate of the actual degree of association. This idea has lead to the use of a corrected coefficient of determination,

$$\bar{R}^2 = 1 - (1 - R^2)\frac{T - 1}{T - K - 1}, \text{ where}$$

$T =$ number of observations and
$K =$ number of independent variables.

$\bar{R}^2$ is also useful in comparing alternate equation specifications. One of the considerations in selecting among alternate specifications of a model is R^2. The user typically would like to have a high R^2 with a large number of observations relative to the number of independent variables. The corrected coefficient of determination takes this idea into account by penalizing the equation with the larger number of independent variables in relation to the number of observations. Thus, adding a new independent variable increases $\bar{R}^2$ only if R^2 increases sufficiently to offset the "penalty" of the adjustment factor for the larger K. Therefore, in comparing the results of alternate model specifications, $\bar{R}^2$ is a more appropriate statistic than R^2.[4]

If the dependent variable is transformed in the process of equation specification, the coefficients of determination are no longer comparable between the transformed and the untransformed versions. In particular, R^2 for an equation transformed to logarithms cannot be directly compared with the R^2 for the untransformed equation. In the logarithmic equation, R^2 estimates the proportion of the variation of the logarithm of Y_t which is associated with the variation of the logarithms of the X_{tk}. This is clearly not the same as measuring the proportion of the variance of the observed Y_t associated with the variation of the observed X_{tk}. The antilogs of the calculated values of log Y_t must be obtained and these values used with the observed Y_t to compute the R^2 value for a direct comparison with the untransformed equations. To re-emphasize the point, a larger R^2 for an equation transformed to logarithms does not necessarily mean that transformation is the preferred alternative. It is not clear without additional computations whether the transformation increases the degree of explanation of the observed Y_t.

Appraising the Results

Tests of Logic

In constructing an econometric model, the researcher typically, but not always, has an idea about the expected signs of the coefficients of the equation. In a demand equation, price and quantity of the commodity are logically inversely related. Thus, the price coef-

---

[4] Explicit statistical tests are available to determine if the added independent variable contributes a "statistically significant" explanation of the dependent variable.

are highly intercorrelated, one may be picking up most of the influence of the two in any case, but retaining both variables in the equation may give a somewhat better estimate of the coefficient of the variable which would have been retained in the alternate specification.

When coefficients are not statistically significant because of high intercorrelation and when there are compelling reasons for including all the intercorrelated variables in the equation, one solution is to obtain additional observations that are less intercorrelated. For instance, it may be possible to pool cross-section data with time-series data for some problems. In other cases, the time series might be extended in the hope that the variables will become less highly correlated. The "solutions" for a given set of data are not very satisfactory. They usually involve taking account of one of the intercorrelated variables indirectly, e.g., by making it part of a ratio or by combining (adding or averaging) the variables. Such procedures simply place restrictions on the parameters of the combined variables; for example, adding two variables restricts each variable to having the same parameter, that is, $\beta(X_1 + X_2)$. The first differences of the observations may be less intercorrelated than the original data, but this transformation of the data makes a special assumption about the error term of the equation (e.g., see Hildreth and Lu, 1960). In sum, when multicollinearity is a problem, any "solution" requires additional information whether it is in the form of more observations or in the form of some restrictions on the parameters in the equation being estimated. In this context, the omission of one of the variables simply restricts its parameter to the value zero.

The t test is strictly applicable only if the independent variables are truly exogenous and if the disturbances are normally distributed with a constant variance and zero covariances. The test is approximately correct if the independent variables include lagged endogenous variables and the assumptions about the disturbances hold.

Tests of null hypotheses are routinely used in applied econometrics, but their importance can be exaggerated. The inclusion of a variable in an equation means that the analyst thinks the variable has a non-zero parameter, and hence the conclusion that a parameter probably is not zero is relatively weak. In principle, other hypotheses such as $\beta_k = 1$ may be tested, but generally the analyst wants the best possible estimate of the unknown parameter. Statistical tests and obtaining "best" estimates are conditional upon a correctly specified model and the use of an appropriate estimation method. Great weight is placed on correct model specification.

Specification Error

Since model specification involves many choices, the possibilities for error are also numerous. For instance, the analyst may specify a recursive system (and use the estimation method of least squares) when a simultaneous system is more appropriate, or an incorrect functional form may be used. In appraising results, the analyst should review model specification relative to the objectives of the research and the intended applications of the analysis. In this subsection, we illustrate the consequences of some of the more frequent types of specification error.

In selecting a particular time period for analysis, the researcher usually assumes that the parameters have not changed within that time period (i.e., no structural change). If the structure has changed, then the estimated equation would be a hybrid not applicable either to the period before or to the period after the structural change. Still, the equation might be incorrectly judged to be acceptable using conventional statistical tests.

For example, the authors estimated a retail-level demand equation for beef for the years 1949–1969. The coefficient relating quantity to price is −1.19 (a one pound per capita change in quantity is related inversely to a 1.19 cents per pound change in price); the coefficient is plausible and highly significant by the conventional t test. Also, $R^2 = .90$, a relatively high coefficient of determination. A scatter diagram of observations was examined, and this suggested a change in the price-quantity relationship between 1957 and 1958. Hence, the equation was re-estimated for two time periods. The price-quantity coefficient increased to −1.35 for the first period (1949–1957) and declined to −0.84 for the second period (1958–1969). The coefficient of the income variable also decreased almost 50 per cent.

Perhaps the most frequent type of specification error is related to the specification of the independent variables. A relevant explanatory variable may be omitted from the equation, or an irrelevant or incorrect variable included. To illustrate, the following equation was computed using data for the years 1951–1964 (suggested by an example in Waugh, 1966).

$$\hat{Y}_t = 31.031 - 0.813\, X_t,$$
$$\quad\;\; (5.387)\;\; (0.385)$$

where Y_t = farm price of beef cattle, dollars per hundredweight, and

X_t = U.S. beef production, billion pounds.

The coefficient of X_t is highly significant, suggesting production and price are closely related, but it also seems likely that other variables are important in understanding the farm price of beef cattle.

An examination of residuals (defined as $Y_t - \hat{Y}_t = u_t$) can be helpful in analyzing various types of specification error. In the beef cattle example, the current residuals are plotted against the residuals lagged one year (Figure 16-1). A positive relationship exists; the residuals are said to be serially correlated. It is also possible to have negative serial correlation (Hildreth and Lu, 1960). Statistical tests exist for testing the hypothesis of zero first-order serial (or auto) correlation. Perhaps the most commonly used is the Durbin-Watson test (Friedman and Foote, 1957, p. 77; Wonnacott and Wonnacott, 1970, pp. 142f.)

Serial correlation in the residuals can arise from using an incorrect functional form and from the omission of a relevant independent variable as well as other reasons (Foote, 1958, p. 148). In our example, it seems likely that several relevant variables have been omitted, but for simplicity we use a first different transformation of the data to introduce a linear trend as a second explanatory variable. This gives

$$\Delta\hat{Y} = 1.710 - 3.218\;\; \Delta X,$$
$$\quad\;\; (.460)\;\; (.405)$$

where $\Delta Y = Y_t - Y_{t-1}$ and
$\Delta X = X_t - X_{t-1}$.

The farm price of beef is estimated to be increasing $1.71 per hundredweight per year even if no change in production occurs.

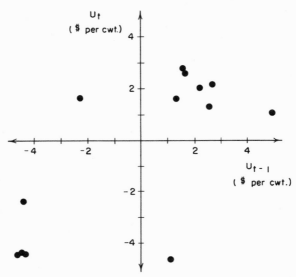

Figure 16-1. Relationship between current and lagged values of residuals in a farm-price-of-beef equation

But the most dramatic effect of introducing the trend variable (through the first difference transformation) is the fourfold increase in the slope coefficient. The net effect of a given change in production on price is estimated to be about four times greater in the second equation than in the first.

The consequences of adding (or deleting) independent variables is further illustrated in Table 16-1. In these equations, the retail price of beef is the dependent variable. If the explanatory variable being added (or deleted) is correlated with the other explanatory variables in the equation, the addition or deletion of that variable will change the coefficients. The coefficient of X_1 in equation (1) would equal the coefficient of X_1 in equation (2) only if the correlation between X_1 and X_3 were zero. In fact, the correlation between X_1 and X_3 was 0.85 in the 1949–1957 period, and consequently the addition of X_3 to the equation influences the estimated coefficient of X_1.[5]

The coefficient of X_2 in equation (3) is smaller than its standard

[5] Multiple regression analysis is (1) unnecessary in the (unlikely) case of zero correlations among all independent variables, (2) unable to estimate the

Table 16-1. Estimated retail price relationships for beef, United States, 1949–1957 *

Equation number	Intercept	Independent variables			
		X_1	X_2	X_3	$\overline{R}^2$
(1)	145.2	−0.899	–	–	.92
	(6.7)†	(0.091)			
(2)	97.3	−1.253	–	0.043	.98
	(10.8)	(0.088)		(0.009)	
(3)	107.2	−1.350	−0.180	0.049	.98
	(16.9)	(0.155)	(0.231)	(0.012)	

* Dependent variable is the retail price of choice beef deflated by the Consumer Price Index. $X_1 =$ consumption of beef, lb. per cap.; $X_2 =$ consumption of pork, lb. per cap.; $X_3 =$ real disposable income, $ per cap.
† Standard errors of respective coefficients shown in parentheses.

error, but the deletion of X_2 from the equation does have some impact on the coefficients of X_1 and X_3. Since pork is a substitute for beef, one can argue that a pork variable logically belongs in the equation. Thus, the coefficient of X_1 in equation (3) may be a better measure of the net effect of X_1 on price than is the coefficient of X_1 in equation (2).

An analysis of a supply relation for cotton for the 1910–1933 period (prior to the price-support program) illustrates the consequences of changing explanatory variables (Tomek, 1972). One plausible model is

$$\hat{A}_t = 6.319 + .566\,P_{t-1} + .565\,A_{t-1} + .271\,t,$$
$$(5.396)\ (.154)\qquad (.150)\qquad (.104)$$
$$\overline{R}^2 = .71,$$

where
$A_t =$ cotton acreage planted, million acres (A_{t-1} same variable lagged one year),

$P_{t-1} =$ season average price of cotton, deflated by the Index of Prices Paid by Farmers, cents per pound,

$t =$ trend ($= 1, 2, \ldots$).

The hypothesis of a zero parameter is rejected for each independent variable, and the results seem reasonable. The coefficient of

separate influences of variables with very high intercorrelations, but (3) applicable to the general case of some intercorrelation among explanatory variables.

the trend variable suggests a positive trend of 271,000 acres per year, net of the effects of the other variables. This may be viewed as a positive shift in supply each year for given levels of price and past acreage.

An inspection of a scatter diagram, however, suggests a large shift in supply from the 1910–1924 to the 1925–1933 period (Figure 16-2). This type of shift can be accommodated by using a zero-one variable (Wonnacott and Wonnacott, 1970, p. 68). The variable D is defined as zero in the years 1910–1924 and as one in the years 1925–1933, and D is substituted for t in the equation.

$$\hat{A}_t = 22.417 + .749\,P_{t-1} + .068\,A_{t-1} + 9.352\,D.$$
$$\phantom{\hat{A}_t =} (4.312)\ (.100) \phantom{P_{t-1} +} (.127) \phantom{A_{t-1} +} (1.321)$$
$$\bar{R}^2 = .89.$$

The coefficient of lagged price is more than 30 per cent higher in the second specification, while the coefficient of lagged acreage declines from 0.565 to 0.068 (and is not significant).

The zero-one variable is interpreted as simply shifting the intercept (level) of the equation. In 1910–1924, $D=0$ and the intercept is 22.417. In 1925–1933, $D=1$ and the intercept is $22.417+9.352=31.769$. The D variable, like the t variable, does not tell why supply changed, but in this example the D variable appears to provide a better method of taking account of the shift. In this sense, the net effect of P_{t-1} on A_t is probably better measured in the second specification.

Accuracy of Forecasts

Another method of appraising results is to use the estimated equation in forecasting forthcoming values of the dependent variable and then to observe whether the forecasts are accurate or not. Obviously, the researcher would like an equation that provides correct forecasts, and if the equation provides good forecasts, it meets a "test" of relevance. The mechanics of forecasting, measures of forecasting precision, and related topics are discussed in a subsequent section.

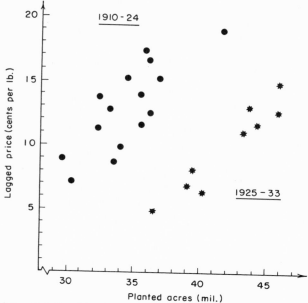

Figure 16-2. Relationship between cotton acreage and lagged deflated price, United States, 1910–1933. Data from U.S. Dept. of Agriculture, *Agricultural Statistics 1937*, pp. 88–89 and p. 399.

In the 1920–1930 period, great emphasis was placed on obtaining a high (close to one) coefficient of determination (Foote, 1958, p. 172), and today with modern computers, it is easy to estimate a large number of alternative equations using a single set of data. This practice may result in an equation specification with a spuriously high R^2; that is, R^2 is large for the particular relationship for the particular sample of data, but this result is not representative of the true population relationship.

Computing and Appraising Elasticities and Flexibilities

Since elasticities play an important role in economics, they are frequently computed from the coefficients of regression equations. Elasticities (or flexibilities) are given directly by the coefficients of equations which are linear in the logarithms of the variables,[6] but for most other functional forms, they must be calculated. A linear demand equation illustrates how elasticities are obtained. Assume we have estimated

$$\hat{Q} = b_0 - b_1 P + \ldots.$$

The coefficient b_1 is an estimate of the net slope relating price (P) and quantity (Q), holding the other independent variables constant. The price elasticity of demand is defined as

$$E = \frac{\Delta Q}{\Delta P} \frac{P}{Q}, \text{ holding other factors constant.}$$

Since b_1 can be viewed as a measure of the change in Q given a one-unit change in P, the ratio $\Delta Q / \Delta P$ equals b_1, where b_1 is negative. Thus, the elasticity is computed from

$$E = b_1 \frac{P}{Q}.$$

The ratio P/Q must represent a point on the estimated demand function; actual observations (from the original sample) cannot be used because such observations typically are not on the regression line. The usual practice is to use the arithmetic means of P and Q, since (1) the least squares fit is known to go through this point and (2) it is a point in the "middle" of the data.

With a demand function that is linear in the original observations, the elasticity varies as the ratio P/Q changes. To compute an elasticity at any point on a linear function, the relevant values of the independent variables are inserted into the equation and the

[6] In the simplest case, the demand equation is

$$\hat{Q} = b_0 P^{b_1}.$$

The derivative is

$$dQ/dP = b_0 b_1 P^{b_1 - 1} = \frac{b_0 b_1 P^{b_1}}{P} = b_1 \frac{Q}{P}.$$

Therefore, $b_1 = \frac{dQ}{dP} \frac{P}{Q}$, the elasticity.

corresponding value of Q on the regression line is computed. The selected level of P and the resulting computed value of Q are then used in the ratio P/Q to obtain the elasticity.

As previously noted, price-dependent equations are frequently estimated for recursive models in agricultural economics.

$$\hat{P} = a_0 - a_1 Q + \dots.$$

In this case, it is natural to estimate flexibility coefficients. The own-price flexibility is

$$F = \frac{\Delta P}{\Delta Q} \frac{Q}{P}, \text{ holding other variables constant.}$$

Thus, the estimated flexibility at the point of means is

$$F = a_1 \left(\frac{\overline{Q}}{\overline{P}} \right).$$

The price elasticity of demand is frequently approximated by using the reciprocal of the flexibility coefficient. As mentioned in Chapter 3, with price-dependent equations, the same variables are not held constant as with quantity-dependent equations; for this and other reasons, the reciprocal of a_1 above does not equal b_1. The reciprocal of the flexibility sets the lower limit of the elasticity. Sometimes a system of price-dependent equations has been developed for a set of substitutes. These equations can be transformed to quantity-dependent variables with prices as the explanatory variables. In this special case, the elasticity can be computed from the transformed equations (computational details are given in Foote, 1958, pp. 87ff.).

Estimates of price elasticities of supply, income elasticities of demand, and flexibility coefficients can be computed from linear equations using analogous procedures. For instance, an acreage response equation for cotton was presented above. The price elasticity of supply is defined as

$$E_s = \frac{\Delta Q}{\Delta P} \frac{P}{Q}.$$

In our equation, $\Delta A/\Delta P = 0.749$, and $\bar{P} = 11.87$ and $\bar{A} = 37.32$. Thus, the estimated supply elasticity, at least in terms of acreage response, at the point of means is

$$E_s = .749 \frac{11.87}{37.32} = .24.$$

Elasticity estimates should not be accepted uncritically, and in appraising elasticity estimates, the procedures used in obtaining the elasticities must be considered. Since some type of statistical analysis usually is the basis for the computed elasticity, the economist must specify and estimate an appropriate relationship. Hence, one question is whether or not the mathematical relationship can be called a "demand curve." As discussed in Chapter 15, simply obtaining observations on prices and quantities does not necessarily specify the slope of the demand curve. It also is obvious that *all* other factors cannot be held constant in a statistical analysis. The economist, at best, will be able to hold some major variables constant. Thus, for this reason alone, the estimated coefficient is an approximation of the theoretical concept. However, these approximations often are useful.

The numerous choices with respect to the data used in demand analysis will affect the magnitude of the elasticity coefficients which are obtained. Elasticities will, of course, vary depending on whether the price-quantity relationship is estimated using farm, wholesale, or retail data. The market area covered and the time period used for the analysis also influence results. This influence on the magnitude of measured elasticities arises, in part, because different demand relationships are involved. One should not be surprised to discover, for example, that the price elasticity of demand for center-cut pork chops at retail in New York City differs from the elasticity of demand for hogs in Iowa.

Elasticity estimates also are influenced by the degree of product aggregation. The more products are combined, the fewer the number of substitutes and therefore the less elastic (or more inelastic) demand is likely to be. For example, there are fewer substitutes for all livestock products combined than for beef alone; hence, one would expect to obtain a lower elasticity estimate for all meat than for beef.

In addition, as the reader may recall, two different samples from the same population are not likely to provide exactly the same estimates of the unknown parameters. Differences arise due to sampling error, and for a particular data set there is no guarantee that the estimated coefficients equal the "true" parameters.

Notwithstanding the above qualifications, empirical elasticities have often displayed some internal consistency. For example, different studies have obtained similar elasticities for retail-level demand equations for meats, such as beef and pork. Farm-level demand relations are typically found to be more price-inelastic than retail-level functions. The important conclusion is that the potential user must select the elasticity which is relevant for his particular problem.

Forecasting from Regression Equations

Mechanics

The actual computations for making a point forecast of the dependent variable in a regression equation are simple. The analyst has presumably estimated an appropriate equation. For example,

$$\hat{Y}_{\circ} = b_0 + b_1 X_{\circ 1} + b_2 X_{\circ 2}.$$

The procedure is to obtain the relevant values of the independent variables for the forecast period (the $X_{\circ k}$), insert them in the equation, and compute the dependent variable.

Once the appropriate equation has been estimated, the major problem remaining is to obtain the relevant values of the independent variables for the forecast period.[7] If the independent variables are predetermined, then their levels are determined by outside or prior events. Nonetheless, obtaining observations to make the forecast may be difficult. For example, in forecasting price, production is predetermined, but it is difficult to know even at harvest the precise level of production.

There are various methods and sources for obtaining estimates of the independent variables for the forecast period. Government agencies sometimes publish relevant estimates. The Crop Reporting

[7] This is sometimes called the problem of making "ancillary forecasts."

Service of the USDA makes monthly preharvest estimates of the
size of many crops. Data are also available on planted acres,
weather conditions, and other factors, so that the analyst might
make his own estimate of crop size. Regular reports are also made
on size of inventories and on expected levels of inventories. Some
variables, like population and income, have rather smooth growth
rates over short periods of time so that reasonable short-term
projections can be made.

Sometimes there is a sufficient time lag between the specified independent variables and the dependent variable that the analyst
can wait until the independent variables are observed before making the forecast. When an equation is part of a recursive model, its
sequential nature is helpful in obtaining estimates of independent
variables in successive equations. For example, supply next year
may depend on current or recent past prices and costs. These observations can be used to forecast supply. The forecast level of supply, then, can be used to help forecast price in the next period.

Short-run forecasts of supply can take advantage of known fixed
biological relationships in the production process, particularly
those for animals (see, for example, Walters, 1965). Units produced
are limited by the size of the breeding herd or flock; gestation and
hatching periods are known; live chicks hatched per 100 eggs, for
instance, is a well established rate. Thus, a forecast of current
broiler production can be related to the hatch of broiler-type chicks
two or three months earlier. The number of chicks hatched, in
turn, depends on the number of eggs placed in incubators and
their hatchability rate.

The point estimate of the dependent variable based on the estimated regression equation is said to be a conditional forecast. The
computed Y (the forecast), based on a least-squares equation, is an
estimate of the mean of a conditional distribution of Y_t. The assumptions about the disturbance terms imply a probability distribution of Y_t's for each set of X_{tk}. The forecast of Y is based on a
new set of X_{tk}, where the observations are presumably drawn from
the same population as the sample on which the equation is based.
Conceptually, as different levels of X_{tk} are specified, the mean of Y_t
changes. The values selected for X_{tk} for the forecast period imply
a particular distribution with a particular mean. The computed Y

is an estimate of the mean, and it is conditional on the values of X_{tk} selected.

Waugh (1961) argues that least squares is always an appropriate technique for obtaining forecasting equations because of the property of providing unbiased estimates of the mean of the distribution of Y_t for *given* X_{tk}. However, there is great difficulty in selecting a correct set of X_{tk} for the forecast period when one of the X's is simultaneously determined with Y_t. If Y_t and a X_{tk} are truly jointly determined, then by definition they have been simultaneously generated by the underlying population relationships. More than one equation is required to "explain" this joint determination. On the other hand, in forecasting from a single equation, the analyst must specify the level of the X_{tk} to compute Y_t. For a X_{tk} jointly determined with Y_t, the selection must be highly arbitrary. Thus, there is little comfort in knowing that the forecast of Y_t is conditionally correct for the selected X_{tk} when one of the X's cannot be correctly specified in a single equation prior to the forecast period.[8]

Evaluating and Using Forecasts

There are two broad reasons why forecasts may differ from the subsequently observed value. Each reason, however, has several ramifications. First, the equation used in forecasting is an estimate, usually based on historical data, of the true population relation. Assuming that the equation is correctly specified and that least squares is the appropriate estimating technique, the computed Y based on the equation is still just an estimate. In addition, the equation may be imperfectly specified. Or, high intercorrelations in the original sample may obscure the influence of the separate regressors. (The equation can still provide useful forecasts as long as future intercorrelation remains identical to intercorrelation in the sample period.) Further, the population parameters may change

---

[8] There is more to the argument than can be presented here. In essence, using a single equation where a simultaneous system would be more appropriate reduces the amount of information on which the forecast is being made. This reduces the "quality" of the forecast relative to the model which uses the additional information.

with the passage of time, and consequently the equation is no longer an estimate of the current population relation.

Even if the equation is a good estimate of the current population relation, a second major reason for inexact forecasts is that the X_{tk} for the forecast period are not the same as those on which the equation is based. The equation is based on a unique sample; the X_{tk} values for the forecast period usually are not replicates of previous values.

There are related practical problems. One is that the ancillary forecasts of the independent variables simply may be wrong. Incorrect values for the independent variables in the forecast period result in incorrect forecasts of the dependent variable. Further, with the growth in the economy, new observations may be outside the range of historical experience. The relationship based on historical time series may not hold outside of the observed range.

In sum, forecasting error arises from two general sources. One is the error in estimating the population relationship from the historical (sample) data. A second factor is that the new observations and conditions for the forecast period need not—in fact, probably will not—result in a value of Y_t which is the mean of the implied distribution of the Y_t. It is possible, however, to compute a confidence interval around the point forecast; the interval must be based on the standard error of forecast (Ezekiel and Fox, 1959; Wonnacott and Wonnacott, 1970).

While forecasts made from equations may be imprecise, they are likely to represent an improvement over forecasts based on the "guesses" of knowledgeable observers. Judgment is essential in making any forecast, but judgments usually can be improved if they are based on quantifiable relationships.

Estimated equations can be subjected to a number of tests which give the analyst clues as to the equation's usefulness in forecasting. Naturally, the equation should provide forecasts which are numerically close to the subsequently observed values. An R^2 fairly close to one is desirable but not a sufficient condition for good forecasts.[9]

[9] It is impossible to specify a level of R^2, say 0.75, which will provide forecasts satisfactory to the user. The necessary precision of the prediction depends on the needs of the user. In addition, the forecasting equation may not be as good as the user would like but still may be better than other available forecasting techniques.

A second test is whether or not the equation can correctly forecast changes of direction of the dependent variable. R^2 is not necessarily a good measure of this attribute. For example, a linear trend line fitted to a variable with a strong trend will have an R^2 near one, but a trend line does not catch changes of direction.

A third test is how well the equation captures "extreme" movements of the dependent variable. This is especially important for those users of forecasts who may be greatly affected by large movements in price (or other variable). The equation will not be very satisfactory for forecasting in this situation if it cannot explain past changes which were relatively large.

A comparison of the computed values $(\hat{Y}_t)$ with the observed values (Y_t) of the dependent variable is a helpful tool in appraising the ability of an equation to capture changes in direction and extreme values (Figure 16-3). For example, observed Y_t may move upward for five successive years and then move down in the sixth year. If computed Y_t moved upward in all six periods, it is correct five out of six times but has missed the important change in direction.

It is also sometimes useful to graph the residuals against time and plot scatter diagrams of u_t against u_{t-1} (Figure 16-1). An objective is to see if the residuals have behaved randomly in the period of analysis. The analyst also would be interested in identifying

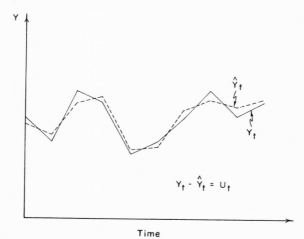

Figure 16-3. An illustration of plotting observed and computed values of dependent variable against time

years with large residuals and in observing whether recent residuals have a mean of approximately zero. A non-zero mean in the residuals in recent years suggests that a new factor may be influencing the dependent variable and that it may be incorrect to assume a zero disturbance for the forecast period. Crom (1972) illustrates how logical assumptions about institutional and behavioral changes can be incorporated into a model to improve projections.

The ultimate test, of course, is to forecast beyond the period of the original sample. This can take two forms. One is to use all available recent data to estimate the equation and to make "actual" forecasts for future time periods. The second is to omit the last one or two periods' observations from the original fit and then see how the equation forecasts using the observed but not included observations. This is an *ex post* forecast. It has the advantage of providing an immediate test of the equation's forecasting ability. However, such forecasts differ from the typical forecasting situation in the sense that the values of the independent variables are exactly known at the time the forecast is made. There is no problem of making ancillary forecasts for an *ex post* forecasting test. For an "actual" forecast, the values of certain independent variables for the forecast period may not be precisely known. As we have indicated, forecasts can be wrong because incorrect values are assigned to the independent variables for the forecast period. Therefore, *ex post* forecasting tests can overstate the accuracy of expected predictions in actual forecasting situations.

Assuming the equation has been used for making forecasts, numerous descriptive measures of the accuracy of the forecasts might be used. The forecasts vary around the subsequently observed values, and consequently measures of variability can be developed. One, for instance, is the average absolute error of forecast, which is simply an average of the absolute deviations of the forecasts from the subsequently observed values.

$$\text{Average absolute error} = \frac{\sum\limits_{i=1}^{I} \left| \text{forecast } Y_i - \text{observed } Y_i \right|}{I},$$

where I = number of comparisons.

Naturally, we prefer not to have large errors. But, descriptive measures of forecasting error are difficult to interpret in terms of judging the accuracy of a forecasting equation. What is the source of a poor forecast? A measure of the error is not meaningful unless we know whether the conditions imposed at the time the forecast was made actually prevailed. Perhaps the equation with a large forecasting error would have provided an accurate forecast if correct ancillary information had been available at the time the forecast was made.

Also, a descriptive statistic for a single equation does not provide a standard of comparison. In judging the accuracy of a forecasting equation, the real issue is whether it is better than alternative forecasting methods. For example, is the equation better (or worse) than forecasting from a "naive model"? How does the equation compare with a consensus, noneconometric prediction of professional forecasters? Forecasts from an equation conceivably could have moderately large errors and still be improvements over other methods.

The Economic Consequences of Forecasts

The payoff to an individual firm from making an accurate forecast can be high if the manager has sufficient time to alter decisions in response to the forecast. The public also may gain through improved resource allocation if accurate forecasts are made of long-run equilibrium prices. Costs associated with variable production and the variable use of marketing facilities can be quite high, and accurate price forecasts may help to smooth production. The government also needs to have accurate forecasts of how producers and consumers are likely to react to alternative price or subsidy programs if rational decisions are to be made.

Short-run public forecasting of prices, however, presents a serious dilemma. If the forecast is made sufficiently far in advance to enable producers to alter production plans, it may turn out to be inaccurate. For example, if the government forecasts a rise in hog prices over the next eighteen months, prices may begin to fall before the expiration of that period because a sufficient number of producers have taken the forecast seriously and have increased production. Forecasts of prices made after the time production decisions can be altered are likely to be more accurate, but less useful to producers. By then it is too late for producers to use the information generated by forecasts; however, such forecasts may still be useful to those involved in processing and marketing or price determination.

The longer forecasts are made into the future, the more important it is to take account of the "feedback" effect of the forecast on subsequent decisions. This again emphasizes the need to develop recursive or sequential models in agriculture which make it possible to take account of the effects of decisions made in one period on outcomes in another. These, in turn, affect future decisions. Hopefully, the theory and techniques discussed in this and the preceding chapter will contribute to improved forecasts by making such relationships explicit and quantifiable.

References

Crom, Richard J. 1972. "Economic Projections Using a Behavior Model," *Ag. Econ. Res.*, 24:9–15.

Ezekiel, Mordecai, and Karl A. Fox. 1959. *Methods of Correlation and Regression Analysis.* 3d ed. New York: John Wiley and Sons.

Foote, Richard J. 1958. *Analytical Tools for Studying Demand and Price Structures.* Econ. Res. Ser., USDA Ag. Hb. 146.

Friedman, Joan, and Richard J. Foote. 1957. *Computational Methods for Handling Systems of Simultaneous Equations.* Econ. Res. Ser., USDA Ag. Hb. 94.

Hildreth, Clifford, and John Y. Lu. 1960. *Demand Relations with Autocorrelated Disturbances.* Mich. State Univ. Tech. Bul. 276.

Manderscheid, Lester V. 1965. "Significance Level—0.05, 0.01, or ?," *J. Farm Econ.*, 47:1381–1385.

Suits, Daniel B., and Susumu Koizumi. 1956. "The Dynamics of the Onion Market," *J. Farm Econ.*, 38:475–484.

Tomek, William G. 1972. "Distributed Lag Models of Cotton Acreage Response: A Further Result," *Am. J. Ag. Econ.*, 54:108–110.

Walters, Forrest. 1965. "Predicting the Beef Cattle Inventory," *Ag. Econ. Res.*, 17:10–18.

Waugh, Frederick F. 1961. "The Place of Least Squares in Econometrics," *Econometrica*, 29:386–396.

——. 1966. *Graphic Analysis: Applications in Agricultural Economics,* Econ. Res. Ser., USDA Ag. Hb. 326.

Wonnacott, Ronald J., and Thomas H. Wonnacott. 1970. *Econometrics.* New York: John Wiley and Sons.

Author Index

Subject Index

Administered prices, 229-231
Aggregate farm prices:
  behavior, alternate explanations, 196-200
  elasticities, aggregate demand and supply, 197
  historical changes, 192-194
Agricultural policy, *see* Price instability, Price policy objectives, *and* Price supports
Agricultural prices, distinguishing characteristics, 1-2, 196-200
Algebraic forms of equations, 334-336
Annual price variation, 89, 172, 249-251, 255
Asset fixity, 74
Auctions, *see* Organized markets

Bargaining, *see* Negotiating prices
Basis, 240-242
Beef:
  retail demand functions, 12, 352-353
  retail-farm price spread, 114
Buffer stocks, 281-285

Capital rationing, 279
Cobweb model:
  description, 176-179, 187-189
  limitations, 179-182
  modifications and applications, 182-186
Coefficients of determination, 343-344
  see also Regression analysis
Commodity agreements, *see* International commodity agreements
Commodity Credit Corporation, 284, 292
Commodity Exchange Authority, 272-273

Complementary commodities, 18, 35-36
Cost curves, 60-62
Cotton supply functions, 353-354
Cyclical behavior in prices, 174-176

Daily price changes, 164-165, 246, 254
Deficiency payments, 298-301
Deflating (a variable), 210, 330-332
Demand:
  aggregate farm products, 15, 197
  changes in demand, 13-19
  derived demand, 23-25, 44-47, 110
  elasticity, *see* Elasticities of demand
  function and schedule defined, 10
  long run, 20-22
  speculative, 19-20
Devaluation of currency, 202-203
Discriminatory pricing, *see* Price discrimination
Distributed lag, concept of, 23

Econometric models, 311-315
  see also Price analysis
Elasticities of demand:
  cross elasticity, 34-36
  empirical estimates, 54-56, 197, 355-359
  income elasticity, 31-34
  price elasticity, 27-31
  relationships among, 36-49
  total elasticity, 49-51
  see also Flexibility coefficients
Elasticities of supply:
  empirical estimates, 64, 197
  price elasticity defined, 62-63
Engel aggregation condition, 41
Engel curve, 17, 31
Equilibrium price, 83

373

AGRICULTURAL PRODUCT PRICES

Designed by R. E. Rosenbaum.
Composed by Vail-Ballou Press, Inc.,
in 11 point linofilm Caledonia, 3 points leaded,
with display lines in Helvetica.
Printed offset by Vail-Ballou Press.
Bound by Vail-Ballou Press
in Columbia book cloth
and stamped in All Purpose foil.

Library of Congress Cataloging in Publication Data
(For library cataloging purposes only)

Tomek, William G.   date.
    Agricultural product prices.

    Includes bibliographies.
    1. Agricultural prices.   I. Robinson, Kenneth
L   date.   joint author.   II. Title.
HD9000.5.T65   338.1'3   73-4872
ISBN 0-8014-0748-6